THE EIGHTY-SECOND ANNUAL MEETING OF THE AMERICAN ACADEMY OF POLITICAL AND SOCIAL SCIENCE

APRIL 7 AND 8, 1978
THE BENJAMIN FRANKLIN HOTEL
PHILADELPHIA, PENNSYLVANIA

The Annual Meeting will be addressed at each session by prominent scholars and officials and will be devoted to

PLANNING FOR THE ELDERLY

Approximately 800 persons will be in attendance sometime during the two days of sessions, representing a wide variety of cultural, civic and scientific organizations.

Members are cordially invited to attend and will automatically receive full information.

- Proceedings of this 82nd Annual Meeting will be published as the July issue of THE ANNALS

- FOR DETAILS WRITE TO: THE AMERICAN ACADEMY OF POLITICAL AND SOCIAL SCIENCE • BUSINESS OFFICE • 3937 CHESTNUT STREET. PHILADELPHIA, PENNSYLVANIA 19104

VOLUME 436   MARCH 1978

THE ANNALS

of The American Academy *of* Political
and Social Science

RICHARD D. LAMBERT, *Editor*

ALAN W. HESTON, *Assistant Editor*

AMERICAN INDIANS TODAY

Special Editors of This Volume

J. MILTON YINGER

Professor of Sociology and Anthropology

Oberlin College
Oberlin, Ohio

and

GEORGE EATON SIMPSON

*Professor Emeritus of Sociology
and Anthropology*

Oberlin College
Oberlin, Ohio

PHILADELPHIA

78-1398

MARION M. WILLIAMS, *Copy Editor*

The articles appearing in THE ANNALS are indexed in the
Book Review Index, the *Public Affairs Information Service Bulletin, Social Sciences Index*, and *Current Contents: Behavioral, Social, Management Sciences* and *Combined Retrospective Index Sets*. They are also abstracted and indexed in *ABC Pol Sci, Historical Abstracts, United States Political Science Documents, Social Work Research & Abstracts, International Political Science Abstracts* and/or *America: History and Life*.

International Standard Book Numbers (ISBN)

ISBN 0-87761-225-0, vol. 436, 1978; paper—$4.50
ISBN 0-87761-224-2, vol. 436, 1978; cloth—$5.50

Issued bimonthly by The American Academy of Political and Social Science at 3937 Chestnut St., Philadelphia, Pennsylvania 19104. Cost per year: $18.00 paperbound; $23.00 clothbound. Add $2.00 to above rates for membership outside U.S.A. Second-class postage paid at Philadelphia and at additional mailing offices.

Claims for undelivered copies must be made within the month following the regular month of publication. The publisher will supply missing copies when losses have been sustained in transit and when the reserve stock will permit.

Editorial and Business Offices, 3937 Chestnut Street, Philadelphia, Pennsylvania 19104.

CONTENTS

iii

BOOK DEPARTMENT

CONTENTS

ECONOMICS

FOREWORD

A great many changes have occurred in American society and among Native Americans since the appearance of an earlier issue of THE ANNALS (May 1957) devoted to an examination of "American Indians and American Life." The Indian population has grown rapidly and has become urban even more rapidly. A civil rights movement has swept over the country, dramatically changing the legal framework within which racial and cultural contacts occur and heightening the sense of group identity of America's minorities. Significant changes in the economic, political, and educational opportunities of the members of minority races have occurred, but these changes only reveal more clearly the great inequalities and the discrimination that remain. These have been years of conflict, as claims have been pressed—in the face of resistance—by various forms of black power, brown power, and red power.

The articles in this issue of THE ANNALS examine many aspects of these changes among American Indians and in the relationships of Indians to the government and the larger society. Our aim, in selecting the authors— distinguished students of Native American life—has been to focus on the recent developments. Yet we are struck also by the continuity. This can best be shown, perhaps, simply by repeating the foreword that we wrote for the 1957 volume, for it may suggest the distance we have yet to go before the country has truly redefined its racial and ethnic practices. It may also emphasize the importance of the study of those practices for an understanding of American society:

White Americans seem continually to be rediscovering the Indians. In the last few years, a growing Indian population on a limited land base, a vigorous national controversy over desegregation, a turn in the Indian policy of the federal government, and world-wide attention to questions of colonialism and minorities have been among the forces renewing America's interest in her Indian citizens.

The student of Indian affairs recognizes that to some degree the status of Indians in American society is similar to the status of other minorities. To a significant degree, however, Indian experience has been different, for unlike any other minority group in the nation, they were here, living in unified societies, when the European settlers came. Their response to invasion may have as much in common with the minorities in Eastern Europe as with the willing and unwilling migrants to America, torn as they were from their cultural roots.

There is scarcely a major issue of policy in the United States that has not been involved in the relationships of Indians and whites. Questions of universal citizenship and franchise; of land use and conservation; of the "melting pot" versus pluralism; of prejudice, discrimination, and segregation; of colonialism; of the separation of church and state; of private property and communal property; and of the extent and nature of government responsibility for education—to mention several basic issues—have all involved policy questions concerning Indians.

We need scarcely stress the importance and value of a study of the place of American Indians in American life. To the social scientist, it offers a valuable field for the testing of theories of social and cultural change, of acculturation, of personality development, and the like. To the policy maker, "the Indian question" is a key test of democracy with which our society has struggled for generations. To the student of international affairs, it offers experience— much of it negative, of course—and an important testing ground for the study of the results of culture contact between highly industrialized and "underdeveloped" societies. And in its own right, as a problem with difficult questions of justice and equality involving a large group of human beings, the analysis of the status of American Indians challenges us all.

Clearly the authors of this volume do not agree on all aspects of the question of the place of American Indians in American life. There are some disagreements in interpretation of facts, in method, and even in objective. While we have not sought to have all possible points of view represented—for our aim has been a scholarly review of several aspects of Indian life today, not a policy debate—we nevertheless welcome the several points of view that naturally appeared as the various authors explored their subjects. Each author writes from a wealth of experience. The interaction of their views can bring us to a more adequate understanding of American Indians and toward a resolution of the difficult questions still before us in establishing full equality and freedom for Indians.

J. MILTON YINGER
GEORGE EATON SIMPSON

ANNALS, AAPSS, **436**, Mar. 1978

The Economic Basis of Indian Life

By ALAN L. SORKIN

ABSTRACT: This paper focuses on trends in the economic position of the American Indian and discusses programs to spur Indian development. The rapid growth in Indian income and occupational status in comparison to blacks and whites is indicated. However, these gains have been made primarily by urban, as opposed to reservation, Indians. Despite economic progress, 50 percent of reservation Indians and 20 percent of urban Indians obtained incomes below the poverty level. The biggest economic problem on Indian reservations is unemployment which has averaged 40 percent of the labor force for the past 20 years. Manpower and industrial development programs, while bringing benefits to a few, have done little to make the reservations economically viable. Moreover, the manpower programs operated by the Bureau of Indian Affairs and Department of Labor overlap and should be coordinated to prevent duplication of effort. Agricultural development has lagged partly due to inadequate technical assistance and financial aid and the fractionated nature of Indian land. The most productive acreage is often sold or leased to whites. Indian centers may hold the key to the integration of native Americans into the social and economic life of urban America.

Alan L. Sorkin is Professor and Chairman of the Department of Economics, University of Maryland-Baltimore County and Associate in the Department of International Health at the Johns Hopkins School of Public Health. He received the Ph.D. in economics from Johns Hopkins in 1966. He is the author of American Indians and Federal Aid *(The Brookings Institution, 1971), as well as a number of articles concerning manpower and industrial development programs for native Americans. He is presently undertaking a study of the economic and social development of the urban American Indian.*

1

THE PURPOSE of this paper is to indicate trends in the economic position of the American Indian as well as to discuss the various programs developed by the Bureau of Indian Affairs (BIA) and other federal agencies to accelerate development of Indian resources. Whenever possible a distinction will be made between data relating to reservation Indians and those concerning nonreservation (urban) Indians. In order to place this information in proper perspective the economic progress of American Indians will be compared with that of white and black Americans.

INCOME

Many reservation Indians receive incomes which are below the poverty level. According to the most recent figures available, approximately one-half of all reservation Indians and one-fifth of all urban Indian families earned less than $4,000 a year (the income level which separated poor families of average size from nonpoor in 1969). Income statistics for Indian, black and white males for 1939–69 are presented in table 1.

While the income of male Indians rose much faster than that of white males over the 1949–69 period, the former was less than one-half of the latter in 1969. The statistics also indicate the widening income gap between reservation and urban Indians. In 1949 the median income of Indians on reservations was 80 percent of that of Indians living in urban areas; in 1969 the figure had dropped to 57 percent. The increased disparity results from the migration of many relatively well-educated and highly skilled Indians from reservations to major urban centers over that 20-year period. In the metropolitan areas better-paying jobs, more com-

mensurate with the level of education and training of the Indians seeking them, were available. At the same time the reservation economy remained comparatively stagnant, and as a result incomes grew slowly.

From 1939 to 1969 the median income of reservation Indians grew slightly faster than the median income of black males (see table 1). In recent years, however, the average income of black males has been double that of reservation Indians. Finally, in 1969 the median income of black males and urban male Indians was almost the same, although the latter had increased nearly three times as rapidly as the former in median income from 1949 to 1969.

Reservation Indians are heavily dependent on government for jobs and income. In 1972, nearly 40 percent of reservation Indian earnings was accounted for by the federal government with an additional 20 percent coming from tribal and state and local government. In addition, 20 percent of income was obtained from commercial and industrial employment, 12 percent from agriculture and 8 percent from forestry, minerals and outdoor recreation.[1]

Such heavy reliance on government employment could become a source of difficulty for reservation Indians. In the event of even a moderate cutback in federal Indian programs, several tribes, which already face severe unemployment problems, would find themselves in

1. Keith Fay, *Developing Indian Employment Opportunities* (Washington, D.C.: Bureau of Indian Affairs, 1974), p. 100. In addition to earned income about 20 percent of all Indian families receive welfare income, compared with only about 5 percent for the total United States population. The average income from this source is $1,200 per Indian family.

TABLE 1

MEDIAN INCOME FOR MALE INDIANS, BLACKS, AND WHITES, 1939–69* (1969 DOLLARS)

YEAR	ALL INDIANS	URBAN INDIANS	RESERVATION INDIANS	BLACKS	WHITES
1939	—	—	$ 576	$1,066	$2,035
1944	—	—	760	1,843	3,506
1949	$1,094	$1,198	950	2,218	3,780
1959	2,218	2,961	1,699	3,398	5,229
1964	—	—	2,074	3,947	6,743
1969	3,509	4,568	2,603	4,508	7,759
Percentage Increase 1939–69	—	—	352	323	281
Percentage Increase 1949–69	220	281	174	103	105

SOURCE: U.S. Bureau of the Census, *Current Population Reports*, Series P–60, nos. 5, 7, and 47, *Income of Families and Persons in the United States* (1965), pp. 51–51; U.S. Bureau of Indian Affairs, "Reservation Income, 1939" (unpublished); Bureau of the Census, 1940 Census of Population, *The Labor Force*, table 71, p. 116 and the volume on *Education*, table 31, p. 161; U.S. Bureau of the Census, 1950 Census of Population, *Nonwhite Population by Race* (1953), table 10, p. 32, and table 21, p. 72, *Occupational Characteristics* (1956), table 10, p. 183, and table 21, p. 215; U.S. Bureau of the Census, 1960 Census of Population, *Nonwhite Population by Race*, table 33, p. 104, *Occupational Characteristics*, table 25, p. 296, and table 26, p. 215; Bureau of Indian Affairs, "Selected Data on Indian Reservations Eligible for Designation under Public Works and Economic Development Act" (mimeographed, 1966); U.S. Bureau of the Census, 1970 Census of Population, *American Indians* (1973), table 13, pp. 161–63, and *Education* (1973), table 7, pp. 149–51.
* Data include all males and all sources of income, whether earned or unearned.

a crisis situation. For example on the Pine Ridge reservation 65 percent of all employed Indians work for the federal government; on the Fort Belknap reservation the figure is 72 percent.[2]

There is great variation in income among reservations. Median family income in 1969 ranged from $2,500 on the Papago reservation in Arizona to $6,115 on the Laguna Pueblo in New Mexico.[3] Even within a state the difference is sizable. For example in Montana, the median family income varied from $4,258 on the Blackfeet reservation to $5,278 on the Northern Cheyenne reserva-

tion. Differences in income levels are more closely related to variations in off-reservation employment opportunities and reservation labor force participation rates than to levels of reservation development.

OCCUPATIONAL STATUS

The distribution of the Indian labor force by occupation reveals a concentration among the lowest paying positions (see table 2). However, the occupational status of Indians in 1970 was more favorable than that of blacks, with higher proportions of the former classified as professionals, managers, and craftsmen, and with fewer enumerated as operatives, laborers, and service workers than the latter.

The most significant occupational change among Indians has been the rapid decline in agricultural employ-

2. Bureau of Indian Affairs, "BIA Program Planning Output Data" (Unpublished tabulation, Bureau of Indian Affairs, December 1972).

3. U.S. Bureau of Census, 1970 Census of Population, *American Indians* (Washington, D.C.: USGPO, 1973), table 14, pp. 171–73.

TABLE 2

PERCENT DISTRIBUTION OF INDIAN, BLACK, AND WHITE MALES BY OCCUPATION
GROUP, 1940, 1960, 1970

OCCUPATION GROUP	INDIAN					BLACK			WHITE		
	1940	1960	TOTAL 1970	URBAN 1970	RURAL 1970	1940	1960	1970	1940	1960	1970
Professional and technical	2.2	4.9	9.2	11.4	6.8	1.8	3.4	5.7	5.9	11.6	14.9
Managers, Officials and Proprietors except Farmers	1.4	2.8	5.0	5.8	4.2	1.3	1.9	2.8	10.7	12.1	12.4
Clerical and Sales	2.0	4.9	8.1	7.3	3.9	2.0	7.0	10.0	14.0	15.1	14.8
Craftsmen and Foremen	5.7	15.5	22.1	23.1	20.9	4.4	10.7	15.4	15.7	21.1	21.9
Operatives	6.2	21.9	23.9	25.6	22.1	12.6	26.7	29.5	18.9	20.1	18.8
Laborers	11.4	20.2	13.2	10.8	15.8	21.4	22.2	16.1	7.5	6.0	6.0
Service Workers	2.6	6.3	10.4	10.8	10.1	15.3	16.0	15.9	6.0	5.7	7.3
Farmers and Managers	46.7	9.5	2.3	0.2	4.6	21.2	4.7	0.9	14.1	5.8	2.8
Farm laborers	21.7	14.0	5.7	1.8	10.2	19.9	7.5	3.6	7.0	2.5	1.5

SOURCE: 1940 Census, *Characteristics of the Nonwhite Population By Race*, table 26, pp. 83–84, and *The Labor Force*, table 62, pp. 88–89; 1960 Census, *Nonwhite Population By Race*, table 33, p. 104, and *Occupational Characteristics*, table 2, pp. 11–20, and table 3, pp. 21–30; 1970 Census of Population, *American Indians*, table 7, p. 86, and U.S. Bureau of the Census, *The Social and Economic Status of Negroes in the United States*, 1970, table 48, p. 60.

ment. Nearly half of all Indian males were classified as farmers or farm managers in 1940, but only 2 percent were so classified in 1970. The principal reason for this decline has been the pressure of competition from non-Indian farmers, whose greater capital resources and technical skill have made farming unprofitable for many Indians. Thus Indian farmers earn only about 60 percent as much as reservation Indian males engaged in other occupations, encouraging an exodus from agriculture as well as the leasing of a large part of the most productive land to whites.

There has been a rapid expansion in the proportion of skilled and semiskilled workers. Nearly half of all Indian males were employed as carftsmen or operatives in 1970 compared to 12 percent of the Indian labor force in 1940. The rapid growth in skilled and semiskilled employment of Indians has been associated with the migration during the 1950s and 1960s of younger Indians from the reservations to urban centers in the West. Many of these migrants were participating in training and relocation programs operated by the Bureau of Indian affairs.

Finally there has been a considerable increase in the proportion of Indian males employed as professional workers or managers and proprietors. Less than 4 percent of

TABLE 3

Unemployment Rates, Indian, Black, and White Males, 1940–1975*

	INDIANS				
YEAR	ALL	URBAN	RESER-VATION†	BLACKS	WHITES
			(IN PERCENT)		
1940	32.9	—	—	18.0	14.8
1950		15.1	—	9.6	5.9
1958			43.5	13.8	6.1
1960	38.2	12.1	51.3	10.7	4.8
1962			43.4	10.9	4.6
1965			41.9	7.4	3.6
1967			37.3	6.0	2.7
1970	28.6	9.4	41.0	8.2	4.0
1973			36.5	7.6	3.7
1975			39.8	13.7	7.2

Source: Black and White Males, 1950–75, *Employment and Training Report of the President*, 1976, table A–20, p. 242; 1940 Census, *Characteristics of the Nonwhite Population by Race*, table 25, p. 82, and *The Labor Force*, table 4, p. 18; 1950 Census, *Nonwhite Population by Race*, table 10, p. 32; 1960 Census, *Nonwhite Population by Race*, table 33, p. 104; *Indian Unemployment Survey* (1963); Bureau of Indian Affairs, unpublished tabulation December, 1967; Bureau of Indian Affairs, "Estimates of Resident Indian Population and Labor Force Status by State and Reservation, March, 1973 and April, 1975" (mimeographed, 1973 and 1975).

* Data for Indians 1940–70 and blacks and whites in 1940 include those 14 years old and over; all other data include males 16 years old and over.

† The Bureau of Indian Affairs considers an individual who is not in school or working as unemployed whether the person is actually looking for a job or not. The Department of Labor, in its calculation of national unemployment rates, excludes persons who are not looking for work from the labor force.

Indian males were so classified in 1940 compared to 14 percent in 1970. The latter figure was nearly twice the percentage of black males employed in professional and managerial jobs.

Many of the Indian professionals are employed as school teachers, both on the reservations and in urban areas where a sizable proportion of the public school students are descendents of the first Americans.[4] Moreover, the Bureau of Indian Affairs and the Indian Health Service have made important gains in placing native Americans in relatively well-paid professional jobs. For example, in 1970 more than one-third of the professional positions in those agencies paying $8,000 or more per annum were held by Indians.[5]

MANPOWER UTILIZATION

The very low levels of Indian income are associated with unemployment rates several times those of non-Indians (see table 3). While the unemployment rates for blacks and whites fell sharply between 1940 and 1960, the rate for Indians rose 16 percent. This increase was chiefly a result of the great exodus of Indians from agriculture in search of better-paid employment. Since many of them lacked training and education, they were restricted to unskilled occupations with high rates of joblessness, particularly in reser-

4. However, only one-sixth of the teachers employed in reservation schools are Indian.

5. Sar A. Levitan and Barbara Hetrick, *Big Brothers Indian Programs: With Reservations* (New York: McGraw Hill, 1971), p. 12.

vation areas where there had been little industrialization.

That the Indian unemployment rate is far above acceptable levels is apparent in a comparison with the rate for males during the Great Depression, which reached 25 percent in 1933. Throughout the 1958–75 period the unemployment rate of reservation Indians was far higher. While the male unemployment rate on reservations has been somewhat lower from 1967–75 than from 1958–65, progress has been painfully slow. Furthermore the jobless rate of reservation Indians seems relatively insensitive to movements of the business cycle. While there was a decrease of more than 50 percent in the unemployment rates of white and black males from 1961 to 1967 (a period of increasing prosperity), the decrease for reservation Indians was only 25 percent. Similarly the relative rise in unemployment during the severe 1973–75 recession was only 10 percent for reservation Indians while the unemployment rates for blacks and whites nearly doubled (see table 3).

Nonreservation Indians have unemployment rates approximately 10 to 15 percent higher than blacks. Both populations are highly urbanized (with 70 percent of all blacks and over 90 percent of nonreservation Indians living in urban areas) and have roughly similar employment and income levels. Many of the reservation Indians, newly arrived in cities, have adjustment problems very similar to those of southern blacks who have migrated to a northern urban center.

Between 1950 and 1970 the unemployment rate for nonreservation Indians fell by nearly 40 percent in spite of a major migration from the reservation to urban areas. This reflects some tendency for migrants to enter cities with relatively tight labor markets.

On some reservations more than half of all males in the labor force are unemployed. Unemployment averaged 67 percent in 1975 among Indians in the Bethel, Alaska area, 78 percent on the Havasupai Reservation in Arizona, and 62 percent on the Ute Mountain Reservation in Utah and Colorado.[6] Jobless rates on most reservations are even higher during the winter when agricultural and other outside activities are at a low ebb.

RESERVATION DEVELOPMENT PROGRAMS

In order to accelerate economic development on the reservations and to provide urban Indians with economic opportunities the Bureau of Indian Affairs and other federal agencies have developed a variety of programs in the areas of manpower training, business and industrial development, and natural resource utilization. Programs in each of these three areas will be discussed in turn.

Manpower training

To ameliorate the problems of poverty and surplus labor on the reservations, the Bureau of Indian Affairs has established a variety of manpower programs which emphasize training and/or relocation of participants. These include direct employment (relocation), on-the-job training, adult vocational training, and the deployment of Indian action teams.

An Indian participating in the direct employment program is either

6. Bureau of Indian Affairs, "Estimates of Resident Indian Population and Labor Force status (16 years and over) by State and Reservation: April, 1975," mimeographed (1975).

placed in a job near the reservation or transported at government
expense to major western and mid-
western cities. He or she is found
employment and generally receives
BIA counseling and other follow-up
services for a year.

Many Indians prefer to remain on
the reservation regardless of the
economic consequences. The Indian Vocational Training Act au-
thorizes the Secretary of the Interior
to contract with private industry to
provide subsidized on the job training (OJT) for Indians 18 to 35 years
of age. Given the present minimum
wage of $2.30 per hour the BIA
pays $1.15 an hour subsidy while
the person is in training. This program not only provides reservation
Indians with a chance to learn a skill,
but through the training subsidy offers an inducement for businessmen
to locate factories on reservations.

Partly because of the concentration of Indians in unskilled and semiskilled positions, the BIA provides
a wide variety of advanced vocational training courses in schools
located within urban centers and
near reservations.[7] Upon comple-
tion of the vocational training course
the enrollee receives job placement
services. Between 1952 and 1975
nearly 150,000 reservation Indians
participated in these three BIA manpower programs.[8] The total level of
funding for these programs in 1975
was $35 million.

While benefit-cost studies[9] show

that these programs have raised the
income of the average participant
substantially, each program has been
plagued by a high dropout and/or
reservation returnee rate. Partly
because of the latter the BIA has
changed the emphasis of the direct
employment and adult vocational
training programs. For example, in
1968, only one-third of the job place-
ments were on or near the reservation with the remaining two-thirds
in urban locations. In 1975, nearly 75
percent of program participants
were found jobs on or near the reservations.[10] With placement close to
home, adjustment problems are less
severe, and the reservation employment assistance officer can maintain
contact with the program participant
and provide effective follow-up
services.

In order to expand employment
opportunities quickly on the reservations, a new training and employment concept has been developed
by the BIA—the Indian Action Team
Program. It provides funds to tribes
that train and employ Indians in construction work on reservations. Training is provided by the Indians themselves, who are generally BIA employees skilled in carpentry, plumb-
ing, bulldozer operation, and other
construction occupations. As the ap-
prentices become trained, they obtain jobs as foremen or supervisors
and in turn teach their skills to additional trainees on a part-time basis.
This program not only gives Indians
the responsibility for construction,
maintenance, and management of
reservation roads and buildings,
but provides them with the skills
necessary to accelerate reservation
development and improve the qual-

7. Bureau of Indian Affairs, "Employment
Assistance Programs" (Unpublished manuscript, 1972), p. 9.
8. Bureau of Indian Affairs, "Statistical
Summary of Activities From Inception of
Program through June 30, 1975" (Unpublished tabulation).
9. See Alan Sorkin, *American Indians and
Federal Aid* (Washington, D.C.: The Brookings Institution, 1971), pp. 104–35.

10. Bureau of Indian Affairs (Unpublished
tabulation, 1976).

TABLE 4

FACTORIES ON INDIAN RESERVATIONS AND TOTAL EMPLOYMENT BY FISCAL YEAR

YEAR	PLANTS ESTABLISHED	PLANTS CLOSED DOWN	TOTAL PLANTS IN OPERATION (END OF YEAR)	TOTAL EMPLOYMENT (END OF YEAR)	
				INDIAN	NON-INDIAN
1957–59	4	1	3	391	171
1960	3	0	6	525	156
1962	5	1	14	887	600
1964	14	7	25	1668	2286
1966	21	4	57	3044	3244
1968	36	3	110	4112	4365
1970	28	4	162	6443	7051
1972	37	1	225	7339	9093
1974	21	4	250	6173	9390

SOURCE: Data for 1957–68 from Bureau of Indian Affairs, "Summary Record of Plants Established as a Result of the Indian Industrial Development Program" (unpublished tabulation, 1968); Idem., "Summary of Plant Closings" (unpublished tabulation, 1968). Data for 1970–72 from Idem., "Employment in Industrial and Commercial Enterprises Established in Indian Labor Force Areas" (unpublished tabulation, 1972). Data for 1974 from Idem., "Employment in Industrial and Commercial Enterprises Established in Indian Labor Force Areas" (unpublished tabulation, 1974).

ity of reservation life.[11] In 1975 about half the reservations had Indian Action Team programs, their total cost coming to about $15 million.[12]

Between 1970 and 1975 the Department of Labor rapidly expanded the number of Indians enrolled in the national programs supported by that agency. During 1975, nearly 52,000 Indians participated in the manpower programs offered under the Comprehensive Employment and Training Act. About three-fourths were reservation Indians. Of the total about 56 percent were in work experience assignments, 18 percent in public service employment, 12 percent in classroom training and 10 percent in on-the-job-

training.[13] Job placement and drop-out rates were comparable to that of BIA programs.

In terms of manpower development there is clear overlap between BIA and Department of Labor Programs. It is imperative that these agencies strive to coordinate their programs and eliminate duplication of effort.

Business and industrial development

Industrial development of Indian reservations is a comparatively recent phenomenon. Prior to 1960 there were only four plants located on Indian land. The number of factories in operation and total employment are shown in table 4. The efforts of the BIA and the Economic Development Administration have

11. Helen Johnson, *American Indians in Transition* (Washington, D.C.: U.S. Department of Agriculture, Economic Research Service, report no. 283, April 1975), pp. 24–25.

12. Bureau of Indian Affairs, "List of Indian Action Team Contractors" (Unpublished tabulation, 1975).

13. U.S. Department of Labor and Department of Health Education and Welfare, *Employment and Training Report of the President, 1976* (Washington, D.C.: USGPO, 1976), p. 106.

succeeded in attracting an increasing number of enterprises; in 1974 there were 250 on the reservations.

As indicated in table 4 the industrial growth of Indian reservations proceeded swiftly from 1957–72, with the Indian labor force more than eight times greater in 1972 than it was a decade earlier. However, only 5 percent of the Indian labor force was employed in reservation factories during 1972. From 1972–74 Indian employment fell by one-sixth. The recession, which began in 1973, was primarily to blame for this situation. With many of these firms being marginal enterprises, a severe downturn in the national economy resulted in substantial layoffs among the Indian employees.

In recent years an increasing proportion of the workers in reservation factories have been non-Indian. This situation has occurred for two reasons. First, many of the expanding industrial plants have been located near the reservation boundaries. These firms recruit Indian workers residing on the reservations as well as non-Indians living elsewhere. Second, due to the high turnover and absenteeism of Indian employees, a few plants have found it necessary to reduce the number of Indians employed. For example, a manufacturer of styrofoam cups at the Gila River Reservation in Arizona claimed he had intended to hire only Indian labor, but found it too unstable and had to fill about half the work force with non-Indians. The manager stated that some Indians had quit and had been rehired ten times.[14] In a carpet mill located on the Crow Reservation in Montana, 60 percent of those Indians hired had quit within one year.[15] However, a large electronics plant on the Navajo Reservation reported that turnover had decreased from 8.8 percent in 1966 to 3.4 percent in 1971.[16]

Economic Development Administration programs

The Economic Development Administration (EDA) recognizes that one of the major barriers to industrial development is the lack of social overhead capital. Thus an important feature of the EDA program is grants of up to 50 percent for the costs of water, sewage disposal, and community building projects. In addition supplementary grants of up to 80 percent of project costs are permitted for distressed communities that have difficulty raising local matching funds.

The EDA also makes public works and business loans at below market interest rates. With regard to the latter, the borrower has 25 years to repay.

From 1966 to 1975 the EDA spent nearly $150 million on Indian reservations with the bulk of the funding for public works grants. Many of these grants have been utilized for the creation of industrial parks. For example in 1975 the Swinomish tribe in Washington received $313,000 for an industrial park and the Cherokee in Oklahoma received $196,000.

However, in spite of expenditures of nearly $150,000,000, including $17 million for industrial parks, not

14. Monroe E. Price and Reid P. Chambers, "The Role of the Interior Department in the Leasing of Indian Lands" (Unpublished paper, 1972), p. 117.

15. Bureau of Indian Affairs, Division of Employment Assistance, "Annual Statistical Summary, 1971," processed, p. 113.

16. Fay, *Employment Opportunities*, pp. 174–75.

more than 2,000 Indians are presently employed due to EDA efforts, including 1,213 working in industrial parks.[17] A 1975 survey indicated that of 3,487 acres of land available for plant sites in industrial parks, only 455 had been leased.[18]

Tribal assistance

Indian tribes provide several types of assistance to potential manufacturers. Tribal land is provided as an industrial site; and in many cases, a plant is built to employer specifications by the tribe at no cost to the firm. The building and grounds are leased to the company (Indian trust property cannot be sold to a non-Indian). These firms pay no property tax, because lands are held in trust by the federal government and treaties exempt them from this tax. Some tribes have provided capital by investing in industrial enterprises, with approximately $25 million being invested in 1971. The Indian Financing Act of 1974, which provided an additional $50 million[19] in guaranteed loans as well as subsidies to loans by private lenders, should stimulate an increase in commercial and industrial investment by the tribes.

The Indian Business Development Fund

The Indian Business Development Fund was initiated by the BIA in 1971 and received a 3.4 million dollar appropriation. The purpose of the program was to stimulate Indian entrepreneurship and employment by providing nonreimbursable capital grants to Indian individuals, tribes, and associations to establish Indian owned businesses. The IBDF grant was designed to provide the necessary equity financing to induce leaders to provide Indian business loans. The program has had enormous leverage in generating capital from customary lenders. Thus in 1971 nearly five dollars in loans was obtained for every dollar of grant money.[20]

During its first year of operation the program was quite successful generating over 3,000 Indian jobs at a cost of less than one-fourth the cost of EDA industrial development programs.[21] The program, in spite of its success, was suspended until 1974, when it was revived following passage of the Indian Financing Act. During 1975 it received an appropriation of $10 million.[22]

Agriculture

Three general categories of farming and ranching are significant sources of Indian income. Grazing which is the least intensive land usage, takes place on nearly 45 million acres of open and forest land; dry farming is practiced on 1.6 million acres, and 600,000 acres are irrigated.[23] Not only are large proportions of the most productive acreage

17. Economic Development Administration, "Indian Industrial Parks Funded by EDA" (Unpublished tabulation, January, 1976).

18. Ibid.

19. Levitan and Johnston, *Big Brothers Indian Programs*, p. 33.

20. Bureau of Indian Affairs, "Indian Business Development Fund: A Briefing Report," processed (April 1972), p. 4.

21. Bureau of Indian Affairs, "Indian Business Development Fund: A Briefing Report," processed (April 1972), p. 11.

22. Interview with Gordon Evans, Bureau of Indian Affairs, July 20, 1976. A 1972 survey indicates that there are 773 Indian-owned businesses employing 5,819 native Americans.

23. Levitan and Johnston, *Big Brothers Indian Programs*, p. 21.

leased to non-Indians, but the returns per acre are smaller on Indian operated farms than reservation farms owned or operated by non-Indians. Thus the dollar return per acre on grazing land is $2 for Indians and $6 for non-Indians; for row crops $96 per acre for Indians and $192 for non-Indians; and for hay, $38 per acre for Indians and $50 for non-Indians.[24]

In addition to poorer land quality, there are several reasons for lower productivity on Indian farms. One problem is that Indian management of farms tends to be inefficient. Poor planning and negligent care reduce Indian crop and livestock yields, in part because of inadequate education and technical assistance, but also because most tribes do not have agricultural traditions and have not adapted readily to farming and ranching. It is unfortunate that vocational agriculture was removed from the curriculum of Indian schools nearly 20 years ago.

Besides these problems of management, most Indians lack sufficient capital to make the investments in machinery, feed, fertilizer, and buildings that are necessary for efficient agriculture. Although the BIA operates a revolving farm loan fund, the level of appropriation is completely inadequate. About $12 million was available in 1973, while needs for agriculture were estimated at more than $89 million.[25]

In addition many Indian landholders are too small to be efficient. The chief obstacle to reallocating land in tracts of economic size is

that land ownership has become quite fractionated over the years owing to the cumulative effects of the 1887 allotment act. This law provided that the federal government must hold land in trust for all heirs of deceased land owners, rather than assign it to one person or subdivide it. As a result, only two-fifths of allotted Indian lands have only one owner, and 17 percent have 11 or more.

Federal efforts to improve Indian agricultural productivity range from technical assistance in soil and water conservation to range management and legal assistance in the consolidation of divided landholdings. The most important efforts in terms of economic potential are irrigation projects. With 600,000 acres presently irrigated, the BIA estimated that another 400,000 could be profitably supplied with water. In 1973, the BIA spent $1.6 million on maintenance of irrigation systems and $16.8 million for the construction of new facilities, $10.2 million of which was earmarked for the large Navajo irrigation project in New Mexico.

Minerals

In recent years, most of the income from minerals has come from oil and gas leases, with much smaller revenues accruing from coal, asbestos, phosphate, uranium, vanadium, and copper. Mineral income is very unequally distributed with about nine reservations receiving 85 percent of the royalties from oil and gas.[26]

It is possible that Indian tribes will receive increasing income from mineral deposits. Recent energy

24. Ibid., p. 22.
25. U.S. Congress, House, Committee on Appropriations, *Department of the Interior and Related Agencies for 1975*, pt. 4, 93rd Cong., 2nd sess., (Washington, D.C.: USGPO, 1973), pp. 244–45.

26. Levitan and Johnston, *Big Brothers Indian Programs*, p. 27.

shortages have intensified the search for fuel reserves, and the BIA has proposed a comprehensive survey of Indian mineral resources.

URBAN INDIAN DEVELOPMENT

Since the end of World War II more than 300,000 reservation Indians have left their communities and settled primarily in urban areas. In the cities they find adjustment difficult because of language problems, alien customs, and poor housing. In the last several years, about 80 Indian centers have been established to assist in finding jobs, housing, and social services provided by federal, state, and local government.[27] One of the major

27. Johnson, *American Indians in Transition*, p. 25.

adjustment problems of urban indians results from their breaking of ties with both their Indian communities and the BIA.

An urban Indian project in Minneapolis–St. Paul, where nearly 10,000 Indians reside, focuses on improving Indian access to health facilities and services. With financial assistance from the Indian Health Service, the Indian Health Board of Minneapolis was established. It is a nonprofit corporation made up of 21 Indian organizations to determine what health resources are available and how to use them. Both state and county health departments have cooperated in the project. By taking the initiative, Indians in this Minneapolis project have located the individuals and groups who are able to solve some of the health problems of Indians living there.

ANNALS, AAPSS, **436**, Mar. 1978

Indian Education Since 1960

By ROBERT J. HAVIGHURST

ABSTRACT: Since 1960 there has been a growing policy of Indian self-determination in the field of education of Indian youth. Two major federal government laws have put money behind this policy—The Indian Education Act (1972) and the Indian Self-Determination and Educational Assistance Act (1975). This leads to a policy of local self-determination for Indian tribes and Indian communities, and to greater responsibility of Indians as teachers and administrators. During this same period there has been a rapid expansion of the number of Indian students in college, most of them aided by government scholarship funds. There has also been a growth of schools on reservations, which are operated by local native school boards, with government funds.

There remains the question of the basic goal of the education of Indian youth—assimilation into the Anglo society or separate economic and social activity, based on tribal culture and tradition. Some form of cultural pluralism will be worked out, located between these two poles. The American Indian Policy Review Commission, established by Congress for the 1975–77 period, has recommended a maximum of self-determination for Indians in their economic, social, and educational life. For the next 20 years, it appears that the Indian tribes and communities will be finding their places in a permissive American society. However, the fact that more and more Indians are moving to large cities and trying to find a place in urban society, will tend to favor a degree of assimilation in the mainstream of economic and social life.

An especially important and significant situation is provided by the Alaska Native Land Claims Settlement, which gives Alaskan Eskimos, Aleuts, and Indians a relatively large amount of money and land in return for the oil and minerals

...id land which has been and will be taken by the Anglo economy. Here, in contrast to nineteenth century dealings between the United States government and Indian tribes, the native Americans are receiving a fairly large amount of money and property, which goes to them as members of native corporations, or regional resident groups. What forms of personal and village or communal life will emerge from this situation?

Professor Robert J. Havighurst has been Professor of Education and Human Development at the University of Chicago since 1941. He has specialized in research in human development and behavior in a variety of societies, and at all age levels. His own research activities have combined methods of sociology, social anthropology, psychology, and education. Between 1942 and 1950, he devoted much of his time to studying the development of Indian children in six tribes of the Southwest and the Dakotas. From 1968 to 1971 he was Director of the National Study of Indian Education, financed by the U.S. Office of Education. Field work for this project was carried on by teams from seven universities studying 26 Indian communities and 39 schools.

THE EDUCATIONAL experience of American Indians saw greater change and greater growth in the period from 1960 to 1977 than had occurred in any earlier period. An official government policy of assimilation of Indians into the mainstream of American culture was changed to a policy of cultural pluralism.

Already, during the New Deal days of the 1930s, Congress had passed the Indian Reorganization Act, and John Collier, Commissioner of Indian Affairs, had worked effectively to increase the power of Indian tribes to govern themselves. Their elected tribal councils were given more powers of local self-government. Many more day schools on reservations were introduced, and they were expected to replace boarding schools. But educational change was at first slow to come. And there was a reaction in Congress against government economic assistance to Indian tribes during the 1950s, which resulted in termination of several reservations, including the relatively large and economically valuable Klamath and Menominee Reservations, a policy aimed to "get the government out of the Indian business." This closing of reservations and division of tribal property among the individual members of the tribe was aimed to encourage Indians to merge into the broader society.

Most Indian leaders and Indian tribes wanted self-determination, as tribes, but did not want to give up the rights and privileges they had in their tax-exempt reservation land. They looked to the new President, John F. Kennedy, who assumed office in 1960 for assistance. The Secretary of the Interior, Stewart Udall, in 1961 appointed a Task Force to advise him on Indian policy.

This was followed in 1966 by a White House Task Force on Indian Affairs, appointed by President Johnson. At that time Senator George McGovern of South Dakota introduced a concurrent resolution in the Congress which stressed a policy of Indian self-determination and economic development. In March 1968, President Johnson sent a message to Congress on Indian Affairs which stressed the government's policy of supporting a stronger Indian voice in Indian affairs, directed the Bureau of Indian Affairs (BIA) to establish school boards at all federal schools, and created a National Commission on Indian Opportunity made up of Indian leaders. At this time the United States Senate appointed a Special Subcommittee on Indian Education, headed by Senator Robert Kennedy, and later by Senator Edward Kennedy. This committee had hearings for 18 months and issued a report urging increased Indian control over education.

Meanwhile, other events and publications relating to Indian affairs were going on: The American Indian Chicago Conference published *The Voice of the American Indian: Declaration of Indian Purpose* (Chicago: University of Chicago Press, 1961); The Commission on Rights, Liberties, and Responsibilities of the American Indian, financed by the Fund for the Republic, of the Ford Foundation produced a report entitled *A Program for Indian Citizens* in 1961; and A National Study of Indian Education, financed by the U.S. Office of Education, directed by Professor Robert J. Havighurst of the University of Chicago, and involving teams from seven universities studying 26 Indian communities and 39 schools, was conducted from 1968 through 1970.

The 1970 Presidential Message on Indian Affairs

The almost complete official acceptance of a policy of self-determination was laid out in detail in President Nixon's message to Congress on July 8, 1970. Before this date there had been much action by individual tribes in their negotiations with the Bureau of Indian Affairs. Most thoroughgoing was the series of contracts made by the Zuni Tribe of New Mexico earlier in 1970, which empowered the tribe to administer all the programs formerly operated by the Bureau of Indian Affairs. The President's Message commences with such general statements as: "It is long past time that the Indian policies of the Federal Government began to recognize and build upon the capacities and insights of the Indian people." The main points of the Message are:

—The Indian tribes should have self-determination over their own affairs without termination of their reservation status and their tribal unity. The Indian tribes should have the right to control and operate federal programs, including schools;
—The federal government should assist financially in projects for economic development of Indian groups;
—A substantial increase in funding of the U.S. Public Health Service for Indians should be made; and
—Assistance to urban Indians through the operation of service centers in major cities should be forthcoming.

The Commissioners of Indian Affairs, who directed the Bureau of Indian Affairs, under Presidents Johnson and his successors were for the first time Indians: Robert Bennett, a member of the Oneida Tribe; Louis R. Bruce, Mohawk-Sioux; Morris Thompson, Athabascan from Alaska; and Forrest Gerrard, Blackfeet.

Cultural pluralism as the basic policy

Education of Indians since 1965 has been powerfully influenced by the broad policy, known as cultural pluralism, which has dominated American interethnic relations. More in the limelight have been the forces working for recognition of the rights and privileges of the two largest ethnic groups—the blacks and the Spanish-origin people. There has also been a rising chorus of voices of European ethnic groups from the east and south of Europe—the Poles, Slavs, Italians, and Greeks. These movements have been antagonistic toward the melting pot ideal which would reduce ethnic differences in America. They have advocated, instead, cultural pluralism, which has three principal characteristics:

1. Mutual respect and appreciation for each cultural group by other groups.
2. Collaboration in government and economic affairs of the country.
3. Self-determination in all matters of importance, as far as possible, and without infringing the rights of other groups.

On a line extending from the extreme of the melting pot at one end and ethnic separatism at the other end, cultural pluralism falls somewhere toward the middle, with the exact location depending on the wishes of the people of a given group, and some assessment on their part of the advantages and the disadvantages of one or another position on the line.

The educational program wanted by a particular ethnic subgroup depends on the solution it works out for itself on the scale of cultural pluralism. Most cultural subgroups have differences of opinion and differences of interest within their ranks with respect to the most desirable solution. There generally is a trade-off between income and economic advantages on the one side, and close harmony of ethnic identity on the other side. The principal issues and problems with respect to education for native Americans lie in their efforts to work out a viable position on the cultural pluralism continuum.

STATUS OF NATIVE AMERICAN EDUCATION AS OF 1970–78

Since 1960 there has been a rapid growth of school and college enrollments of Indian youth, together with tentative movements toward greater initiative and responsibility by Indian communities for the administration of their schools. An example of what this policy signified to a responsible Indian leader is given in the following statement by the former Tribal Chairman of the Northern Cheyenne, Mr. John Woodenlegs, in 1970:

For over a year I have spent most of my time working on education, serving as a member of the National Indian Education Advisory Committee, as an education field worker for the American Association on Indian Affairs, as a member of one public school board, and an ex-officio member of an advisory school board.

Our goals have been:
1. To educate our schools and the local communities to the idea of community

schools, serving the needs of the local people over and above daily education of children.

2. To encourage parents to be more concerned and involved with the schools, including active membership on school boards.

3. To help teachers get more knowledge of the Cheyennes, their past history and culture and present life.

4. To encourage Cheyenne resource people to go into classrooms to talk on history and culture.

We feel our children need education which gives the best of both cultures. We feel that many of the values of our past Cheyenne society can still serve us well in this modern world. We feel we need this to give us understanding and pride in our past, just as other Americans learn their history for the same reason.[1]

Types of schools attended by Indian youth

In 1978 there are about 275,000 Indians aged 6–17, inclusive, and about 90 percent of them are enrolled in school. There are four categories or types of schools. Except for the first category, these are not official and there are no official data on the numbers of students, but they can be estimated with reasonable accuracy. The types, with numbers of Indian pupils, are:[2]

	Enrollment	Percent of Total Group
A. Schools with practically all-Indian enrollment:	47,000	17
BIA-operated boarding and day schools; Indian-Controlled School Boards:		
Contract with BIA (estimated)	2,500	1
Mission or other private schools	9,000	3
Public schools operating on or contiguous to reservations	30,000	11
B. Public Schools with 50 to 90 percent Indian enrollment:		
Contiguous to Indian reservations or in native communities	105,000	38
C. Public schools with 10 to 50 percent Indian enrollment:		
Mainly in rural communities and small cities	50,000	18
D. Public schools with 1 to 10 percent Indian enrollment:		
Mainly in large cities	30,000	11

Thus the educational picture is very complicated. But one thing should be clear. Practically all native Americans between the ages of 6 and 17 inclusive have access to schools and attend schools almost as fully, in terms of proportions attending school by age, as do the

1. Estelle Fuchs and Robert J. Havighurst, *To Live on This Earth: American Indian Education* (Garden City, N.Y.: Doubleday, 1972), p. 20.

2. Here and elsewhere in this article we include Alaskan Eskimos and Aleuts in the numbers, and sometimes we speak of native Americans to remind ourselves that we do include approximately 7,000 Aleuts,

Anglos, the Spanish descent groups, and the blacks. The proportion of Indians who graduate from high school is smaller than the proportion of all American students, but this is more a matter of socioeconomic status than of ethnicity, and the proportion of Indians graduating from high school is approximately the same as the proportions of other ethnic groups which have a similar socioeconomic or income composition.

School achievement and mental ability of Indian youth

On standard tests of school achievement, Indian pupils fall below national averages, as a group. Starting with the third grade, Indian pupils achieve at a level about one year below national averages; and they achieve about two years below national averages at the senior high school ages. This relatively low academic achievement is not because Indian children are less intelligent than white children. Several studies based on intelligence tests which do not require reading ability show Indian children to be at or slightly above the level of white children.

For example, on the Goodenough Draw-a-Man Intelligence Test, which is a test of mental alertness that does not require language facility, Indian children show about the same level of achievement as white children. The 1,700 Indian children who took this test in 1969 under the auspices of the National Study of American Indian Educa-

tion showed an average IQ of 101.5, which is slightly superior to the average of white children. On the Grace Arthur Performance Test of Intelligence (a battery of nonverbal tests), in a study made in 1942, a representative sample of Indian pupils from six tribes showed an average IQ score of 100.2. As part of the latter study, a group of 30 Sioux pupils on the Pine Ridge Reservation showed an average IQ score of 102.8, but the same group, tested a year later with the Kuhlmann-Anderson, a verbal test requiring reading ability, showed an average IQ score of 82.5.[3]

There is abundant evidence that the school achievement of children depends to a large extent on their experience in their family and their local community or neighborhood. If their parents read widely, read to them, use large vocabularies while conversing at home, take them to museums, provide children's encyclopedias in the home, and set examples of educated behavior, the children will generally follow in their footsteps. On the other hand, if the parents do not read or read very little, do not speak English, do not use complex sentences or express themselves in complicated ways, their children are likely to be slow in learning to read English and consequently retarded in the other school subjects. They are even more likely to achieve poorly in school if they live in a community or neighborhood characterized by poverty.

Teachers of Indian pupils

Since the majority of Indian pupils attend public schools with white

28,000 Eskimos, and 16,000 Indians, in Alaska, from the 1970 census. This is especially important, from the point of view of cultural pluralism, since these three groups have very different cultures and languages. The Eskimos and Indians have a number of different tribes or subgroups.

3. Fuchs and Havighurst, *To Live on This Earth*, chaps, 4 and 5.

pupils and are taught in classes with white children, both groups have the same teachers. These are probably a cross-section of teachers in the small cities and rural parts of the country west of the Mississippi, and a similar cross-section of teachers in the 20 or more big cities that have relatively large Indian populations.

However, the schools operated by the Bureau of Indian Affairs have about 1,800 teachers who have passed a federal civil service examination and have been assigned to BIA schools. The BIA made a study of its teachers in 1968, from which the following facts are drawn. There were 1,772 teachers, 61 percent women. Among the teachers, 15 percent were Indian. Salaries in 1968 ranged from $6,176 to $15,119, depending on amount of training, standing in university class, and amount of teacher experience. These teachers are on duty for 12 months, with the three summer months taken up with in-service education, student home visits, preparation for the following year, and vacation. Employment in Alaska is accompanied by a 25 percent cost of living supplement.

Indian teachers tend to stay longer in service than non-Indians. It is likely that substantially more Indians will seek teaching jobs, both in BIA schools and in local public schools, as their numbers of college graduates increase. Of school administrators in BIA schools, 28 percent are Indian.

Postsecondary education of Indians

There has been a very rapid increase in the numbers of Indian youth who enter a university and who finish a four-year course. Before about 1960, the number who

completed high school was small, and most of them did not go on to college. A substantial fraction went into a one- to two-year vocational training program such as that of the Haskell Institute, maintained by the Bureau of Indian Affairs at Lawrence, Kansas. The Institute provided secretarial and trade training, and its graduates had a good record of employment.

After 1960, larger proportions of Indian youth began to attend postsecondary institutions. This proportion probably multiplied fivefold between 1960 and 1970. Approximately 8,000 Indian students were in universities or postsecondary colleges in 1970. This constituted about 12 percent of the number in the Indian age group from 18 through 21. At that date, about 35 percent of an age group finished secondary school, 20 percent entered a university level institution and another 10 percent entered a postsecondary institution for vocational training; and 5 percent graduated from universities with a bachelor's degree based on four years of study. These are all rather high figures, compared with other American groups with low family incomes. A major reason was the availability of money to help pay for this kind of education—money provided both by the federal government and by a number of tribal councils. The BIA in 1969 awarded scholarship grants to 3,432 young people, with an average of $868 per student. By 1975 the number of scholarship awards had increased to 15,000 with an average of $1,750 per student. In that year there were 1,497 graduates from four-year colleges who had received BIA scholarships. Of this number, 335 had been trained for teaching, and 198 for health service work. The BIA had a record of 48 Indian studies programs in as many colleges and universities in 1971. The following institutions all had fifty or more Indian students per year in the period 1966–70: University of Alaska, Northern Arizona University (Flagstaff), Fort Lewis College (Colorado), University of New Mexico, Phoenix (Arizona) Community College, Pembroke State University (North Carolina), University of Montana, Northern Montana College, Central Washington State College, Northeastern State College of Oklahoma, Brigham Young University (Utah), and the Navaho Community College.

The Navaho Community College is a creation of the Navaho tribe, and is not supported financially by the federal government. Founded in 1968, the College has been built amid sage brush, pinon and juniper trees on the arid Arizona landscape, with the Lukachukai Mountains in the background. Navaho Community College accepts and recognizes the reality of and the persistence of Indian culture and institutions. It holds that uniquely Indian values, skills, and insights are highly functional in the modern world today, and, just as Indian knowledge contributed to the survival of European settlers in the New World, so today, Indians have much to contribute to the survival of American and world society. Navaho Community College is based upon the assumption that not only is it possible for Navahos to direct and control their own institutions, but that this is the only way they ever will be able to assume total responsibility and self-support, at least as a group.

The College is ruled by a Board of Regents consisting of ten Navahos, one from each of the five administrative areas of the Reservation, two members elected at large and ap-

pointed by the Tribal Chairman, and three members ex officio: the chairman of the tribe, the chairman of the Navaho Education Committee, and the president of the college student body. The Indian faculty members have organized a Curriculum Committee to search out and formulate a Navaho philosophy of education, in which the present and future are rooted in the values of the traditional past. Ned A. Hatathli, first president of the College, said,

If we can blend these and come up with a philosophy this would be a stepping stone for the Navaho tribe. There is something good in Navaho values, in their way of rearing children. The Navaho have existed for centuries and we have seen the growth of the people. Medicine men, the elders, are helping us search for the things that have sustained the Navaho.[4]

A further impetus to higher education for Indians came in 1976, when $500,000 was provided for 50 fellowships for students who had been accepted for professional study by universities. This money comes from the Indian Education Act, and has been allocated for the academic year of 1976–77 to cover tuition costs and subsistence for students who have been accepted for programs in engineering, law, medicine, business, forestry, and fields related to one of these areas. The fellowships will be continued for four years of study for successful students.

CONTEMPORARY EDUCATIONAL ISSUES

Early in the 1970s, the federal government provided funds which would assist native Americans to re-

4. Ibid., p. 288.

form and direct their educational systems. The Indian Education Act of 1972 and its successor, the Indian Self-Determination and Educational Assistance Act of 1975 provide money and require Indian direction and Indian responsibility for the design of program. The Bilingual Education Act, part of the Elementary and Secondary Education Act since 1967, provides funds for the employment of teaching staff who speak the local home language in Indian and Eskimo communities.

The Indian community is itself divided on the kind of education it wants for Indian youth, recognizing that Indian-oriented education is central to the establishment and maintenance of a viable cultural pluralism. The two extremes of assimilation and separatism have their proponents. For example, an exchange between Robert A. Manners and John Collier was published in the journal *Indigena*, which enabled Manners to state forcefully the case for assimilation. He wrote: "The aim should be not to protect the American Indians against the risks to which most white members of our society are subject, but to elevate them to a status and a competence in which they are equipped to face those risks with the same chances of 'success' as the whites. . . ." We should "provide the Indian with the tools he will need for voluntary assimilation."[5]

At the opposite pole, we have strong Indian voices arguing against "Anglo-conformity," and for Indian self-determination. One of the most eloquent was that of Clyde Warrior,

a Ponca living in Oklahoma, and President of the National Indian Youth Council, speaking in 1967:

Perhaps, the National Indian Youth Council's real criticism is against a structure created by bureaucratic administrators who are caught in this American myth that all people assimilate into American society, that economics dictates assimilation and integration. From the experience of the National Indian Youth Council, and in reality, we cannot emphasize and recommend strongly enough the fact that no one integrates and disappears into American society. What ethnic groups do is not integrate into American society and economy individually, but enter into the mainstream of American society as a people, and in particular as communities of people. The solution to Indian poverty is not "government programs" but in the competence of the person and his people. The real solution to poverty is encouraging the competence of the community as a whole.

[The] National Indian Youth Council recommends for "openers" that to really give these people "the poor, the dispossessed, the Indians," complete freedom and responsibility is to let it become a reality, not a much-heard-about dream and let the poor decide for once, what is best for themselves. . . .[6]

In another vein, there is a growing number of Indian and Eskimo teachers who are teaching in native communities where the home language is not English and where there is a local community desire to preserve the traditional way of life, including the language. The writer experienced this directly when teaching at the University of Alaska, where some Eskimo village school teachers were working for a University degree. For them, an

5. Robert A. Manners and John Collier, "Pluralism and the American Indian," in *The North American Indians: A Sourcebook*, eds. Roger C. Owen, James J. F. Deetz, and Anthony D. Fisher (New York: Macmillan, 1967).

6. Alvin M. Josephy, Jr., ed., *Red Power: The American Indians Fight for Freedom* (New York: American Heritage Press, 1971), p. 77.

Eskimo language was essential as the language of instruction in the village school, and as a means of preserving and maintaining the Eskimo culture. They, personally, had been subjected to an Anglo-dominated educational program, with the problems that arose from having teachers who did not understand their language or their culture.

Self-determination of educational program as the dominant policy

In 1975 the Congress created the American Indian Policy Review Commission and instructed it to formulate a perspective on the status of American Indians in the United States. The Commission made its final report in the summer of 1977. The five Indian leaders and six members of Congress on the Commission were:

Indian Commissioners
John Borbridge, Jr., Tlingit-Haida
Louis Bruce, Mohawk, Oglala Sioux
Ada Deer, Menominee
Adolph Dial, Lumbee
Jake Whitecrow, Quapaw,
  Seneca-Cayuga

Members of Congress
James Abourezk, South Dakota
Lloyd Meeds, Washington
Lee Metcalf, Montana
Mark O. Hatfield, Oregon
Sidney R. Yates, Illinois
Sam Steiger, Arizona

The work of the Commission was done by eleven task forces, including one on Indian education, which consisted of four Indian educators and staff members.

The Commission recommended that all government-aided Indian programs should be brought together under a federal Indian Department or independent agency, reporting to the Office of the President. The Congress should enact legislation that would aid tribal governments and Indian communities to take responsibility for control of education in accordance with their desires. Among other objectives is that of recruiting and training Indians to serve as teachers in practically all schools with a predominantly Indian enrollment.

Initiative has already been taken by several hundred Indian organizations which have sought and received money from the federal government for educational programs. For example, under the Indian Education Act and for fiscal year 1976, approximately $18 million was given to school and tribal education projects in the form of 210 separate grants, aimed to supplement existing education programs and to train Indian personnel for work in the schools.

This amplifies the program which was started in the late 1960s, whereby the Bureau of Indian Affairs contracted with a local Indian school board on a reservation to give the money that would have gone to pay expenses of a BIA-operated school to the Indian Board which would take responsibility for the school. The first and best-known of these contract schools is the Rough Rock School on the Navaho Reservation. This school is governed by a five-person school board, all Navahos, with only one having any schooling. The school starts teaching in the Navaho language, and devotes a good deal of attention to Navaho tradition and Navaho arts. John Dick, one of the first school board members, said:

We want our children to be proud of being Navajos. We want them to know who they are. . . . In the future they will have to be able to make many choices and do many different things. They need a modern education to make their way, but they have to know both worlds—and being Navajo will give them strength.[7]

By 1975 there were 15 of these Indian-contracted school boards, which had banded together into a Coalition of Indian Controlled School Boards.

The Alaska native land claims and education

December 18, 1971 marked the most comprehensive and favorable legal settlement of native people's claims to land and its resources yet seen—the Alaska Native Claims Settlement Act. The educational implications and results of this Act have profound significance for Alaskan natives and for the question of the viability of a policy of cultural pluralism for Indians.

Here, for the first time, very large economic resources are placed in the hands of native people with very few external controls over the way they use those resources. The United States Congress recognized the right of Alaskan natives to land and mineral resources, restored 40 million acres of land to native ownership, and promised to pay $962.5 million for land taken over by the state and federal governments. There are approximately 55,000 Eskimos, Aleuts, and Indians living in Alaska, and another 20,000 living outside of Alaska, having one-fourth or more Alaska Indian, Aleut, or Eskimo ancestry. As of the date of passage of the Act, there were approximately 76,500 "Alaskan natives" of all ages entitled to equal shares of the land and money. These

people as individuals will not receive large money grants. Over the 20-year period from 1971 to 1991, most of them will receive less than $1,500 apiece. The valuable thing they receive is 100 shares in one of 12 Native Regional Corporations which take title to the land and which keep for investment purposes 90 percent of the money paid under the Act. Also, the Regional Corporations must distribute almost half of their income to some 200 native villages which will form corporations to select land, possibly invest money, or use money income to provide services to village residents.

The Regional Corporations were formed as quickly as possible after the passage of the Act, and have been using the approximately $200 million they received from the government in the first five years to invest in productive enterprises such as hotels, supermarkets, mineral exploration, reindeer herds, and fish canneries. The stock in the Regional Corporations cannot be sold in the market until 1991, 20 years after the passage of the Act. At that time, the youngest stock holder will be 20 years old (having been born on or before the day of the passage of the Act by Congress). The money value of the stock will then depend on the investment experience of the corporations, just as it does for any other business corporation. Since every Indian, Aleut, and Eskimo in Alaska has become a "capitalist" by virtue of the Act, there will be a need to understand this complicated process. One educational consequence has been the publication of a high school textbook, *Alaska Native Land Claims*, by economist-educator Robert D. Arnold, sponsored by the Alaska Native Foundation.

Educational effects of the Act are

7. Fuchs and Havighurst, *To Live on This Earth*, p. 253.

already seen in the training of employees of the Regional and Village Corporations, in the Corporations' selection of officers who have some business or technological experience or training. Several vocational schools have come into existence — such as the school at Barrow, farthest north settlement in the United States, and capital city of the Arctic Slope Regional Corporation. Furthermore, an Eskimo university, Inupiaq University, was founded at Barrow, to serve as a kind of community college, with representatives in a dozen villages on the Arctic Slope. Correspondence courses are offered for those who cannot get to classes.

Informed opinion is divided concerning the educational consequences of the Land Claims Settlement. Some say they will result inevitably in the assimilation of the Alaska native people into the economic and cultural mainstream. Others say that the Eskimo culture, with its emphasis on community action and cooperation, will be active in the form of a cooperative society culture, and that the Eskimo language will be kept alive in the villages, which will not grow very much because life in them requires hunting, fishing, and adjustment to the arctic climate, a life style which few Anglos will choose.

In the upper Yukon River region, inhabited by Athabaskan Indians, the Tanana Chiefs Conference is an organization of tribal leaders with headquarters at Tanana, on the Yukon. They have organized two educational projects in response to the Land Claims Act. One is the Tanana Chiefs Land Claims College, to help villagers work effectively with the resources of the Act; the other is the Tanana Chiefs Survival School, aimed at working for the maintenance of the Athabaskan culture.

Bilingual programs and issues

The Bilingual Education Act has a major application in Indian education. It emphasizes the use of the child's home language in his learning to read. Since he already has a speaking vocabulary in his home language, he can learn to read this language without the difficulty of having to learn a new vocabulary at the same time. This sensible procedure has been used with Navaho children, where there has been a Navaho orthography (set of signs for the sounds of the language) for some years, and children's books have been printed in Navaho. With this method, Navaho pupils can progress in reading as rapidly as Anglo pupils can. Soon after entering school, Navaho students start to learn English as a second language, just as Anglo pupils might commence to study Spanish or French in the elementary school. The goal of this method is to teach reading efficiently, and, at the same time, enable the pupil to see that his home language is of value in the school.

For Indian children who speak English at home, the tribal language is treated as a second language to be learned after the pupil has been using English in the school. This has as its basic aim the teaching of respect and familiarity with the native culture and tradition. In an English-speaking community, bilingual education means having bilingual teachers who accept whatever language the child seems to prefer and who will begin a program of the native language, as a second language, when students are nine or ten years old. On the other hand, if the native language predominates in the local community, a bilingual program tends to emphasize English in the school after children have reached the age of nine or ten.

Courses in Indian history and culture

Nearly everybody working in the field of Indian education favors the study of Indian history and culture in the elementary school and junior high school curriculum. This is thought to be effective in promoting mutual understanding and appreciation of the various native cultures by the bearers of the various cultures. However, there are some problems.

Where there is primary concern for helping Indian youth to understand and appreciate their own tribal history and culture, reading material that deals explicitly with the local tribe, if the tribe maintains a collection of such materials, as many Indian tribes do, is of great importance. Such material can be supplemented by bringing pupils into contact with elders of the tribe, who can tell stories and exhibit crafts which they have practiced. This may be called the "ethnocentric approach" to teaching the local history and culture. In schools where the Indian pupils are in a majority this approach turns out well, especially if native teachers, who are increasing in numbers, are in charge.

However, there is a serious problem of teaching general Indian history and cultures accurately and with enough detail to make the material interesting and effective with respect to "understanding and appreciation" for Anglo pupils and for the wide variety of native American tribes. Very few history or social studies text books for use in the mid-

dle school grades or the high school give accurate and balanced information. The National Study of American Indian Education commented as follows:

. . . One author, after examining more than a hundred history texts, concluded that the American Indians have been obliterated, defamed, disparaged, and disembodied. The notion of the blood-curdling, perilous, massacring savage is common[8]

The writing and production of scrupulously honest textbooks are of prime importance.

The 1977 frontier of Indian education

We have noted that approximately 30 percent of Indian youth are in schools where they are in the minority—often a small minority. There is no likelihood that this proportion will decrease; it will probably increase. Whether these young people become Indian-Americans or mainstream Americans will depend somewhat on the quality of the education they experience. The Indian Education Act makes money available for educational programs in such communities. Whether the local school board tries to do anything for these youth, as Indians, will depend largely upon initiative taken by Indian adults and others who are interested in cultural pluralism.

With respect to the 70 percent of Indian youth in communities where Indians are the largest cultural group, Indians are gaining greater control over programs and policies. They will have to decide how far the schools should go in pushing Indian youth toward assimilation into the dominant culture. They will

8. Ibid., p. 216.

have to decide how the native languages should be treated in the schools, and how much attention should be given to the history and culture of Indians and of the local tribe.

The policy of the federal government, and the policies of state and local school districts, will be to maintain schools which encourage freedom of choice for Indians. This is stated clearly in the 1975 Indian Self-Determination and Educational Assistance Act. That is, Indian tribes and Indian individuals will be encouraged to make the decisions that determine their future, supported somewhat better than they have been in the past by the wider society in which they live.

ANNALS, AAPSS, **436**, Mar. 1978

Religion Among American Indians

By MURRAY L. WAX AND ROSALIE H. WAX

ABSTRACT: The traditional worldview of North American Indians is outlined as a basis for explicating the central tribal ceremonials and for comprehending the tribal response to prolonged missionization from Christian denominations. The missionaries operated in a context of authoritarian superiority, and most conceived of themselves as bearing civilization, rather than a plain scriptural message; hence, there was little concern to modify Euro-Christianity to fit with native rituals and values. Today, most Indians are Christians, at least nominally; but, in many cases, the Christianity is integrated with the native worldview, and the individual participates in a variety of both Christian and neotraditional rituals. The destructive impact of the European invasions stimulated millenarian movements, such as the Ghost Dance; the continued vitality of these movements was expressed in the recent occupation of Wounded Knee, which should be comprehended as a religious, rather than a political, action. The Peyote Cult, organized as the Native American Church, constitutes a syncretism of Christian and traditional rites and attitudes, and it is widespread as intertribal and pan-Indian. Further pan-Indian, neotraditional, revivalistic, and millenarian movements may be anticipated.

Murray L. Wax and Rosalie H. Wax are professors in the Departments of Sociology and Anthropology, Washington University at St. Louis. Together, they have performed major field research projects with the Oglala Sioux of Pine Ridge and the Tribal Cherokee of eastern Oklahoma; they have also worked with various other tribal and national Indian groupings. Their joint fieldwork and Rosalie Wax's work earlier in the relocation centers where the Japanese-Americans were confined during World War II are described frankly in her book Doing Fieldwork: Warnings and Advice *(University of Chicago Press). In addition to the area of religion, magic, and worldview, their interests also include the study of education and the ethical and methodological problems of fieldwork.*

SUCCESSIVELY, we discuss traditional worldview and ceremonials, Christian missionization,
the consequent religious system
upon a modern Plains reservation,
Indian millenarianism, and the Peyote cult. The reader is reminded
that the traditional religious system
of any one tribe, such as the Navajo,
Iroquois, or Pawnee, could easily require several monographs for eluci-
dation; the modern system of such a
tribe could require another several.
Restricted, as we are, to the brief
compass of this essay, we must omit,
compress, and cite selectively. If the
several pieces of the essay do not
fit together as neatly as we should
like, and if our coverage of religious
matters is far from complete, this but
reflects the diversity among tribal
groups, the heterogeneity within
what were once religiously and culturally homogeneous communities,
and the overall complexity of the
subject matter.

We have tended to illustrate and
develop our arguments from among
the tribal groups we know best, because it is for those that we can make
the most accurate judgments as to
the reliability and significance of the
ethnohistorical and ethnographic
sources. In particular, we refer most
often to the Oglala Sioux (or Teton
Dakota) of the Pine Ridge Reservation, while making occasional references to the Pawnee and to the
Cherokee. We believe that this con-
sistency of focus will help the
reader, even though we realize that
the resultant coverage is less than
encyclopedic. While details of religious systems have varied and continue to vary among the tribes of
North America, nonetheless kindred
social and religious processes have
been at work during the years, and
we hope that our presentation will
have the virtue of exhibiting common themes.

TRADITIONAL WORLDVIEW AND RELIGIOUS CEREMONIALS

As viewed by the traditional Indian, the world was composed of a
variety of sentient beings who were
responsive socially and emotionally
to the conduct of humans. Unlike the
scientistic Western vision, which
perceives man as if he were part of
a system of molecular structures
amidst a universe of other such structures, all governed by abstract laws
of physical reaction, the Indian view
was of a world inhabited by beings.
The Lakota word, *oyate*, seems to
designate "people," but "includes
not only man but each blade of
grass and leaf and living creature on
this earth." Thus, as the Buffalo Virgin Calf instructed the Sioux, when
she gave them the sacred pipe, "All
these people and all these things are
joined to you who smoke the pipe—
all send their voices to Wakan Tanka.
When you pray with this pipe, you
pray for and with everything."[1]
"Everything" could include, not
only living things—plants and animals—but even rocks and other en-
tities which modern Western man
considers as inanimate, that is without soul or spirit.

The myths, or holy tales, of the
Pawnee depict the animals as if they
were different tribes of human beings. When a human hero en-
counters an animal, the two may con-
verse, share a pipe, perform a ritual,
or engage in a contest. If the hero
and the animal are of opposite sex,
they may marry, establish a household, and have children. Several
Pawnee stories describe how human

1. Joseph Epes Brown, ed., *The Sacred
Pipe: Black Elk's Account of the Seven Rites
of the Oglala Sioux* (Baltimore, Md: Penguin
Books, 1972), pp. 6–7; Gayla Twiss, "The
Role of the Pipe in Dakota Religion," *Pine
Ridge Research Bulletin*, no. 10 (August
1969), p. 11.

beings came to hunt the buffalo (bison); this is never presented as a technological achievement (involving horses, bows and arrows, or guns), but as a social treaty arising from such adventures as a marriage between a human and a buffalo cow, followed by a ritual contest between the human and the protagonists of the buffalo people:

A witch-woman and her grandson live on the prairie. Although he is a great hunter, she is a cannibal and prefers the delicate flesh of human beings. The buffalo are angered at this slaughter of man, and they send two young cows to lure the boy to them so that they might kill him. When the trio reach the herd, the boy finds them all hostile, except for one wise chief who knows that he has acted at the behest of his grandmother and has not himself partaken of human flesh. There are now contests between the boy, aided by a small friendly faction of buffalo, and the hostile majority. The magic and strength of the boy and his helpers prove the more potent: he can blow smoke higher; he can drink more; and he can run faster.

Enraged by their defeat, the hostile faction attacks the boy, but his grandmother and her dogs now come to his aid. She tastes buffalo meat and finds it superior to human. They separate: she going north, bearing seeds and agricultural implements; he going south to become a warrior.

The buffalo hold a great council: "The people will live and they will kill many buffalo and eat of our meat. . . . In all things we were beaten by the boy. In smoking the boy beat us; so the people will do the smoking, and they will send us only whiffs of smoke.

In drinking of the water from the pond, the boy was given horns to help him drink the water; so from this time the people shall make spoons from our horns, and eat with them. . . ."[2]

The various tribes (or species) of beings, and the different individuals among them, each may possess distinctive kinds of power. (In Shakespearian English, it would have been spoken of as virtue, an inherent power or efficacy, as in a phrase such as "a medicine of great virtue.") In many North American myths, beaver and loons were thought to have great therapeutic powers, while eagles had great powers of vision, mice had powers for stealth and concealment, and so on. Such powers were not a simple by-product of physiology, but were sustained by ritual and could be transferred from being to being. Thus, many tribes, especially of the Plains, had a Vision Quest, in which an individual would isolate himself, perhaps on a hilltop, where he would fast and pray for as many as four days and nights; in some cases he would mutilate or scarify himself. If he were fortunate, he would experience a vision; and, if he were especially fortunate, in the vision he would encounter a being who would become a spiritual helper, granting him some particular kind of power that might assist him in warfare, or healing, or gambling, or love. By such a vision, a great runner might have acquired power from horses or wolves; a person gifted at finding lost objects might have acquired power from eagles or hawks; while a great buffalo hunter might have acquired from that species the gift of calling them and bringing a herd to himself.[3]

3. Descriptions of *hanble ceya* ("crying for a dream"), the ritual of crying for a vision among the Oglala Sioux, may be found in Stephen E. Feraca, *Wakinyan: Contemporary Teton Dakota Religion*, Studies in Plains Anthropology and History, no. 2 (Browning, Montana: Museum of the Plains Indian, 1963), pp. 20–25; also in Brown, *The Sacred Pipe* pp. 44–66. Feraca has read this manuscript and noted several errors, which we have corrected; we are grateful to him for his coun-

2. Condensed from "The Cannibal Witch and the Boy Who Conquered the Buffalo," in *The Pawnee: Mythology*, ed. George A. Dorsey (Washington, D.C.: Carnegie Institution, publication no. 59, 1906), pp. 72–82.

To modern Americans, the foregoing depiction of an animate world with a dynamic of power may sound mystic, and there may be a tendency to associate power with the more dramatic and unusual of natural events. In opposition to this view, it should be emphasized that for the traditional Indian, any variety of prosperity or success was a manifestation of some particular kind of power: a healthy birth; a successful hunt; a profitable war party; a winning streak at gambling; a good harvest. Good health and vitality were manifestations of power; illness and weakness were signs of the absence of power, or that some being was directing its power against one's self. Consequently, therapy was not a matter of readjusting the homeostatic equilibrium of the biochemical organism, but a matter of reestablishing harmonious relationships between the afflicted person and the human and other beings of his environment (note the comments about the RedBird Smith movement among the Cherokee).

The conceptual fashions and developments of the 1960s have in some ways assisted the communication of this traditional worldview, but in other ways they have muddied Western perceptions. Thus, the emphasis upon altering or expanding consciousness, or upon "finding the self," whether through drugs or rituals, misdirects our attention. The young man on a Vision Quest was not seeking to enlarge his consciousness; he sought a vision in order to establish a relationship that would confer power; and he sought power because only by possessing power could he become an adult of stature

and respect. The man (or woman) who vowed to participate in the Sun Dance, and who then prayed, fasted, danced, and tortured him (or her) self during the several days of its performance, would be seeking to restore or maintain health and prosperity to family and kin.

The theology of this traditional world is addressed to the notion of maintaining a proper balance and harmony among its beings and powers. Thus, many peoples had great annual ceremonials which were designed to replicate—or move the world toward—the organization that it was given by the deities cosmogenically. From the revered Pawnee priest, Running Scout, Dorsey collected a poetic account of the creation, with similarities to the opening paragraphs of Genesis:

In the beginning was Tirawahut (the Universe-and-Everything-Inside); and the chief in Tirawahut was Tirawa, the All-Powerful, and his spouse was Atira (Vault-of-the-Sky). Around them sat the gods in council. Then Tirawa told them where they should stand. . . .

Each of you gods I am to station in the heavens; and each of you shall receive certain powers from me, for I am about to create people who shall be like myself. They shall be under your care. I will give them your land to live upon, and with your assistance they shall be cared for. You (pointing to Sakuru, the Sun) shall stand in the east. You shall give light, and warmth, to all beings and to earth. . . . Teuperekata, Bright-Star (Evening Star), you shall stand in the west. You shall be known as Mother of all things; for through you all beings shall be created.

After the gods are assigned their stations and duties, the earth and its beings are created by the joint activity of the gods under the leadership of Tirawa, and first man and first woman set upon it. They multiply and the people number many vil-

---

sel, while occasionally deviating from his interpretations of contemporary religions among the Oglala Sioux.

lages. Eventually, almost all the villages are called together for a great ceremony led by the priests:

Mother Bright-Star told this man that now they were to hold a ceremony in imitation of Tirawa, when he first made up his mind to make earth, people, and animals to live on the earth; that the gods who sat in council with him had been given certain stations in the heavens; that each of these bundles was to be dedicated to those certain gods, stars in the heavens; and that in this ceremony they were to have the same relative positions as the gods in the heavens, who had given them the bundles. . . .

And so the people replicate the great actions of creation.[4]

This tale, concerns, not merely blessings (or magical power), which culture heroes have received from divine and other beings, but the proper, harmonious structure or pattern of the universe, most strikingly illustrated by Tirawa's stationing of the stellar deities. Narrowly conceived, the purpose of the rite is the symbolic recreation of the situation described in the myth, where the hero obtained magical power, so that ritual participants may now be blessed, as was he. Broadly conceived, as might a philosophically minded Pawnee, the purpose is to recreate a desirable pattern of relationships among the beings of the universe—human, divine, and other —so that each may give to the others. In an unpublished manuscript Dorsey, himself, interpreted all Skidi Pawnee ceremonies as having a significance much like the broader one we have inferred from his data: "In theory the Skidi Pawnee ceremonies all have as their object the performance either through

drama or through ritual of the acts which were performed in the mythological age."[5]

To Dorsey's words, we would add only that "performance" must not be understood as if it were imitation or commemoration but rather as re-presentation. The performance is not a play-acting of a past, it is the re-creation now of the harmonious order of the universe.[6]

CHRISTIAN MISSIONIZATION

From the sixteenth century, when the Spanish brought Roman Catholic missionaries into the Caribbean, until the present date, the Indians of North America have been the repeated target of Christian missions. Catholic missionaries accompanied the Spanish into Mexico and New Mexico, where they proselytized the Pueblo peoples; they also accompanied the French explorers, traders, and trappers into northeastern North America, up the St. Lawrence River and across the Great Lakes onto the prairies. Russian missionaries of Greek Orthodox faith labored among the Indians and Eskimo of Alaska, until it was purchased by the United States. Moravians, Methodists, and Baptists were working among the tribes of the Southeast early in the nineteenth century. And more recent decades have seen intensive efforts by the Church of Latter Day Saints, Seventh Day Adventists, and Pentecostal sects.

In general, the missionaries bore an ethnic self-confidence of such magnitude as to constitute arro-

4. George A. Dorsey, ed., *Traditions of the Skidi Pawnee*, Memoirs of the American Folk-Lore Society, vol. VIII, (Boston, Mass.: Houghton-Mifflin, 1904), pp. 1–12.

5. Cited in Ralph Linton, "The Origins of the Skidi Sacrifice to the Morning Star," *American Anthropologist*, vol. 28 (1956), p. 457.
6. Cf. Murray L. Wax and Rosalie H. Wax, "The Magical World View," *Journal for the Scientific Study of Religion*, vol. I, no. 2 (Spring 1962), pp. 179–88.

gance. They felt that they were dealing with a people who were not only pagan, but inferior to such degree that they had totally to be transformed. As Stephen Riggs, the Sioux missionary was to write in 1846:

As tribes and nations the Indians must perish and live only as men! With this impression of the tendency of God's purposes as they are being developed year after year, I would labor to prepare them to fall in with Christian civilization that is destined to cover the earth.[7]

With this attitude it is not surprising, but nonetheless noteworthy, that after 36 years of work among the Cherokee, none of the missionaries of the American Board was capable in 1851 of preaching in that native language.[8]

This gulf in status and authority—and therefore in culture and language—between missionary and missionized made it difficult for Christianity to be ethnically modified and adapted, as it had been for example, during the prolonged medieval missionization of northern Europe. It also increased the likelihood that, as nationalistic tendencies reemerged among Indians, they would be expressed in revitalizations of traditional religions, rather than in "reformations" and other revisions or purifications of the Christian gospel. (Note that Deloria, who was trained in a Christian seminary, and whose family has closely been associated with Christian denominations, has come to reject Christianity and to advocate a return to traditional Indian beliefs.)[9]

The relationship between the missionaries and the federal government continued to be close for many years, and in 1865 the government contracted with the missionary societies for the maintenance of schools for teaching agricultural and mechanical arts to Indians. To eliminate denominational competition, the various Indian agencies were allocated exclusively among the missionary societies (with the exception of the Catholics). Thus in 1870, the Pawnee, Omaha, Winnebago, and other Nebraska tribes were under the jurisdiction of the Hicksite Friends (Quakers); the Yakima, Skokomish, Quinault, and other northwestern tribes under the Methodists; and RedCloud's band of Sioux under the Episcopalians.[10]

Originally, the Catholic Church had been indifferent to the plans of the federal government for containing and assimilating the Indians, but when its missionaries found themselves excluded from Indian territories it was not slow to respond. The Sioux had long been exposed to Catholic missionaries, and Red-Cloud was discontented with the relationship the federal government had established for his band with the Episcopalians. He kept pressuring the Indian agents to admit "the Black Robes." Meanwhile the Board of Indian Commissioners—Protestant in its composition and ideologically committed to tolerance—became in 1881 the recipient of a Presbyterian memorial asking that "Indians be granted the same religious liberty which we claim for ourselves.[11] So it was that in 1888 the Jesuits were able to establish a mis-

7. Cited in Robert F. Berkhofer, Jr., Salvation and the Savage: An Analysis of Protestant Missions and American Indian Response, 1787–1862 (Lexington: University of Kentucky Press, 1965), p. 7.

8. Ibid., p. 49.

9. Vine Deloria, Jr., God Is Red (New York: Dell, 1973).

10. Henry E. Fritz, The Movement for Indian Assimilation, 1860–1890 (Philadelphia, Pa.: University of Pennsylvania Press), pp. 56; 76–79.

11. Ibid., p. 103.

sion on the Pine Ridge Reservation. (Nevertheless, tolerance was confined to Christian denominations, and indigenous rituals, such as the Sun Dance, were long under federal ban. While public revival of the Sun Dance may be dated to the 1930s, it was not until 1959 that the piercing rituals were publicly reinstituted.)

The Jesuits of Pine Ridge included scholars who devoted themselves to the conscientious study of the Lakota language and Siouan traditions. Initially, their interest was evangelical and they dismissed traditional rituals as heathen and therefore to be extirpated. But, by the mid-1960s some of the Fathers had become ethnologically more sophisticated and religiously more catholic. Thus, Paul Steinmetz advocated the transformation of the Sacred Pipe into "a Christian prayer instrument," and he spoke of the Pipe reverently as "a type of Christ because it is the instrument of the mediator in the Sioux Religion."[12] So deep was the break between himself and the earlier generation of Jesuits that he encountered resistance from the more devout among his parishioners, "there will be good Catholic Indians who will not want to accept the Pipe because it has been condemned by some Fathers,"[13] but he felt confident enough to develop a liturgy for the Pipe. Even so, his proposal remains quite conservative in that the Pipe does not have in his service the central and symbolic role which it has in either the traditional Sioux rituals or some Plains versions of the modern Peyote Cult. Rather, during the service which Steinmetz

outlines, the Pipe is used in gesture and movement, but it is not communally smoked. He suggests that, if the Pipe is to be smoked—and passed from person to person as in traditional rituals—that this be done at the conclusion of the prayers, when it becomes a part of the social aspect of Holy Communion. With these qualifications, we may note that, not only among the Jesuits of the Catholic Church, but also among Protestant missionaries, there has been a recent movement toward reevaluating the native practices of exotic peoples, rather than dismissing them all as "heathen." This reorientation has come to affect the attitude toward such Plains ceremonials as the Sun Dance, and the observer will now encounter Christian ministers willing to bless its participants, whilst more fundamentalist evangelicals denounce them as engaging in pagan and heathen rites.

A MODERN PLAINS RESERVATION

Pine Ridge, South Dakota, is representative in many ways of Plains Indian reservations. Except for the congestion of the Agency town, the Indian population of about 10,000 people is thinly scattered across an area approximately the size of the state of Connecticut. Natural resources are modest, and the population is characterized by poverty, underemployment, unemployment, and a variety of related problems. Although the Sioux have been missionized for decades and their children enrolled in schools where English is the sole accepted language, nonetheless Lakota remains the primary domestic and communal language for many persons and English is a foreign language, which only a minority handle with skill and comfort. (Lakota is the Siouan dialect

12. Paul Steinmetz, "Explanation of the Sacred Pipe as a Prayer Instrument," *Pine Ridge Research Bulletin*, no. 10 (August 1969), p. 20.
13. Ibid., p. 21.

TABLE 1

PRIMARY RELIGIOUS AFFILIATION OF INDIANS
OF PINE RIDGE, BY PERCENTAGE
OF INDIAN BLOOD

DENOMINATION	PERCENT FULLBLOOD	PERCENT MIXEDBLOOD
Episcopalian	47	27
Roman Catholic	33	58
Presbyterian	11	6
Body of Christ	3	1
Latter Day Saints	1	0.4
Other	5	7.6
Total	100	100

spoken by the Oglala of Pine Ridge.)[14]

In the late 1960s a baseline data survey was conducted on Pine Ridge. Fullblood Oglalas comprised 45.6 percent, mixedblood Oglalas comprised 48.7 percent, and Indians from other tribes 5.6 percent of the total Indian population. The survey also inquired as to membership or affiliation with religious denominations.[15] In percent, the findings are shown in table I. Other denominations together with percentage of reservation adherents include: Native American Church (0.8 percent), Seventh Day Adventists (0.6 per-

cent), Church of God (0.4 percent), Lutheran (0.3 percent), Gospel Missionary Union (0.3 percent), Congregational (0.3 percent), Methodist (0.2 percent), and Baptists (0.1 percent).

These figures of denominational membership would not look out of place for many other small towns of mid-America. Nevertheless, Pine Ridge is in fact very different from non-Indian communities of mid-America. While less than one percent of Indians list the Native American Church (Peyote cult) as their primary religious affiliation, nevertheless, 11 percent of fullbloods and 6 percent of mixedbloods acknowledge attending its meetings. And, while no figures were obtained as to attendance at the great Sun Dances, sponsored annually by the Oglala Sioux Tribal Government during the late 1960s, the count would have numbered several thousands. Also, many families who consider themselves members in good standing of Christian denominations, nonetheless participate in the small cultic ceremonials known usually and generally as *yuwipi*. And, in addition, there are many other cults or ceremonials, and corresponding types of shamans, medicinemen, or holymen, or other initiates.[16]

14. Descriptions of the Pine Ridge Reservation, as of the 1960s, may be found in Eileen Maynard and Gayla Twiss, *That These People May Live: Conditions among the Oglala Sioux of the Pine Ridge Reservation* (Pine Ridge, S.D.: Indian Health Service, U.S. Public Health Service, 1969); also in Murray L. Wax, Rosalie H. Wax, and Robert V. Dumont, *Formal Education in an American Indian Community*, Monograph #1, Society for the Study of Social Problems, Supplement to *Social Problems*, vol. XI, no. 4 (1964), especially chaps. 2 and 3.

15. The baseline data survey was reported in a number of issues of the *Pine Ridge Research Bulletin*, and in Maynard and Twiss, *That These People May Live*. Of special utility here is the anonymous essay, "Some Denominational Preferences among the Oglalas" in *Pine Ridge Research Bulletin*, no. 10 (August 1969), pp. 1–6.

16. In addition to the ceremonials already mentioned—*wiwanyank wacipi* ("sun gazing as they dance"), the Sundance; the *yuwipi* and *wanbli* rituals; and *hanble ceya*, the vision quest—there are *inikagapi*, the rite of purification via the sweat lodge; *išna ta awi ča lowan*, puberty rite at menarche; *šunkwaci*, horse dance; and others. Sacred to the entire Sioux nation is Ptehincala Canunpa, the Buffalo Virgin Calf Pipe, held in trust by a shaman on the Cheyenne River Reservation; it has not been displayed nor used publicly for some time. Among priests and practitioners, there are *wicaša wakan*, holy man; *wapiye wicaša*, doctor man; *pejuta wicaša*, medicine man; *pejuta winyela*, medicine woman; as well as

Between February and May of
1973, a group of Indians, mainly
Sioux, and variously affiliated with
the American Indian Movement
(AIM), occupied and assumed politi-
cal-military control over the hamlet
of Wounded Knee. Their activities
were opposed by the recognized
tribal government and by the Nixon
administration. There were great
shows of force on both sides, some
casualties, and much coverage in the
mass media. The incident has come to
be known as Wounded Knee II, in
commemoration of the terrible slaughter inflicted upon the Sioux in the
same locale in 1890. In retrospect, it is
hard to take WK-II seriously as a
pragmatic political act, and it is noteworthy that in the next election to
the Oglala Sioux Tribal executive,
AIM spokesman Russell Means
could not secure a majority of the
vote. Nevertheless, one should not
underestimate WK-II as a symbolic
statement or religious ceremonial.
Indians from all over North America
made pilgrimages to the besieged
camp at Wounded Knee, bringing
gifts and blessings. Medicinemen
are known to have journeyed with
their sacred bundles through the en-
trenchments in order to perform rites
which they had not otherwise thought
appropriate in modern times. For
many Indians, at that moment in
time, Wounded Knee had become
the locus of an epiphany.[17]

the shamans who perform *wanbli* (*wanbli
wapiye*). For further details on the above,
consult Feraca, *Wakinyan* and Brown, *The
Sacred Pipe.*

17. A portrait of Wounded Knee-II may be
found in Vine Deloria, Jr., *Behind the Trail
of Broken Treaties: An Indian Declaration of
Independence* (New York: Dell, 1974). See
also, Philip D. Roos *et al.*, "The Impact of
the American Indian Movement on the Pine
Ridge Reservation," (Paper delivered at the
annual meetings of the Society for the Study
of Social Problems, 1977).

MILLENARIANISM

The 1890 massacre at Wounded
Knee was precipitated by the spread
to the Sioux of the Ghost Dance movement. Originating with a prophet
among the Northern Paiute, the
Ghost Dance swept like a prairie
fire across the Plains, bringing to Indians a message of hope and trans-
figuration. Once lords of the Plains,
proud and untrammeled horse-no-
mads, their needs supplied from
their great hunts of the buffalo, the
Plains tribes in a few decades had
been decimated by disease, emaci-
ated by starvation, and confined to
idleness in reservation settings under alien and authoritarian governance. Traditional religious ceremonials had appeared useless to cope
with the new disasters; only too often the revered possessors of sacred
lore had gone to their deaths without
being able to transmit their skills and
rituals to the next generation.

The Ghost Dance was but one of a
number of movements that have affected various of the North American
tribes. Its prophet, Wovoka, preached
that the world would be returned to
its state prior to the coming of the
Whites and that the dead Indians
and vanished game would reappear.
Associated with his message were
various rituals, especially a round
dance which, when performed, led
some of the participants to lose consciousness and journey spiritually to
the land of the dead, where they encountered their ancestors and the
ecological conditions of their childhood.[18]

Some observers believed that the

18. There have been many studies and anal-
yses of the Ghost Dance, but the fullest ethno-
graphic account was given in 1896 by James
Mooney and is reprinted now as *The Ghost-
Dance Religion and Wounded Knee* (N.Y.:
Dover, 1973).

Ghost Dance movement had ceased with the Wounded Knee massacre. But, 40 years later, Alexander Lesser found the Ghost Dance cult was still influential among the Pawnee.[19] Alice Kehoe, working among Canadian Dakota during the 1960s found remnants of its cult.[20] Whether or not the movement still persists among the Oglala is a matter for argumentation. Among the older generation, there are many who cherish the hope for the return of the Black Hills. Several decades ago, such hopes might have been classified as millenarian, especially when held tenaciously by a people without funds, political power, or legal skills. Yet in an age when tribes elsewhere are having success with a court suit over rights to much of the real estate of Maine, there is a genuine question as to how to categorize the hopes for the return of the Black Hills. For some Sioux who are highly assimilated to non-Indian culture, that return would simply constitute an heirship claim, representing a cash payment for a swindle performed upon their ancestors; but for many Sioux of traditional attitudes, the Black Hills constitute a sacred symbol of the vitality of the Sioux people and of their relationship to the larger universe.

Among the Tribal Cherokee of eastern Oklahoma, a kindred type of vision persists: the resurrection of the sovereign and independent Cherokee nation. Such a nation existed from the time of their removal from the southeast (under the presidency of Andrew Jackson) until the turn of the century, when Congress forcibly dissolved it. The dissolution and the accompanying division of the Cherokee lands, with their allotment in severalty, represented catastrophe for the Tribal (or fullblood) Cherokee. In these hours of tribulation, a spiritual leader, RedBird Smith, directed their attention to the traditional Cherokee way—the white path of harmony—and rekindled the fires of the stompground for the Nighthawk Cult.[21] As of 1963, there were in eastern Oklahoma six functioning Nighthawk stomp grounds, each a cultic center for a local fullblood community. (There were also 42 churches in the Cherokee Indian Baptist Association, 9 Cherokee Methodist Churches, 3 Cherokee-Creek Baptist Churches, and 3 other Cherokee churches, each of these also functioning as a cultic center for a local Cherokee-speaking community.)[22] Explicitly for the Nighthawk Cult, but also for many of the members of the Christian churches, the restoration of the sovereign Cherokee nation remains a cherished goal. To the typical outsider who observes the extent of the intrusion into Cherokee lands of the Whites and their governmental agencies, the hope for a revived sovereignty must appear millenialist and utopian. Nevertheless, it is precisely the restoration of sovereignty of Indian tribes and nations that is intrinsic to much of contemporary Indian nationalism (as manifested in AIM and in the writings of such spokesmen as Vine Deloria, Jr.)

19. Alexander Lesser, *The Pawnee Ghost Dance Hand Game*, Columbia University Contributions to Anthropology, vol. XVI, (New York: Columbia University Press, 1933), pp. 1–337.

20. Alice B. Kehoe, "The Ghost Dance Religion in Saskatchewan, Canada," *Plains Anthropologist*, pt. 1(1968), pp. 13–42.

21. Robert K. Thomas, "The Origin and Development of the RedBird Smith Movement" (M.A. thesis, University of Arizona, 1954).

22. Albert Wahrhaftig, "The Tribal Cherokee Population of Eastern Oklahoma," *Current Anthropology*, vol. IX, no. 5 (December 1968), pp. 510–18.

THE PEYOTE CULT[23]

For centuries peyote has been used sacramentally by the peoples of Middle America. Like the wine in the communion chalice of the Christian Eucharist, its status is freighted with symbolism, emotion, and tradition. The Huichol Indians of Mexico annually perform a lengthy pilgrimage in order to gather peyote for their ritual use.[24] Plains Indians will perform individual pilgrimages to the regions where it is found and will recite prayers on encountering the first specimen. Thus peyote is no more to be interpreted in terms of its biochemical composition than is the wine in the chalice. For its communicants, peyote is a beneficient and potent deity, capable of healing and of conferring a variety of blessings and benefits.

Among North American Indians, the cult developed during the past century. It can especially be found among the tribes who were native to the southern plains during the nineteenth century and were then settled in western Oklahoma. But the cult has spread widely throughout the West, from the Winnebago of the Great Lakes to the Paiute of the Great Basin, and from the Arapaho of the northern Plains to the Navajo of the Southwest. It seems evident that the cult took root among these peoples as they lost their more traditional religious practices during the latter half of the nineteenth century and the earlier part of the present century. While there are significant differences between the cults as practices by the Huichol and by

Plains Indians, there are notable similarities, such as the journey or pilgrimage for peyote, the nighttime ceremonial, and the presence in the morning meal of corn (maize).

Peyote grows wild in the Rio Grande River valley and southwestward. *Lophophora williamsii* is a small, carrot-shaped cactus whose top is harvested to become the "peyote button" that will be ingested. Chemically, the button is complex and contains a variety of alkaloids, some with effects like strychnine and others with effects like mescaline. The taste is bitter, and even habituees may be subject to vomiting. A variety of effects seem to follow digestion. Excitement and exhilaration are followed by alterations in the sense of time and by optical visions such as brilliance of colors, and auditory hallucinations. The toxic effects seem minor, and the plant is not addictive.

The spread of peyote among North American Indians coincided with the Prohibition movement, and peyote became the subject of religious and governmental attacks. The accusations were based more upon fantasy than on knowledge, but legislation against the consumption of peyote was introduced in both the Congress and some state legislatures. Partly in an effort to accommodate the sacramental usage to Euro-American religious traditions, and to provide themselves with the religious protections of the federal constitution, some Indians began a process of formal organization. In 1914, the "First-born Church of Christ" was organized under the laws of Oklahoma. Since strong Christian elements pervade the Plains ritual, the title was not a misnomer; but, nevertheless, many peyotists were uncomfortable about it, and, within a few years, some organized them-

23. The principal source for this section is Weston La Barre, *The Peyote Cult*, 4th ed., enl. (New York: Schocken Books, 1975).
24. Fernando Benitez, *In the Magic Land of Peyote*, trans. John Upton (New York: Warner Books, 1968).

selves as the Native American Church (NAC). That title, which symbolizes the intertribal and aboriginal nature of the cult, has proved more popular and durable. The church has since been established and incorporated in a number of states, but the general organizational structure is congregational and federal rather than bureaucratic and centralized; or, to be more exact, the structure is loose and decentralized in the fashion characteristic of Plains or intertribal associations. (It may be illuminating to compare the discussion by Gerlach and Hine of the strength and resilience of a similar type of anarchic or decentralized structure in the cases of the Pentecostal and Black Power movements.)[25]

Typically, the religious service of an NAC group begins on Saturday night and continues until Sunday morning. For Plains Indians, the location may be a tipi; for Navajo, a hogan; but in practice, the service can be held anywhere so long as there is space for a central altar, including a fire (or coals), about which the participants will be seated. At midnight and dawn there are ceremonies involving water; and, in the morning, there is a ritual breakfast which will include corn (maize), fruit, and boneless meat. During the service, peyote is passed among the communicants, and in the Plains ritual, each usually consumes at least four buttons. Likewise a water-drum and other ritual paraphernalia are passed about the circle, and in turn each person sings four peyote songs, while accompanied on the drum by the person on his right. The service

may vary, depending upon the tribe and the leader. In some cases there may be a sermon; and in some cases there may be reading from the Bible, which is present in the central altar.[26]

In addition to the services beginning on Saturday night, others may be held on holidays, or at times of stress or illness, or to express gratitude or thanksgiving for a special event like the birth of a healthy child. Whether among Mexican or North American Indians, doctoring (healing) is a major rationale for a cultic ceremony, and peyote is regarded as a powerful therapist. Among Plains Indians, services will also be sponsored for the purposes of securing a vision that will confer blessings and power upon the supplicant.

CONCLUSION

We began this essay with a review of traditional religious worldview and ceremonials. These ceremonials were an aspect of the integration of community and tribe. Belief was not an issue, and participation flowed from membership in the tribe and its voluntary associations (medicine societies). Centuries of missionization and of intercourse with a variety of non-Indian peoples have fractured this religious and cultural unity. A tribal unit of 10,000 persons now contains a multiplicity of denominations and of cultic practices, some mutually consistent, others mutually inconsistent. Moreover,

25. Luther P. Gerlach and Virginia H. Hine, *People, Power, Change: Movements of Social Transformation* (Indianapolis, Ind.: Bobbs-Merrill, 1970).

26. An informal but accurate account of a peyote service with an intertribal composition, held on the Navajo Reservation, can be found in Peter Nabokov, "The Peyote Road" reprinted in *Solving "The Indian Problem,"* eds. Murray L. Wax and Robert W. Buchanan (New York: New Viewpoints, 1975), pp. 197–210.

there has also been the emergence of intertribal, yet distinctively Indian, religions such as the Native American Church.[27] The major directions of change seem to be toward millenarianism—as expressed in a drive to reclaim lands and regain sovereignty—and toward reviving or revitalizing traditional cults. Christian denominations also are moving toward a more catholic recognition of the virtues of the traditional cults and ceremonials.

27. For a discussion of these issues see Murray L. Wax, *Indian Americans: Unity and Diversity* (Englewood Cliffs, N.J.: Prentice-Hall, 1971).

ANNALS, AAPSS, **436**, Mar. 1978

Hippocrates Was A Medicine Man: The Health Care Of Native Americans In The Twentieth Century

By Patricia D. Mail

ABSTRACT: The provision of health and medical care to American Indians and Alaska Natives has undergone major changes in the 150 years during which the federal government has assumed responsibility for these services. Significant legislation leading to present programs and directions is reviewed to place current programs in the perspective of historic evolution. The changing patterns of disease indicate that Indian health status is rapidly approaching that of the Western world, with a reduction in infectious diseases and an increase in psychosocial problems and chronic conditions. In order to provide quality health care under isolated, rural conditions, the Indian Health Service is exploring innovative uses of paraprofessionals and the application of modern space technology to primary care settings.

Patricia D. Mail is a Public Health Educator and Community Health Representative (CHR) Coordinator with the U.S. Public Health Service, Indian Health Service. She holds a Masters in Public Health from Yale University, an M.S. degree from Smith College, and an M.A. degree in Anthropology from the University of Arizona. She is currently working with Indians of the Pacific Northwest, and has had experience with the Papago and Apache peoples in Arizona. She teaches a course in cross-cultural counseling as a part of Seattle University's Alcohol Studies Program, and is an advisory board member for the Seattle Indian Alcohol Program.

40

THE health of the Native American is a complex and many-sided realm. The roots of Indian health practice are lost in antiquity, and the present delivery of health and medical care involves, in some instances, the most modern space technology. Some concepts about Indian health belong to the contemporary folklore, such as the stereotype of the "drunken Indian," which reflects a widely held belief that Indian people are somehow different and cannot drink like normal people. Yet recent research has suggested that this is not the case.[1] Other elements in Indian health are still largely unexplored, such as the understanding of the success of native practitioners and ceremonials. And with this is the mostly Indian-transmitted knowledge of power and the persistence of native belief systems. Indian health is a rapidly changing, politically impacted, and culturally important field. Very briefly, an overview of its many dimensions will be considered.

STEPS TO THE PRESENT

The provision of medical care to native peoples was, at one time, an empirically refined and exclusively practiced art independent of Western man. Native practitioners were called by many names, but all strove to maintain and promote the well-being of individuals and to maintain their native societies. Armed with an extensive pharmacopoeia[2] and considerable faith, they endeavored to minister to the needs of people in both a physical and mental environment.

Indian health today is largely dependent on Western-trained practitioners and the vagaries of politicians. The transition between independence and dependence is a long and intricate history, interwoven with the history of the gradual domination of Indian peoples by the relentless European westward migration.

When Indian land had been secured and reservations established, treaties provided for minimal medical care in the person of a "physician to reside at said central agency, who shall furnish medicine and advice to their sick, and shall vaccinate them."[3] On the Great Plains, the War Department became involved in the administration of medical services to Indians largely to protect American soldiers from infectious diseases. Congress authorized the appropriation of monies to vaccinate against smallpox in 1832. In 1849, the responsibility for Indian health was transferred, along with other Indian concerns, to the newly created Bureau of Indian Affairs, Department of the Interior. Medical care for Indians passed from military to civilian control.[4] In 1954, the responsibility for Indian health was

1. L. Bennion and T. Li, "Alcohol metabolism in American Indians and Whites," *New England Journal of Medicine*, vol. 294, no. 1 (1 January 1976), pp. 9–13. J. H. Leland, *Firewater Myths*, Monograph no. 11 (Rutgers Center for Alcohol Studies, 1976). J. E. Levy and S. J. Kunitz, *Indian Drinking* (New York: John Wiley, 1974).

2. V. J. Vogel, *American Indian Medicine* (New York: John Wiley, 1974).

3. V. Deloria and K. Kickingbird, *Treaties and Agreements of the Indian Tribes of the Pacific Northwest* (Washington, D.C.: The Institute for the Development of Indian Law, n.d.) p. 14.

4. Felix Cohen, *Handbook of Federal Indian Law* (Albuquerque: University of New Mexico Press, 1942), p. 243.

transferred to the Department of Health, Education, and Welfare, U.S. Public Health Service. However, authority for the provision of medical services to Indians had been broadly established in 1921 with the passage of the Snyder Act, which provided for appropriations to assist Indians in the "conservation of health" and for the "employment of . . . physicians." In 1954, P.L. 83–568 provided the authority to transfer "all functions, responsibilities, authorities, and duties . . . relating to the maintenance of the health of Indians . . ." to the U.S. Public Health Service, under the Direction of the Surgeon General.[5] Since 1954, the Indian Health Service has grown from a budget of $34.5 million and a staff of 2900 to its present 1975 level of staffing at 7400 individuals and an annual appropriation in excess of $200 million.[6]

Health and medical care for the American Indians and Alaska Natives is currently available in 24 western states through a network of 51 hospitals, 83 health centers, and over 300 health stations.[7] In addition to direct medical care through outpatient installations and inpatient facilities, the Indian health service also saw the passage of significant environmental health legislation in P.L. 86–121, which provided a separate authorization for the construction of sanitation facilities on reservations where there had never been running water or sanitary waste disposal. This legislation, coupled with more recent Housing and Urban Development (HUD) grants, has permitted a vastly improved physical environment for many Indian peoples.[8]

In 1975 and 1976, two complementary pieces of major Indian-oriented legislation were passed into law, the implications of which herald major changes for medical service delivery and perhaps mark the greatest legislative impact on Indian tribes since the Indian Reorganization Act of 1934. These bills are: P.L. 93–638, the Indian Self-Determination and Education Assistance Act (January 4, 1975), and P.L. 94–437, the Indian Health Care Improvement Act (September 30, 1976). This last is one of the most comprehensive documents spelling out the obligations of the federal government with respect to the needs of Indian peoples yet promulgated. This is not to imply that it fully meets the needs of Indian people, or that it does not have some drawbacks.

The Self-Determination Act provides the legal framework within which an Indian tribe may contract with the federal government for the operation of various health programs which are managed by the tribe itself. And the Indian Health Care Improvement Act delineates a number of program areas in which Indian people may manage contracts: training programs, specific health services, health facilities, waste disposal programs, and urban Indian clinics. The latter is a most important inclusion, because it is the first time that those Indian peoples residing off-reservation have had their health needs formally recognized by legislation.

5. "DHEW, PHS, Provision of Contract Health Services," in *Federal Register*, 41(206): 46792 (22 October 1976).

6. D. J. Press, D. Sakiestewa and R. D. Kane, *A Study of the Indian Health Service and Indian Tribal Involvement in Health* (Arlington, Virginia: Urban Associates, 1974) p. 3. Prepared for the Office of Special Concerns, DHEW.

7. Ibid., p. 142.

8. Ibid., p. 11.

TABLE 1

INDIAN HEALTH SERVICE PROGRAM ACCOMPLISHMENTS

HEALTH IMPROVEMENTS	1955 RATE	1974 RATE	PERCENT DECREASE
Death Rates:			
Infant	62.5	18.7	70
Neonatal	22.7	9.4	59
Postneonatal	39.8	9.3	77
Maternal	82.6	16.4	80
Influenza and pneumonia	89.8	29.7	67
Certain diseases of infancy	67.7	21.0	69
Tuberculosis, all forms	55.1	7.5	86
Gastroenteritis, etc.	39.2	6.6	83
Congenital malformations	19.0	8.5	55
Incidence Rates:			
New active tuberculosis	257.7*	79.8	69
Trachoma	1712.7**	388.8	77

SOURCE: Indian Health Service, Analysis and Statistical Branch, "Program Accomplishments." (A package of charts and materials prepared for the congressional budget hearings of March 8 and March 10, 1976.)
* 1962 Rate
** 1966 Rate

THE CHANGING PATTERNS OF DISEASE

One should make a distinction between health problems and medical problems. Increasingly among nonmedical professionals, as well as tribal employees, health problems are being defined as those sociocultural and physical-environmental elements which have a negative effect on the physical and emotional well-being of people: (1) inadequate housing; (2) poor nutrition; (3) a lack of job opportunities; (4) inferior educational opportunities; and (5) lack of recreational outlets. Clinical personnel still tend to define medical problems as those diseases and states of ill-health which are encountered in the clinic setting, and which lend themselves to reporting on the various medical records forms. But the medical problems are symptomatic of the health problems, so efforts directed at Indian health improvement are two-fold: preventive and curative.

Since the Indian Health Service began to keep records on Indian medical problems in calendar year 1955, there has been a major improvement in the health of native peoples, as indicated by selected morbidity and mortality rates and the percent decrease in these rates through calendar year 1974. These are summarized in table 1.

Until very recently, Native Americans died in larger numbers from diseases which did not cause high mortality in the rest of the population: infectious diseases and conditions relating to poverty. However, an examination of the leading causes of death for Indians and Alaska Natives in 24 reservation states would suggest that Indians' general health status and living circumstances are catching up with the rest of the nation. More native people are dying from accidents and chronic conditions, while a glance at the reduction in rates in table 1 indicates that infectious disease is coming more and more under control. In calendar

year 1971, the Indian Health Service listed the top ten causes of death
for Indians as: accidents, diseases of
the heart, malignant neoplasms,
cirrhosis of the liver, cerebrovascu-
lar disease, influenza and pneu-
monia, diseases of infancy (unspeci-
fied), diabetes mellitus, homicide,
and suicide.[9] Four of these conditions are related to the heavy use of
alcohol among reservation residents:
accidents, cirrhosis, homicide, and
suicide. Regardless of whether or
not the Indian has a genetic suscep-
tibility to alcohol intoxication, there
is an overwhelming abundance of
evidence to indicate that alcohol
abuse among native peoples is a serious problem. In a widely quoted
study, the Indian Health Service
noted that alcohol abuse was the
number one health problem of
American Indians.[10] Yet that same
agency has no overall policy for dealing with this health problem and
professionals within the agency often appear reluctant to plan for treatment or intervention. It is of interest to note that the National Institute
for Alcohol Abuse and Alcoholism,
a separate HEW agency, has some
$24 million in funds for Indian al-
cohol programs.

When the U.S. Public Health Service first examined the beneficiary
population it had inherited from
the Bureau of Indian Affairs, the major causes of mortality and morbidity
were infectious diseases. In the first
decade of health services delivery
to Indian people, the sources and

causes of morbidity and mortality
were vigorously attacked by the Division of Indian Health personnel.
Not only medical staff, but allied
health manpower as well, worked
together to develop a comprehensive approach to the reduction of
disease. Sanitarians, civil engineers,
medical social workers, and health
educators formed a part of the team
which scattered across the reservations to ameliorate existing conditions. The success of this broad-scale
approach to community health has
resulted in a marked reduction of the
infectious diseases. Even tuberculosis and otitis media are no longer
the threats they once were for Indian
people, although there is still considerable fear in the Indian communities about tuberculosis, and
much repairable deafness from otitis
which requires surgical correction.

In the last few years, the chronic
diseases and mental health problems have increasingly required the
attention of medical professionals
and the growing cadre of paraprofessionals. In spite of vague and
fragmented programs, or perhaps because of them, alcohol abuse continues to be held by many tribal
people[11] as well as by federal officials[12] to be the major health problem among Indian people. However,
alcohol abuse is also held by many
to be symptomatic of environmental,
acculturative, and other stresses
which impact heavily on Indian
communities.[13] Levy and Kunitz

9. U.S. Public Health Service, *Indian Health Trends and Services*, DHEW publication no. (HSA) 74–12,009 (Washington, D.C.: USGPO, 1974). p. 32.
10. Indian Health Service Task Force on Alcoholism, *Alcoholism: A High Priority Health Problem*, DHEW publication no. (HSM) 73–12002 (Washington, D.C.: USGPO, 1972.)

11. Arizona Commission of Indian Affairs, Phoenix, *Reservation Survey: Health.* (A series of questionnaires submitted to tribal leaders from 1963–66 asking for Indian perceptions of major health problems. Alcohol was often cited as the number one problem.)
12. Indian Health Service Task Force, *Alcoholism: A High Priority Health Problem.*
13. J. Ablon, "Cultural Conflict in Urban Indians," *Mental Hygiene* 55 (1971), pp.

point out that among Navajo, Apache, and Hopi people there may have been prehistoric cultural configurations which have persisted and which influence present drinking habits,[14] while Lurie notes that Indian-style drinking helps to maintain a sense of "Indianness."[15] Other observers note that there are differences in Indian drinking and that certainly not all Indian drinking constitutes alcoholism or even alcohol abuse.[16] It can be seen that there is much more unknown about this major health problem than is known, and sensitive individuals working in the field of Indian alcohol abuse suggest that it is time to stop the body count of abusers and begin to develop comprehensive, community-based approaches to the problem which incorporate prevention, early identification and intervention, effective treatment, follow-up and rehabilitation, with all of the attendant services implied by these concepts.[17] This would require a multi-agency

cooperative approach, because services to Indian people are seriously fragmented across numerous agencies. However, such an attack is not inherently impossible.

It has been suggested that differential use of health facilities by social class[18] and generational differences in morbidity rates for some diseases result from the strains of acculturation.[19] Certainly it is a mistake to view cultural groups as internally homogeneous,[20] but due to limitations of space it will be necessary to generalize about Indian people and trends, keeping in mind that there are always exceptions. A partial solution to dealing with the cultural differences which affect utilization of health services, as well as influence the health behavior of Indian people, is to increase the utilization of indigenous personnel, most especially therapists who deal with emotional and social problems. It has been suggested that effective medical care delivery would be enhanced if health professionals could modify their etiological concepts of causation of psychosocial disturbances, and if native practitioners could also achieve a better understanding of contemporary medical concepts and be assisted to integrate these into the indigenous concepts of disease causation.[21]

199–205. W. V. Curlee, "Suicide and Self-destructive Behavior on the Cheyenne River Reservation," in *Suicide Among the American Indians* (Washington, D.C.: U.S. Public Health Service, publication no. 1908, June 1969), pp. 34–36. E. P. Dozier, "Problem Drinking among American Indians: The Role of Sociocultural deprivation," *Quarterly Journal of Studies on Alcohol*, vol. 27, no. 1 (1966), pp. 72–87.

14. Levy and Kunitz, *Indian Drinking*.
15. N. O. Lurie, "The World's Oldest Ongoing Protest Demonstration: North American Indian Drinking Patterns," *Pacific Historical Review*, vol. 40, no. 3 (1971), pp. 311–32.
16. F. N. Ferguson, "Navajo Drinking: Some Tentative Hypotheses," *Human Organization* 27 (1968), pp. 159–67. J. J. Westermeyer, "Options Regarding Alcohol Use Among the Chippewa," *American Journal of Orthopsychiatry*, vol. 42, no. 3 (1972), pp. 398–403.
17. Personal communication with Ernest J. Turner, Director, Seattle Indian Alcoholism Program, November 1976.

18. E. L. Koos, *The Health of Regionville* (New York: Columbia University Press, 1954). p. 160.
19. S. Graham, "Ethnic Background and Illness in a Pennsylvania County," *Social Problems*, vol. 4, no. 1 (1956), pp. 76–82.
20. P. Kunstadter, "Culture Change, Social Structure, and Health Behavior: A Quantitative Study of Clinic Use Among the Apaches of the Mescalero Reservation" (Ph.D. diss. University of Michigan, 1960), p. 409.
21. E. F. Torrey, "Mental Health Services for American Indians and Eskimos," *Community Mental Health Journal*, vol. 6, no. 6 (1970), pp. 455–63.

This brings up the question of who is currently providing care for Indian people. The traditional doctor-patient relationship is undergoing some interesting and innovative alterations in an attempt to better meet the health needs of a rural, often isolated, frequently bilingual, and culturally distinct people.

INNOVATIONS AND NEW DIRECTIONS

Almost from the time of the transfer of responsibility from the Bureau of Indian Affairs to the Public Health Service, professionals within the health delivery system began to consider innovations and changes in the traditional medical model in order to provide a comprehensive program of medical and health services to the Indian people. Confronted with major manpower shortages, a very rural and scattered population, language differences, and distinct value and cultural differences, not to mention the isolation of professionals, antiquated facilities and inadequate congressional appropriations, the administrators of the Division of Indian Health began to explore a then new approach to service delivery: the paraprofessional. The earliest groundwork was laid by the Navajo-Cornell Field Health Research Project, which in 1955 began to explore ways to develop effective cross-cultural health delivery. The development of a cadre of Health Visitors, who worked as a part of a medical team to help bridge cultural and linguistic gaps, laid the foundation for the burgeoning paraprofessional programs which exist today.[22] Medical teams in Alaska were de-

veloping the Village Aide programs, training indigenous individuals in isolated native villages to provide a range of primary care functions. The importance of indigenous first-contact people became a major concern of Indian Health Service staff. Thus, in 1968 a training center and research station was established on the Arizona desert in Tucson. This multicomponent program consisted of a national training center, Desert Willow, whose function was to provide basic training to tribally-hired and-employed outreach workers known as Community Health Representatives. The Health Program Systems Center began to explore ways to facilitate the delivery of health services, and the Office of Research and Development, in cooperation with the National Aeronautics and Space Administration, sought ways to bring space technology down to earth to improve medical care delivery in remote corners of Indian reservations. And with the growing recognition of the capabilities of physician-extenders, the Indian Health Service established, in 1970, a Community Health Medic training program to produce Indian physician assistants.[23]

In addition to these paraprofessionals, there is a growing cadre of other allied health workers within the IHS, including trained native people who concentrate in the areas of nutrition, maternal and child health, senior citizen programs, alcohol abuse counseling, and other social service areas. Many of these individuals are not directly employed by the IHS, but are hired by tribes and agencies under federal contracts. The biggest program with as yet

22. J. Adair and K. W. Deuschle, *The People's Health* (New York: Appleton-Century-Crofts, 1970).

23. *Community Health Medic of the Indian Health Service*. (Tucson, Arizona: Health Program Systems Center, April 1971).

largely unrealized potential is the Community Health Representative program, which employed nearly 1,500 paraprofessionals by the end of fiscal year 1976. Because these individuals are employed by their respective tribal governments, and their work assignments are largely developed to meet local needs, the program allows for a flexible approach that few other programs can manage. The tribe sets the employment criteria, so that education, age, and previous experience vary widely. Although the program initially saw itself as independent of the IHS professionals, since 1970 there has been a growing sense of teamwork, and more and more reservation health needs are being identified and met as a result of the community outreach provided by the CHRs. The program is operated through a contract mechanism, whereby the IHS contracts with individual tribes or Indian agencies for services, and the tribes hire and administer the employees. Current funding for this program alone is in excess of $15 million dollars. But while the program is a tribal program, the IHS has a definite responsibility for ongoing training, support, and advice on program planning and evaluation.

One of the major benefits of the CHR program is that the existence of trained paraprofessionals not only increases the reach of health services and contributes to community education, but the CHRs can also provide important cross-cultural training and orientation to Indian health professionals as the non-Indian staff undergoes its annual change-over of physicians. Certainly one of the continuing problems for Western-trained professionals is the necessity to make some accommodations in accepted medical practice to meet cultural expectations about

appropriate and acceptable medical care. The CHR can advise the physician, as well as explain to the patient necessary procedures, thereby establishing a very important link in the chain of services.[24]

Although it is too early to really assess the impact of these new programs, the Indian Health Service is exploring new directions in health service delivery which have important implications for the rest of the nation. One program which has possible benefits for most of Alaska and many other isolated populations is the STARPAHC program (Space Technology Applied to Rural Papago Advanced Health Care).[25] By utilizing sophisticated telemetry, a communications link (which could someday be beamed via satellite), and mobile health centers, the IHS is exploring ways for a physician and physician assistant to communicate with patients when the physician is located in a medical center at some distance from the patient. By television and radio the physician can direct the physician assistant and patient to assess immediate medical problems and make recommendations for further care.

Also being explored are new ways

24. W. Brodt, "Implications for Training Curriculums from a Task Inventory Survey of Indian Community Health Representatives," *Public Health Reports*, vol. 90, no. 6 (November–December 1975), pp. 552–60. N. H. Rund, R. D. Myhre, and M. Fuchs, *Community Health Representative: A Changing Philosophy of Indian Involvement* (Tucson, Arizona: Office of Program Development, Indian Health Service. February 1970). Patricia D. Mail, "Professionalism: The Paraprofessional View" (Paper prepared for the 11th annual meeting of the USPHS Professional Association, New Orleans, May 1976).

25. *Space Technology in Remote Health Care*, National Aeronautics and Space Administration, publication no. JCS–09161 (Houston, Texas: August 1974).

to deal with patient records, and the Health Information System is a project which provides physicians with a computer-based medical record designed to reflect sociocultural data as well as pertinent medical history. Special training of paraprofessionals in early disease intervention is also producing significant results in the reduction of such major health problems as infant diarrheas and streptococcal infections.[26]

Aside from programs within the federal government, there has been a growth of urban Indian outpatient and social service programs in many cities where there is a substantial Indian population. Such cities as Seattle, San Francisco, Los Angeles, Chicago, and Minneapolis have seen the growth and development of Indian clinics, many of which had their origins in volunteer services until state and finally federal funding could be obtained to maintain and increase services. The urban Indian programs have predominantly Indian staffs, and frequently tend to siphon off from the reservations skilled Indian professionals. The impact of recent federal legislation which recognized urban Indians has yet to be fully assessed.

SUMMARY AND CONCLUSIONS

Medical services and health care programs for Indians and Alaska Natives have moved from the nineteenth to the twenty-first century in a span of some 25 years. Programs and projects currently being explored by the Indian Health Service have implications for changes in traditional medicine which might point to directions that national health delivery programs should take. The ever-expanding utilization of paraprofessionals and allied health professionals has demonstrated that effective quality care can be achieved with fewer physicians who are, in turn, better utilized. Recent federal legislation has laid a groundwork for the increasing assumption of Indian tribal responsibility for health care, and the Indian population is growing more and more sophisticated with respect to its knowledge, expectations, and understanding of modern medicine. Yet in most Indian communities, there is a renewed interest in the value and worth of traditional practices as well, and Indian students in the health professions are seeking to combine the best of both traditions to provide even better health services to Indian people in the years ahead.

The Indian Health Service is faced with the continuing responsibility to provide effective and comprehensive services to Indian people, and the urban migrant is making increased demands on the federal government to recognize his entitlements, regardless of residence. As the nation's population concentrates in urban centers, recruitment and retention of skilled professionals is an increasing problem for the IHS, with the expanded roles for paraprofessionals providing only a partial solution.

Overall, the health of Indian people is vastly improved from the first measures taken in the late 1950s, but the status of health of Indian people is not yet equivalent to that of the majority population, nor will it be until unemployment, poverty, isolation, discrimination, poor housing, inadequate and inferior education, and federal paternalism give way to genuine Indian participation, management, and assumption of admin-

26. Personal communication with Rice Leach, M.D., Office of Research and Development, Indian Health Service, Tucson, Arizona, June 1976.

istrative responsibility by trained Indian people. The Indian Health Service is working to bring this about, and within the Indian communities there is a growing sense of new pride in being identified as the First Americans.

Western medicine sprang from the traditions of the Greeks, as articulated initially by Hippocrates. Indian medicine, as practiced by the medicine man, is now being integrated with Western medicine to provide a more sensitive and effective approach to bridging the cultural differences between the Old World and the New. From the empirical knowledge of medicine men come the practical approaches of contemporary practitioners, working together to provide accessible, acceptable, and effective medicine designed to improve the status of Indian health.

ANNALS, AAPSS, **436**, Mar. 1978

The Bureau of Indian Affairs: Activities Since 1945

By RAYMOND V. BUTLER

ABSTRACT: The journey from termination, where the federal government was trying to get out of the Indian business, to Indian self-determination, where the federal government is committed to becoming a full partner to the Indian tribes, is the major theme of Indian affairs over the past several decades. The impact of Indian self-determination on the future operations of the Bureau of Indian Affairs cannot be predicted at this time. The particular nature of and direction of the change will depend upon how totally the tribes embrace its philosophy; the commitment of the Congress to the concept outlined in the Indian Self-Determination Act, as reflected in appropriations and supportive legislation; and the conversion of the Bureau from the role of policymaker to technical advisor. Present critical problems involving urban Indians, water, hunting and fishing rights, historic land claims, and the question of federal recognition of heretofore unrecognized Indian groups, will challenge every aspect of the concept of self-determination.

Raymond V. Butler, a Blackfeet Indian, was appointed Acting Commissioner of Indian Affairs in January of 1977 and served in this capacity for most of that year. Since 1972 he has served as head of the Division of Social Services in the Bureau of Indian Affairs (BIA). A graduate of the University of Washington, with a masters degree in social work from Florida State, Butler has worked at the agency, area, and central office levels in the Bureau. He began his career with BIA in 1958.

MEMBERS of the Eighty-third Congress, reflecting years of frustration in trying to solve the "Indian problem," in 1953 unanimously endorsed House Concurrent Resolution 108 which stated:

Whereas it is the policy of Congress, as rapidly as possible to make the Indians within the territorial limits of the United States subject to the same laws and entitled to the same privileges and responsibilities as are applicable to other citizens of the United States, to end their status as wards of the United States, and to grant them all of the rights and prerogatives pertaining to American citizenship; and

Whereas the Indians within the territorial limits of the United States should assume their full responsibilities as American citizens: Now therefore, be it

Resolved by the House of Representatives (the Senate concurring), That it is the sense of Congress that, at the earliest possible time, all of the Indian tribes and individual members thereof... should be freed from Federal supervision and control. . . . It is further declared to be the sense of Congress that, upon the release of such tribes and individual members thereof from such disabilities and limitations, all offices of the Bureau of Indian Affairs . . . whose primary purpose was to serve any Indian tribe or individual Indian freed from Federal supervision should be abolished.[1]

This resolution initiated what has come to be called the "Termination Policy."

On January 4, 1975, President Gerald Ford signed the "Indian Self-Determination and Education Assistance Act." This law states as a "Declaration of Policy" that:

The Congress declares its commitment to the maintenance of the Federal Government's unique and continuing relationship with and responsibility to the Indian people through the establishment of a meaningful Indian self-determination policy which will permit an orderly transition from Federal domination of programs for and services to Indians to effective and meaningful participation by the Indian people in the planning, conduct, and administration of those programs and services.[2]

The journey from termination, where the federal government was trying to get out of the Indian business, to self-determination, where the federal government is committed to becoming a full partner to the Indian tribes, is the major theme of Indian affairs of the past two decades.

TERMINATION

Contrary to many opinions, the termination policy did not spring full-blown from the brows of conservative Congressmen. It was the logical culmination of the historical policy aimed toward the assimilation of the American Indians into the mainstream of American life. From the beginning of its history until 1934, the federal government's Indian policy was based on the understanding that sooner or later all Indians would be assimilated into the American melting pot with all the benefits, as well as the responsibilities, which such a move entailed. The fluctuations of the Indian policy during the nineteenth and early twentieth centuries were manifestations of the differing means. The end, however, was always the complete assimilation of the American Indian. In the 1930s under the administration of President Franklin D. Roosevelt, the Commissioner of Indian Affairs, John Collier, initiated a different

1. U.S. Congress, House, *Concurrent Resolution 108*, 83rd Cong. 1st sess, 1953.

2. 88 *Stat.* 2203, 2204.

approach. The Collier policy was aimed at preserving, as much as possible, Indian culture, tribal identification, and lifestyle. For many, this policy was enunciated in the Indian Reorganization Act (IRA) of 1934. The major purpose of this act was to revitalize weak and, in some cases nonexistent, tribal governments. This was to be accomplished by means of written tribal constitutions and by-laws approved by the Secretary of the Interior.

As a result of a number of circumstances (not the least of which was Collier's inability to sell his policy to a skeptical Congress), toward the end of World War II the feeling was beginning to grow that the New Deal reforms were hampering the Indians in their overall growth and development. The problem appeared to be too much federal interference in the management of the Indians' lives. Many believed that the government, through the Bureau of Indian Affairs, was guilty of preventing the Indians from enjoying the full fruits of American citizenship. If the Indian could be freed from these unnatural constraints, then he, too, would have the enjoyment and responsibilities inherent in the American Dream.

In the immediate postwar period, the movement for termination was accelerated.[3] Some commentators see evidence of termination in the Indian Claims Commission. Claims settlement was viewed as a necessary step to provide the Indians with financial reserves to aid them when they began to manage their own affairs.[4]

House Concurrent Resolution 108 called for the termination of all the Indian tribes within the states of California, Florida, New York, and Texas. In addition, four individual tribes were singled out for immediate action. Subsequently, on June 17, 1954, the Menominee tribe of Wisconsin, one of the four, became the first tribe slated for termination.[5] Between 1954 and 1959 ten more termination acts were passed. The final act was in 1962, and it concerned the Ponca tribe of Nebraska. These acts "freed" 13,263 tribal members and removed over 1,365,800 acres from federal trust status.[6]

Glenn L. Emmons, Commissioner of Indian Affairs from 1953 to 1961, supported the Congressional decisions. At first, however, he expressed apprehension at the possibility that Congress was too impatient in its desire "to write the whole problem off as insoluble and to liquidate it in one sweeping piece of legislation."[7] By 1958, he was one of the chief exponents of the policy ". . . I have no hesitancy whatever in calling it [H. Cong. Res. 108] one of the most valuable and salutary Congressional measures we have had in Indian Affairs for a great many years."[8] Even then, however, Emmons continued to caution that a unilateral immediate termination of all federal relationships with Indians and the destruction of tribal integrity was not the administration policy.

5. Menominee Termination Act. 69 *Stat.* 2150.
6. Taylor, *States and Indian Citizens*, p. 180.
7. Glenn L. Emmons, Address to the Annual Convention of the National Congress of American Indians, Omaha, Nebraska, 1954, cited in Tyler, *History of Indian Policy*, p. 177.
8. Glenn L. Emmons, "Why We Still Have an 'Indian Problem,'" *Sunday Telegram* (Worcester, Mass.), 12 January 1958, cited in Tyler, *History of Indian Policy*, p. 178.

3. Theodore W. Taylor, *The States and Their Indian Citizens* (Washington, D.C.: USGPO, 1972), pp. 53–56.
4. S. Lyman Tyler, *A History of Indian Policy* (Washington, D.C.: USGPO, 1973), p. 150.

... the policy of the present administration does NOT call for hasty termination of Federal trust responsibilities in Indian Affairs. Rather it [the administration] emphasizes the need for thorough study, careful planning, and full consultation with the Indians, tribe by tribe and group by group. It also recognizes and stresses the right of the Indians to continue holding their lands in common and maintaining their tribal organizations for as long as they wish after the Federal trusteeship has been terminated.[9]

The continued fears of the Indians and their allies precipitated a slight shift in the position of Secretary of the Interior Fred E. Seaton. In 1960, in an attempt to allay these apprehensions, he stated that the administration has "no thought whatever of trying to force Indian people off the reservation, or even of subtly persuading them to move against their will."[10] Although this had been the stated position from the beginning of the 1950s, the Indian opponents of termination continued to argue over the reconciliation of the terms "earliest possible time" in H.C.R. 108 and such terms as "force" and "subtly persuading" as in the Secretary's statements.

It would be a mistake to view the termination question as being the government on one side and the Indians on the other. There were vigorous proponents and opponents of termination in both camps. Many tribes were severely divided over the issue of whether or not to seek termination. The reluctance of some of the federal officials to push too hard for such legislation has been mentioned.

It should be reemphasized that the termination policy was directed by Congress to represent the overview of the general direction of Indian policy. It was not, however, the exclusive concern of the Bureau of Indian Affairs. The Bureau still had the responsibility to those tribes, the vast majority, who remained under federal jurisdiction. In this regard, Commissioner Emmons had a four-point program which was the guide to his administration. The four points concerned health, education, economic development, and employment.

The health portion of this program was solved, in part, by the transfer of the Bureau's health programs to the United States Public Health Service in 1955, where it became known as the Indian Health Service. While this move was motivated in part by the desire to bring a wider range of health services and programs to Indian people, it was also part of the plan to dismantle the Bureau of Indian Affairs by transferring its separate functions to the executive departments which handled that specific area. Thus it was thought, for example, that eventually Indian education would be in the Office of Education and law enforcement in the Justice Department. None of these other transfers were consummated. Instead the various executive departments established what became known as "Indian Desks" which occasionally competed with the Bureau offices, performing similar functions on the reservations.

The second area of Commissioner Emmons's concern was with education. The Johnson O'Malley Act[11] continued to be a cornerstone of the Bureau's education program. This Act enabled the Secretary of the Interior to contract with states and public school systems for the education of Indians, including the provi-

9. Ibid.
10. Tyler, *History of Indian Policy*, p. 186.
11. 48 *Stat.* 596.

sion of special programs to meet their needs. Further aid to public education of Indians was provided when the 81st Congress enacted legislation enabling public school districts to count Indians in the formula for reimbursement under the impact aid program (P. L. 874).

Emmons supplemented Indian school programs by initiating an adult education program to provide the opportunity for a basic education to all Indians who desired it. In addition to the traditional forms of education, the Bureau supported legislation enacted in 1956, which authorized vocational education and training to Indians between the ages of 18 and 35.[12] This program rapidly became one of the most important federally supported educational programs.

The commitment to the education of the Indians was not directly concerned with the termination controversy. Many persons, however, were aware that the more the Indians were exposed to the public schools and the values taught there, the greater the possibility for erosion of tribalism within the reservation. For the most part, this was viewed at the time as a positive achievement. It was noted by several commentators that the losses in terms of tribal cohesiveness were more than offset by the gains of the individual in his ability to function in the non-reservation world.

The Vocational Education Training Act of 1956 had a twofold purpose. The first act was to provide useful education opportunities for young adults, but it was also part of Emmons's industrial development program. It would provide a competent manpower pool to attract

industries to the reservations. Unfortunately, like many programs of the period, this program competed with the Relocation Service Program, whose purpose was to remove the Indians to where there were jobs, thereby depleting this same manpower pool.

Manpower was only one of the resources available on the reservation, and in the 1950s efforts to assess the economic potential of the individual reservations were intensified. Land was the most obvious, and on many reservations the only, resource available for development. Public Law 450 made it easier for Indian land owners to obtain loans from banks by permitting them to use their allotted land as collateral.[13] In addition, another law enabled owners to lease their lands for a period of up to 50 years. The advantage of this law to the Indian was that he could now lease his property to persons who were interested in long term improvement and not just immediate exploitation.

THE 1960s

The Kennedy Administration ushered in the New Frontier. It was only natural that the Indian community, major participants in the old frontier, received the attention of the new administration. Immediately after assuming office, Secretary of the Interior Stewart Udall appointed a special task force to study the Indian situation and make its recommendations.[14] The report, submitted in July of the same year, recommended a shift from the historical custodial role of the Bureau to that of entre-

12. P.L. 84-959.

13. P.L. 84-450.
14. Task Force on Indian Affairs, "Report to the Secretary of the Interior," mimeographed (Washington, D.C., 10 July 1961).

preneur. It emphasized the development of the human and natural resources available in Indian country. Although the language was more vigorous and the platform more visible, the Task Force's emphases were very similar to those of the previous administration. It called for a strong effort to attract industries to the reservation, an expanded vocational education and placement program, and special efforts aimed toward the economic development of the reservations. The objectives of the program, dubbed the "New Trail," were maximum Indian economic self-sufficiency and participation of Indians in American life, and equal citizenship rights and responsibilities.

The tools to accomplish these ends were the Area Redevelopment Act, the Housing Act, and the Manpower Development and Training Act. In addition, authorizations for the Indian revolving loan fund were increased from $10 million to $20 million. These acts are indicative of the new place Indian affairs had in the Kennedy and Johnson administrations. The economic and social problems of the Indians and the reservations were no longer considered unique; instead, they were seen as similar to the difficulties of other economically depressed areas. Therefore, according to the New Frontiersmen, a separate law for the manpower problems of the reservations was not necessary. Instead, what was needed was to adapt the provisions of the Manpower Development and Training Act to the Indian community. The advantage of of this outlook was that the Indians could benefit from the experience of the other communities and have a broader scope from which to choose their own solutions to their problems.

Philleo Nash, Commissioner of Indian Affairs during the period, was particularly concerned that the Indian community and the Bureau take advantage of the entire resources of the federal government. It was through his instigation, for example, that the arrangements were made with the Department of Labor to apply the provisions of the Manpower Development and Training Act to Indians. He succeeded in gaining congressional approval for considering Indian reservations as communities in the War on Poverty legislation, thereby increasing the availability of federal resources to the Indian communities. He was also instrumental in impressing upon the Indian leaders the importance of federal grantsmanship; that is, the technique of obtaining federal monetary grants to use on the reservations. The establishment of the Office of Economic Opportunity with its Community Action Project for Indian reservations popularized the concept of Indian Desks in the executive departments. Nash strongly supported this type of program. His policy differed from that of Emmons in that Nash believed that the Indian Desks should serve as technical advisors to the Bureau and not usurp its functions. In this way he hoped to avoid wasteful duplication and competition on the reservations.

To facilitate these changes, in 1962, the Bureau organized the Division of Economic Development. Its purpose was to oversee the utilization of reservation natural resources, encourage business and industrial development, supply technical assistance to the tribes, and assist with land management practices. In addition, the Division handled home building and public works programs.

Indian education was also a major concern of the Nash administration, with special emphasis on vocational education. In 1962, the Congress more than doubled the Bureau's budget for vocational education; it was one of the Bureau's most successful educational efforts. In 1963, Commissioner Nash estimated that 86 percent of those who completed the program were gainfully employed.[15] Unfortunately, two other areas, the high secondary school dropout rate and the low number of college students remained a major cause for concern to the Commissioner. Some of the dropouts were later salvaged by the vocational training programs, but the low college attendance continued to mystify him.[16]

The continued involvement and importance of education programs on the reservation brought increasing demands for the entire operation to be transferred to the Office of Education within the Department of Health, Education, and Welfare. In anticipation of such a change, HEW created an Office of Indian Progress to consolidate the Department's efforts. Indian leaders, however, made it abundantly clear that they did not favor such a wholesale transfer.

In response, the Bureau began a concentrated effort toward upgrading its educational programs, making them more responsive to the local Indian community. Indians were encouraged to become active in the local school districts, to serve on the school boards, and participate in the parent-teacher associations. A large construction program was undertaken

in the early sixties. Between 1962 and 1967 construction was authorized on buildings that would accommodate a student capacity of 20,000.[17] During this period the Bureau broadened its definition of education on two fronts. In cooperation with the Public Health Service, it launched a concentrated effort to identify and educate mentally retarded Indian children. On the other side of the scale, the Bureau continued to operate the Institute of American Arts, designed to attract the gifted Indian artist, in Santa Fe, New Mexico.

While money was literally being poured into Indian country during the early 1960s, many Indian leaders were reluctant to take full advantage of the opportunities offered because of the specter of termination. They feared that if all the tribes seemed to be self-sufficient, the cry for termination would again be heard. At the same time they were aware that much of their so-called prosperity was a direct result of, and based on, the same federal programs which would be withdrawn if the tribe were terminated.

To allay these fears and to encourage greater participation by the tribes in the antipoverty programs, President Lyndon B. Johnson delivered to Congress on March 6, 1968, "The Forgotten American" speech. In it the President called for an end to termination and proposed a "new goal" that stressed self-determination. "I propose, in short, a policy of maximum choice for the American Indian, a policy expressed in programs of self-help, self-development, self-determination."[18] Concurrent

15. Philleo Nash, "Address" to the Annual Convention of the Congress of American Indians, Cherokee, North Carolina, 1962.

16. Philleo Nash, Address to the Annual Meeting of the Governor's Interstate Indian Council, October 15, 1962.

17. *Annual Report of the Commissioner of Indian Affairs* (Washington, D.C.: USGPO, 1966), p. 6.

18. "The Forgotten American," Presidential Message to Congress, 6 March 1968, p. 2.

with this statement, the President established the National Council on Indian Opportunity, headed by the Vice President, and composed of Indian and business community leaders. The purpose of this council was to give greater high level emphasis to finding solutions to the Indians' problems.

Self-determination quickly became the most popular phrase used by both government and tribal officials. But what did President Johnson mean when he uttered the phrase? No one knew precisely and Congress also failed to give any substance to what appeared to many an empty political slogan.

The Congress did produce a negative definition of self-determination with the passage of the Civil Rights Act of 1968.[19] Title II of that act constituted what has been called an "Indian Bill of Rights." It emphasized that Indian tribes are subject to the United States Constitution. Self-government by an Indian tribe does not exempt that tribe from the Constitution's limitations and responsibilities.

NIXON AND FORD YEARS

The theme of Indian self-determination was quickly picked up and used with various interpretations by all those involved in Indian affairs. Richard Nixon, in his presidential campaign of 1968, strongly supported the repeal of termination and the concept of self-determination. He also pledged a greater involvement of Indian people in the federal planning and policy decisions affecting their lives. Underlining these specific policies was Nixon's belief in cultural pluralism. This is important because it illus-

trates an historic shift from assimilation, of which termination was the logical result, toward a policy of recognition and appreciation of the differences among cultures.

Upon assuming the presidency, Nixon continued to pursue the policy announced in his campaign. He appointed Louis R. Bruce as Commissioner of Indian Affairs. Bruce was a vigorous supporter and salesman for the concept of self-determination. He was strongly supported by the Secretary of the Interior Walter J. Hickel. To insure that the Indian view would be heard at the highest level, the President maintained the National Council on Indian Opportunity that was chaired by the Vice President, but reorganized it to include eight Indian members and an equal number of cabinet level officials. The culmination of this effort was President Nixon's Special Message to the Congress on July 8, 1970. This message, while repeating the same general philosophy of President Johnson's earlier message, was much more specific and stronger. Nixon called for an end to termination and at the same time an end to the paternalism, as exercised by the federal government, over the affairs of the Indian people. He called for self-determination, which he defined as strengthening "the Indian's sense of autonomy without threatening his sense of community. . . . And we must make it clear that Indians can become independent of Federal control without being cut off from Federal concern and Federal support."[20]

The specific recommendations of the President to Congress in this message included: 1) a new congressional resolution specifically repealing the termination policy out-

19. P.L. 90–284.

20. *Indian Record* (August 1970), p. 3.

lined in HCR 108 of the 83rd Congress; 2) congressional support for Indian control of Indian programs; 3) recognition of the right of and support for Indian communities to take over their schools; 4) support for the Indian Financing Act of 1970; 5) assistance for Indians living in urban centers; and, 6) the establishment of an Indian Trust Council Authority "to assure independent legal representation for the Indians natural resource right" and to avoid conflicts of interests within federal agencies.[21]

In Commissioner Bruce, President Nixon found a person fully committed to the ideals put forth in the 1970 message. Prior to that message, Bruce had issued a memorandum to Bureau personnel in which he emphasized that under his administration the Bureau would be transformed from a management to a service organization. In other words, he believed in, and would try to implement, the idea of Indian policy being made by the tribes, with the Bureau providing the technical expertise and guidance needed to define and implement tribal policies. He further stated that the tribes should have the option to take over any, or even all, the BIA reservation programs if they should so desire.

Bruce, who was an Indian, believed that one way to insure that the BIA reflect the Indian point of view was to fill its top positions with Indians. Shortly after taking office he realigned the BIA's central office and appointed a new executive staff of 15 Indians. He also believed in working closely with such organizations as the newly formed National Tribal Chairmen's Association (NTCA) and the National Congress of American

Indians (NCAI). In January 1972, the Commissioner released a five point program for his administration.[22] The major thrust of this program was the economic development of the reservation under what was called a Reservation Acceleration Program (RAP). This was a systematic attempt to study each reservation individually to determine its particular capabilities and needs. In addition, Bruce, reemphasized Nixon's desire for Indians to gain increased control over their educational programs.

The restoration of the Blue Lake to the Taos Pueblo in December 1970, and of 21,000 acres to the Yakima were the first concrete results of the Nixon Indian policy. These land transactions were significant. Formerly Indians could only receive cash payments for lands unjustly taken; now, the fact that land had been returned gave new hope to those tribes with similar claims. The Menominee Restoration Act of December 22, 1973, restoring the previously terminated Menominee tribe to federally recognized status, provided concrete evidence that termination was dead.

While the rhetoric of the Nixon administration was producing results as in the restoration acts discussed above, it was, at the same time, increasing the expectations of the Indian community. The gap between results and expectations began to irritate some Indian people who felt that, despite all the administration's efforts to reach Indians, they were still being ignored. This frustration, combined with the radical-activist mood of the late 1960s and early 1970s, contributed to the rise of militancy among the Indian populace. The Indian occupation of Al-

21. Ibid., pp. 4–11.

22. Tyler, *History of Indian Policy*, p. 257.

catraz Island, from the fall of 1969 until the Indians were forceably removed in the summer of 1971, was the first manifestation of Indian militance. The most spectacular was the takeover of the Bureau of Indian Affairs' Central Office Building in Washington, D.C. for six days in November 1972 by a group using the slogan "Trail of Broken Treaties." This action led to the resignation of Commissioner Bruce and most of his executive staff. It was followed the next spring by the Wounded Knee incident on the Pine Ridge Reservation. While these actions were deplored by most responsible Indian leaders, they did serve to emphasize the severe social and economic problems affecting America's Indian population.

Major pieces of legislation affecting Indians were also being passed by the Congress. The most important was the Indian Financing Act of 1974. The act consolidated and increased existing Indian revolving loan funds then being administered by the Bureau and authorized insuring or guaranteeing of commercial loans to members of the Indian community. In addition, it established the Indian Business Development Program designed to provide capital grants to aid and encourage independent Indian businessmen. The importance of this Act was that it not only received the philosophical backing of Congress but its financial support as well.

INDIAN SELF-DETERMINATION ACT

On January 4, 1975, President Gerald Ford signed the Indian Self-Determination and Education Assistance Act. This act was viewed as the most significant piece of Indian legislation since the Indian Reorgani-

zation Act of 1934. It was the legislative embodiment of much of Nixon's 1970 message. It contained a strong statement, not only repudiating the termination policy, but also emphasizing a commitment to the "maintenance of the Federal Government's unique and continuing relationship with Indian people. . . ."[23] It emphasized the federal obligation to the principle of Indian self-determination by fostering Indian involvement and participation in the direction of education and service programs.

Contracting is the process which the act provides for Indian tribes to assert their control over the federal programs. In order to assure the smooth transition of a program from federal to tribal control, the act mandates that the BIA provide any and all technical or other kinds of assistance required by the tribe. Such assistance was designed to lessen the possibility of tribal default on its contracts. Furthermore, if after contracting to administer certain programs, the tribe no longer wishes to continue, it has the right of retrocession. In other words, a tribe retains the right to return a contracted program to the Bureau of Indian Affairs at anytime, and for any reason, without penalty.

Despite these safeguards, the specter of termination made many of the tribes reluctant to avail themselves of the Self-Determination Act's provisions. This remained true despite the continuous effort of the Commissioner of Indian Affairs Morris Thompson. He spent a considerable portion of his time trying to sell the tribal leaders on the advantages of the program. His efforts were hampered somewhat by the failure of appropriations committees of the

23. P.L. 93–638.

Congress to fully fund the grant and technical support provisions of the act.

The impact of the Indian Self-Determination Act on the future operations of the Bureau of Indian Affairs cannot be predicted at this time. It could change the entire concept of Indian affairs. The nature and direction of the change will depend upon how totally the tribes embrace the act and its philosophy, the commitment of the Congress to the act as reflected in appropriations and supportive legislation, and the commitment of the Bureau to its role of technical advisor rather than of policymaker.

In addition to the implementation of the Self-Determination Act, other matters that will have to be addressed in the immediate future are: the position of the Bureau on the urban Indian question; the land claims of eastern seaboard and other Indian groups; definition and protection of Indian water rights; and the question of federal recognition for a number of heretofore ignored Indian groups. As in the past the handling of these matters will involve the interaction of many parties, in and out of government, and on and off the reservation. Today, as a result of the greater social awareness brought to the fore in the 1960s and the commitment to the concept of human rights, the climate is ripe for large strides toward a more responsive era in the field of Indian affairs.

ANNALS, AAPSS, **436,** Mar. 1978

The Bureau of Indian Affairs Since 1945:
An Assessment

By JAMES E. OFFICER

ABSTRACT: Following World War II, the Bureau of Indian Affairs entered one of the most turbulent periods of its history. First arousing Indian ire during the 1950s for its support of the so-called termination policy, it passed through a relatively tranquil decade in the 1960s as many other government agencies began supplying services to Indians, then moved into the 1970s, which have been notable for much favorable legislation and greatly increased appropriations. At the same time the Bureau has been significantly affected by growing Indian frustration and militancy. By late 1976, it was also beginning to feel the effects of an expanding white backlash against Indians in many areas, stemming at least in part from more aggressive Indian espousal of the concept of tribal sovereignty. This backlash has produced changes in the committee structures of Congress which could have negative consequences for Indian legislation and appropriations. Internally, the Bureau since the mid-1970s has experienced considerable tension between Indian and non-Indian employees, the former having been favored by federal court decisions confirming their entitlement to preference in hiring, promotion, and lateral transfer within the BIA and the Indian Health Service. The administration of President Carter faces unprecedented challenges in Indian affairs because of the many changes which have taken place since 1945.

James E. Officer, at present a Professor of Anthropology at the University of Arizona, was U.S. Associate Commissioner of Indian Affairs from 1962–67, and Assistant to Secretary of the Interior Stewart L. Udall in 1967–68. He served on Udall's 1961 Task Force on Indian Affairs and on the 1962 Task Force on Alaska Native Affairs. He holds a Ph.D. in anthropology from the University of Arizona, represents the United States on the Interamerican Indian Institute, and in 1968 received the Department of the Interior Distinguished Service Award.

than three decades have
_ _ passed since John Collier,
considered by many to have been
the greatest of all Indian Commissioners, submitted his resignation to
President Franklin D. Roosevelt.
Through this interval, the Bureau of
Indian Affairs has remained the nation's ranking symbol of the evils of
excessive federal paternalism. Yet,
in many respects, the Bureau of today is very different from that which
Collier headed.

The protective functions of the
agency—founded in treaty, statute,
and court decision—remain, clearer
in extent perhaps than in Collier's
day, but still woefully fuzzy in many
areas. The number of social and economic services provided Indians by
the BIA is greater than when Collier
left office, and the funding which
supports them is infinitely more generous; yet the overall scope of these
services has, in fact, diminished.
Since 1955, another federal agency
in a completely different department
has provided medical attention for
reservation Indians and helped them
build community water and sewage
disposal facilities. For well over a
decade a majority of the social welfare services and most agricultural
extension services have been administered by state agencies. Both the
states and the U.S. Office of Education have assumed major roles in
educating Indian children. A variety
of other agencies—many of which
did not even exist in Collier's day—
now bring to Indian reservations a
host of services differing from or
complementing those provided by
the Bureau of Indian Affairs.

Finally, the BIA itself—which today has Indians in nearly all major
policy positions—has been encouraging tribes to take over administration of many programs heretofore
planned and directed by the Bureau.

Financial support for these services
continues to come from federal
sources, but tribal, rather than federal, bureaucrats administer them.[1]

On the reservations, the economic
emphasis since 1945 has shifted
from agriculture and stock raising
to tourism, industrial development,
and exploitation of mineral resources. Attorneys and other specialists, rather than employees of the
Bureau of Indian Affairs, are often
the principal advisers to tribes in all
these areas of economic endeavor.

Many longstanding controversies
surrounding Indian property and
water rights are now being litigated,
or settled through legislation, as
lawyers for the departments of Justice and the Interior begin to take
more seriously their roles as Indian
advocates; and, even more importantly, as private attorneys with support from foundations and government agencies begin to supply Indians the kinds of legal services not
previously available.

Without question, then, the three
decades since John Collier's resignation have been among the most
dynamic in history for American Indians; and for all its reputation as a
federal agency which still conducts
its business in mid-nineteenth century style, the BIA has not remained
unaffected by the changes going on
within and around it.

INDIAN POLICY AFTER WORLD WAR II

The single most important ingredient in Indian policy following
World War II, and in much of the
period since, has been what is now
widely known as "termination"; that

1. George P. Castille, "Federal Indian Policy and the Sustained Enclave: An Anthropological Perspective," *Human Organization*,
vol. 33, no. 3 (Fall 1974).

is, the elimination of the special relationship between many Indians and the federal government. The foundation for a postwar termination policy was laid in Commissioner Collier's day. During 1943–44, Collier and Secretary of the Interior Harold Ickes engaged in a running battle with the Senate Committee on Indian Affairs over a subcommittee report calling for a termination program more radical in nature and extent than that which Congress endorsed a decade later.[2]

TERMINATION AND INDIAN CLAIMS

One of Collier's sorest disappointments on leaving office was his failure to secure general legislation permitting Indian tribes to sue the federal government for past grievances.[3] William A. Brophy, Collier's hand-picked successor, gave high priority to such legislation, and on August 13, 1946, Congress finally passed an Indian Claims Act.

Brophy's success in obtaining this important legislation was related to the greatly increased strength of the terminationists in Congress. Convinced that the federal government could never withdraw from its special relationship with Indian tribes so long as many obviously legitimate claims went unsettled, these legislators became strong advocates of a claims act.[4] Within six months after its passage, the Indian Bureau was called upon to explain how it might reduce its budget by withdrawing services from Indian groups, and to supply a timetable for achieving this goal.[5] Over the next four years, Congress considered several termination proposals without taking final action on any.

Neither Brophy nor his successor, John R. Nichols, favored termination. In fact, it was not until May 1950, that the first "termination-minded" Commissioner took office. He was Dillon S. Myer, previously head of the War Relocation Authority, who announced shortly after taking over the Commissioner's post that he was setting up a Program Division to prepare proposals for withdrawing special federal services from Indians.[6] Under Myer's stimulus, Congress began looking at a variety of termination-related bills. Although it enacted none, it did push several beyond the hearing stage, and the House even passed a bill to transfer legal jurisdiction over California reservations to the state.

Shortly before leaving office on March 20, 1953, Myer assisted the new Republican administration to draft a policy letter to Congress on Indian affairs. It put the Eisenhower government solidly behind a policy of termination, one which Myer's successor, New Mexico banker Glenn Emmons, endorsed as enthusiastically as Myer.[7]

During the summer of 1953, Congress began work on several pieces of major termination legislation. The

2. Kenneth R. Philp, *John Collier's Crusade for Indian Reform 1920–1954* (Tucson: University of Arizona Press, 1977), p. 208. U.S. Congress, House, Committee on Indian Affairs, *Investigation of Indian Affairs*, 1944, pp. 28 ff.

3. Philp, *Collier's Crusade for Indian Reform*, p. 241, fn. 2.

4. U.S. Congress, House, *Report 1466*, 1945, p. 1351; and U.S. Congress, House, *Report 2503*, 1952, p. 16.

5. William Zimmerman, Jr., "The Role of the Bureau of Indian Affairs Since 1933," *The Annals of the American Academy of Political and Social Science*, (May 1957), pp. 36–37. Also, see *House Report 2503*, pp. 162–79.

6. U.S. Department of the Interior, *Annual Report of the Secretary*, 1952, p. 389.

7. U.S. Department of the Interior, *Annual Report of the Secretary*, 1953, p. 23.

first of these—House Concurrent Resolution 108—was approved on August 1. It confirmed termination as official government policy and specified certain tribes and groups from which special federal services were to be withdrawn "at the earliest possible time."[8] Two weeks later, it enacted Public Law 83–280 bringing Indian lands in California, Minnesota (except for the Red Lake Reservation), Nebraska, Oregon (except for the Warm Springs Reservation), and Wisconsin (except for the Menominee Reservation) under the legal jurisdiction of the states, and authorized other states, whenever they chose to do so, to assume similar jurisdiction in their areas. President Eisenhower reluctantly signed PL 53–280, at the same time urging Congress to amend it to provide for Indian consent.

During its second session in 1954, the 83rd Congress transferred the responsibility for Indian health programs from the BIA to the U.S. Public Health Service, and passed six termination bills, including two which affected tribes with substantial resources (the Klamaths and Menominees). Except for a handful of bills related to a number of small tribes and Indian communities in about half a dozen states, the entire termination record of the 1950s rests with the 83rd Congress.

Contributing to the slower pace of termination legislation after 1955 was the fierce opposition of Indian tribes and defense groups. The National Congress of American Indians, founded a decade before, now had a major issue with which to rally its membership. It quickly moved into the forefront among the organizations lobbying against House Concurrent Resolution 108. Inside Congress, friction developed between those legislators who felt that no tribe should be terminated without its consent, and those who believed that consultation, with or without consent, was sufficient.

By the middle of 1958, the termination thrust had lost its punch. On September 18 of that year Secretary of the Interior Fred Seaton told a radio audience in Flagstaff, Arizona that "no Indian tribe or group should end its relationship with the Federal Government unless such tribe or group has clearly demonstrated— first, that it understands the plan under which such a program should go forward, and second, that the tribe or group affected concurs in and supports the plan proposed."[9]

Although the termination policy resulted in new service programs for Indians (to prepare them for federal withdrawal) and placed increased emphasis on the importance of education and economic development, the most significant legacy of the era was a psychological one. Many Indians by the late 1950s were convinced that the federal government intended to set them adrift without regard for the consequences. "Termination means ex-termination" was a common way of putting it. As a result of their fears, Indians for a time forgot tribal differences to join forces in the fight against termination.

THE KENNEDY–JOHNSON YEARS

Early in August of 1961, President Kennedy appointed Dr. Philleo Nash, an anthropologist cum politician, as Commissioner of Indian Affairs. Dr. Nash had served on an

8. See Edward H. Spicer, A Short History of the Indians of the United States (New York: Van Nostrand, 1969), document no. 18, p. 218.

9. U.S. Department of the Interior, Annual Report of the Secretary, 1958, p. 231.

Indian affairs task force established the previous January by Secretary of the Interior Stewart L. Udall. Although many Indian leaders hoped that Nash would begin with a vigorous effort to secure the repeal of termination legislation, the new Commissioner chose instead to concentrate on obtaining congressional support for several important, but relatively noncontroversial, legislative amendments which could increase Indian employment and stimulate reservation resource development. Even before taking office, Nash had urged the Interior Department to seek increases in the appropriations ceilings for the Indian Revolving Loan Fund and the Adult Vocational Training Program. In September, only a month after taking office, he was successful in persuading Congress to raise these ceilings.

Nash also set out to make certain that Indians shared in the benefits of federal programs designed for all Americans in need. He directed his subordinates to help tribes apply for assistance under the new Area Redevelopment Act, and by the end of his first year in office, he had stimulated the designation of 56 reservations and four Alaska native regions as "Redevelopment Areas" eligible for federal financial aid in formulating Overall Economic Development Programs (OEDPs).[10] He also opened discussions with representatives of the federal housing agencies which resulted in the creation of tribal housing authorities and the beginning of low rent and mutual self-help housing projects. In addition, he initiated conferences with the Department of Labor which led eventually to help for Indians under the Manpower Development and Training

Act. Nash's determination to involve other federal agencies in serving the population of the reservations became a hallmark of his administration and has significantly influenced U.S. Indian policy in subsequent years.

INDIANS AND THE POVERTY PROGRAMS

Apart from the BIA and the Indian Health Service, the federal agency making the greatest impact on the reservations during the 1960s was the Office of Economic Opportunity. By the end of fiscal year 1965, ten Job Corps Conservation Centers had been approved for Indian reservations, 55 Indian communities had applied for assistance under the Neighborhood Youth Corps Program, another 20 had requested funds for Operation Head Start, and 26 applications had been approved for Community Action Programs.[11]

Most OEO programs stressed Indian initiative and provided grants to tribes to develop their own projects. Especially through the Community Action Programs (CAPs), a broad cross-section of tribes began for the first time to assume responsibility for the kind of decisionmaking previously done for them by employees of the BIA.

Hostility between local BIA officials and representatives of the Office of Economic Opportunity was, from the outset, more pronounced than that between BIA employees and colleagues in other federal agencies. The latter were usually willing to defer to BIA personnel as more knowledgeable about Indian ways than

10. U.S. Department of the Interior, *Annual Report of the Secretary*, 1962, p. 10.

11. U.S. Commission on Indian Affairs, *Indian Affairs, 1965, A Progress Report from the Commissioner of Indian Affairs* (Washington, D.C.: USGPO), pp. 20–22.

they. Not so the young, community development-minded representatives of the OEO. To many of them, the Bureau was the "enemy" and they made few concessions to BIA employees, privately branding them as anti-Indian, unimaginative, and overly paternalistic.

Nash's tenure as Commissioner, which ended early in 1966, was not marked by the passage of any major legislation of general character, although he did assist several tribes in obtaining legislation beneficial to them. Attempts to find a legislative solution to the complex land inheritance problem common to many reservations failed in the 87th and 88th Congresses, largely because of opposition from the National Congress of American Indians, whose representatives viewed the proposals under consideration as threats to preservation of the Indian land base.[12]

Following Nash's departure, President Johnson in April 1966, nominated Robert L. Bennett for Commissioner. Bennett, a career BIA employee, and an Oneida from Wisconsin, became the first Indian to serve in the post in nearly a century.

THE NEW THEME: SELF-DETERMINATION

In their report on Bennett's confirmation hearings, members of the Senate Interior Committee criticized the BIA for not following through on congressional directives regarding the termination of several tribes for which withdrawal programs had been requested. The report was a shock to both Indians and

BIA personnel who had come to feel that termination was a dead issue. When Secretary Udall summoned Bureau officials to a policy conference in Santa Fe shortly after Bennett's confirmation and invited representatives from Congress, many tribal leaders became alarmed that a new era of termination was in the offing. The National Congress of American Indians called an emergency executive meeting in Santa Fe and demanded admission to Udall's conference. Indian representatives were finally admitted, but while the Secretary was deliberating on the matter, he was accused in the press of formulating Indian policy without Indian participation.[13]

In fact, Udall had called the meeting to inform BIA officials and congressmen of the work of a team of Interior Department officials, headed by Under Secretary Charles Luce. This group was trying to develop legislative proposals aimed at stimulating Indian reservation resource development within a context that could assure tribal governing bodies more responsibility than they had had previously. Among the proposals under consideration were those which would establish a federal loan guarantee and insurance fund, permit tribes to issue tax exempt bonds, authorize the chartering of Indian corporations, and allow tribal governing bodies to mortgage or sell trust property when a majority of the tribal members felt this step necessary in order to raise development capital. The secretary also wanted to tell those present in Santa Fe of his favorable reaction to a recommendation by one

---

12. U.S. Congress, Senate, Subcommittee on Indian Affairs, *Hearings on S. 1049, A Bill Relating to the Indian Heirship Land Problem*, 88th Cong., 1st Sess, 1963, pt. III.

13. For a somewhat fanciful account of this episode by a nonparticipant, see Stan Steiner, *The New Indians* (New York, Harper & Row, 1968), chap. 18.

ASSESSMENT OF THE BUREAU OF INDIAN AFFAIRS 67

of the BIA superintendents that the Bureau establish a new policy of contracting with tribes so as to permit them to administer service programs traditionally administered by BIA employees. Udall circulated copies of the letter in which the superintendent had made this suggestion.

Unfortunately for the secretary, some of the legislative proposals of the Interior Department team were already known to the Indians because of the leak of an early draft which came into the hands of the NCAI leaders prior to the Santa Fe meeting. Thus, from the outset these proposals were identified with termination and the issue of Indian participation. Over the next ten months, Commissioner Bennett held many meetings with Indians to discuss the proposals, but he could not dispel their doubts. The legislation, with a number of changes based on comments made by Indian leaders, was introduced in Congress in May of 1967 as the "Indian Resources Development Act." In the face of heavy Indian opposition to parts of the bill, Congress took no final action on it.

During late 1966 and early 1967, the Indians also defeated an attempt to transfer the education functions of the BIA to the Office of Education. This effort had the support of such prominent senators as Robert Kennedy, and was also favored by some officials of the Office of Education, but Indian opposition was almost unanimous and the idea was abandoned.

While not able to enlist Indian support for the resources development bill, Bennett did manage to convince Indian leaders that neither he nor Secretary Udall favored a return to the policies of the 83rd Congress. During late 1967 and early 1968, the Interior Department sol-

idly backed efforts to amend Public Law 83–280 so as to require Indian consent before legal jurisdiction over reservations could be transferred to a state. On April 11, 1968, such amendments were included in a civil rights bill passed by Congress.

A month before this important Indian victory over termination, President Johnson sent Congress a message in which he proposed a new policy of maximum choice for the American Indian, "a policy expressed in programs of self-help, self-development, and self-determination."[14] It was one of the strongest presidential messages on Indians in many years.

By early 1969, when President Johnson departed from office, the BIA's traditional role as the Big Daddy of the reservations had been greatly altered. Other federal agencies were channeling millions of dollars annually into Indian communities. Also, several million dollars worth of BIA programs were being administered by the tribes themselves under contract.[15] The legal staff of the Interior Department was assuming a greater advocacy role for Indians, as a result of which Secretary Udall, in the closing days of his administration, was able to take important actions favorable to such Indian groups as those of the Colorado River, Quechan, Salt River, and Palm Springs reservations. He also imposed a freeze on state selection of lands in Alaska which assured that some of the state's better lands would be set aside for the natives

14. "The Forgotten American," Presidential Message to Congress, 6 March 1968.
15. See "Remarks of Secretary of the Interior Rogers C. B. Morton Before the National Tribal Chairmen's Association," (Department of the Interior News Release, August 8, 1972), p. 2.

and hastened the passage of an Alaska native claims act.

THE REPUBLICANS RETURN TO OFFICE

Many Indians were apprehensive early in 1969 that Richard Nixon's return to Washington would lead to a resumption of the hated policies of the 1950s. His choice of Louis R. Bruce in August of 1969 to replace Bennett as commissioner was reassuring since Bruce, a Mohawk-Sioux enrolled at Pine Ridge, was known to be opposed to termination.

At his hearing before the Senate Interior Committee, Bruce announced that he intended to accelerate BIA contracting with tribes, to give special attention to discharge of the Bureau's trust responsibilities, and to undertake a complete restructuring of the BIA.[16] A few months after Bruce's hearings, Secretary of the Interior Walter Hickel announced a reorganization of the Washington office of the Bureau. Important to this effort, he said, was to be the recruitment of a "new team," including established Indian leaders, to occupy the BIA's top management positions.[17]

On July 8, 1970, President Nixon sent Congress a highly significant message in which he repudiated forced termination, and announced that he would propose legislation to expand the authority of the BIA and the Indian Health Service to contract with Indian tribes. "Self-determination without termination" was the slogan Nixon recited.

Responding to the president's message, Congress took steps to retreat from previous termination actions. It repealed legislation which would have terminated the Oklahoma Choctaws, restored the authority of the Five Civilized Tribes to select their own leaders, and authorized the Indians of Annette Island (Alaska) to share legal jurisdiction with the state. But, most important of all, it restored to the Indians of the Taos Pueblo sacred lands previously taken from them and incorporated into a national forest. The Indian Claims Commission had earlier confirmed that these lands, which included a shrine known as Blue Lake, had belonged to the Indians for centuries. However, the Claims Commission could not return the lands to the Pueblo, since its authority provided only for financial compensation. In awarding the Indians land rather than money, Congress repudiated a termination-related policy established more than 20 years before.

In October, 1970, two months before return of the Taos lands, Secretary Hickel announced the appointment of 15 Indians to key posts in the BIA's Washington office. For the most part, they were a totally new breed of BIA Indian, several having worked previously with the Community Action Programs of the Office of Economic Opportunity. Some were even said to be affiliated with the militant new American Indian Movement (AIM).[18]

In his message to Congress, President Nixon had indicated that new legislation would be sought to give

16. "Statement of Louis R. Bruce Before the Committee on Interior and Insular Affairs of the U.S. Senate," 11 August 1969.

17. "Executive Realignment Announced for the Bureau of Indian Affairs," (Department of the Interior News Release, 9 January 1970).

18. "Militant Indians Fight Apathy of Urban Brothers," *Arizona Daily Star*, 13 February 13 1972. See also "26 Indians Arrested in D.C. Protest," *The Washington Post*, 23 September 1971.

the BIA and the Indian Health Service greater contracting authority. This was felt necessary because the only authority of this kind which the Bureau possessed was based on a brief passage in a 1910 act primarily concerned with reservation resource development. Shortly after Nixon's message was delivered, the Interior Department proposed several bills related to contracting.

The members of the new BIA team were enthusiastic about contracting services to the tribes and moved vigorously ahead as if the Bureau already had all the authority necessary. Their exuberance alarmed certain key congressmen and officials of the Office of Management and the Budget. These persons communicated their concern to Secretary Morton, who decided to make some changes in the direction of the BIA which would assure that legal limits were not transgressed in the contracting process. Among these changes was the return to the Bureau of John O. Crow as Deputy Commissioner in charge of the day-to-day operations of the agency. Crow had occupied the same position under Commissioner Nash, but had been transferred in 1966 to the Bureau of Land Management as part of the transaction which eventually led to Nash's replacement by Robert L. Bennett. Although considered an able administrator, Crow was regarded as a conservative who, in the eyes of the new Bruce appointees, symbolized the old BIA. His return split the agency into two camps— the veteran employees, both Indian and non-Indian, who backed Crow and the reform-minded new crowd, who supported Bruce. In September, 1971, a small group of Indians from the National Indian Youth Council and the American Indian Movement attempted a citizens' arrest of Crow which led to an altercation between them and the police.[19]

As the feud seethed, Morton continued his crusade for new legislation. On December 18, 1971, the Alaska natives won a major victory with the passage of an act providing them the means to confirm title to 40 million acres of land, and receive payments of nearly a billion dollars.

INDIAN PROTESTORS OCCUPY THE BIA OFFICES

During the summer and early fall of 1972, leaders of the American Indian Movement recruited persons to go to Washington as part of a caravan called "The Trail of Broken Treaties." The trip was to conclude with presentation to government officials of a list of 20 points, many of them relating to treaties and the concept of Indian tribal sovereignty. Early in November, about 900 Indians reached the capital.

Following a series of misunderstandings and unanticipated incidents, many of the Indians seized and occupied the BIA headquarters building on Constitution Avenue. When threatened with expulsion, they barricaded themselves inside, destroying much of the interior of the building in the process.[20] White House negotiators finally persuaded them to leave, promising more than $66,000 to cover the expenses of returning to their homes.[21] On December 2, three weeks after the de-

19. "John O. Crow Appointed Deputy Commissioner of Indian Affairs," (Department of the Interior News Release, 23 July 1971). Also see "Morton Backs Down in BIA Flap," *Arizona Daily Star*, 18 August 1971.

20. "BIA Takeover Action Defended," *Arizona Daily Star*, 5 December 1972.

21. "BIA Raid Payoff Defended," *Arizona Daily Star*, 6 December 1972.

parture of the demonstrators, Secretary Morton announced that all authority over Indian affairs was being removed from Commissioner Bruce, Deputy Commissioner Crow, and Assistant Secretary Harrison Loesch, the man many Indians held responsible for Crow's return.[22]

For nearly a year after Morton's announcement, the BIA was without a head. During a part of this time, an Oklahoma businessman named Marvin L. Franklin (a member of the Iowa tribe) served as Special Assistant to the Secretary of the Interior for Indian Affairs. Franklin had barely arrived in Washington when a new confrontation broke out between Indian militants and federal marshals at Wounded Knee, South Dakota. White House officials again intervened in late March 1963.[23]

Under Franklin's aegis, the headquarters office of the Bureau was again restructured. Among the innovations was the establishment, for the first time, of an Office of Trust Responsibilities.

On November 28, 1973, the Senate confirmed the appointment of Morris Thompson, a 34-year-old Athapascan Indian from Alaska, as the new commissioner. Less than three weeks later, Congress passed the Menominee Restoration Act, repealing the termination law enacted nearly 20 years before. The following April it passed the Indian Financing Act of 1974, a measure which President Nixon had proposed in his 1970 message.

During Thompson's first year in office, the Interior Department solicitor issued several opinions which provided a legal basis for restoring Colorado riverfront lands to the Chemenuevi and Fort Mohave reservations, and proclaiming exclusive hunting, fishing, and boating rights in Washington's Lake Roosevelt for the Indians of the Colville and Spokane reservations.[24] In the federal courts, also, 1974 was a big year for Indians. Among the major decisions was one by Judge George Boldt which held that Indians who were members of treaty tribes in the state of Washington were entitled to half the massive fish catch from the waters of that area.

As the 93rd Congress prepared to adjourn in January 1975, it enacted two major pieces of Indian legislation. The first created an Indian Policy Review Commission to undertake a two-year study of Indian affairs and to propose revisions in federal policies and programs. The members were to be congressmen and Indians. The second bill was The Indian Self-Determination and Education Assistance Act. It provided new contracting authority for the BIA and the Indian Health Service, and gave Indians greater control over the use of federal funds for educating Indian children in public schools.

During his term as commissioner, which ended in November of 1976, Thompson enjoyed relatively good relations with the Indians—in part, no doubt, because of the impressive legislative record of the period, and the great increase in BIA appropriations, which by fiscal year 1977 had reached nearly $800 million. However, inside the Bureau, things were more chaotic. New positions, created by the numerous reorganizations during the 1970s, were often

22. "Morton Takes Command of Effort to Put Indian Operation Back to Work," (Department of the Interior News Release, 2 December 1972).
23. "Wounded Knee: Where Did It Begin?" Arizona Daily Star, 18 March 1973.
24. Indian Record, 1974, pp. 6–8. (Newsletter of the Bureau of Indian Affairs.)

poorly defined and went unfilled for long periods, or were filled by a succession of persons, none of whom seemed to have a clear notion of what his responsibilities were. Thompson's failure to develop an internal policy to deal with preferential employment rights of Indians contributed to dissension between Indian and non-Indian personnel, relations between the two deteriorating to their worst point in history.

Court decisions of the 1970s, especially those relating to Indian water and mineral rights, created confusion in the minds of BIA employees as to exactly what their trust responsibilities were. To many the idea of trusteeship appeared to conflict with that of Indian self-determination. They found this conflict especially difficult to handle when implementing the new Self-Determination Act. The rules which the BIA promulgated for administration of the act ran to many thousands of words, and Indians complained of the red tape involved.

Early in 1977, the Policy Review Commission completed its work and submitted its final recommendations in May. The various task forces which had been involved in the effort produced a number of different suggestions about the BIA, one of which was to abolish it entirely and replace both it and the Indian Health Service with a new, independent agency.

THE TRIBAL SOVEREIGNTY ISSUE

Encouraged by court decisions of the 1970s, Indian leaders have recently begun to focus on the issue of tribal sovereignty—a highly controversial concept which by early 1977 was creating an anti-Indian backlash in such diverse areas as

Maine and Washington.[25] The Indian Policy Review Commission came down heavily in favor of the full exercise of tribal sovereignty, including tribal right to tax both Indians and non-Indians, to try both in tribal court, and to control waterways, as well as hunting and fishing.

Congressman Lloyd Meeds, Vice Chairman of the Commission, disassociated himself from its views in a lengthy dissenting opinion, and resigned as head of the Indian Affairs Subcommittee of the House. When a new chairman could not be found early in 1977, the parent Interior and Insular Affairs Committee merged the Indian and Public Lands subcommittees, thus leaving the Indians without a subcommittee of their own in the House. James Abourezk, lame duck champion of Indian rights in the Senate, narrowly averted abolition of the Indian Subcommittee of that body by having it set up as a "select" subcommittee with a two year life span.[26]

THE INDIAN BUREAU IN 1977

On July 12, President Carter sent forward to the Senate his nomination of Forrest J. Gerard as Assistant Secretary of the Interior for Indian Affairs, a title which will replace that of Commissioner of Indian Affairs.[27] Not pleased with the nomination, Senator Abourezk delayed until mid-September the scheduling of confirmation hearings.[28] Gerard, a

25. See the March, April, and May, 1977 issues of *Wassaja*, monthly newspaper published by the American Indian Historical Society, 1451 Masonic Avenue, San Francisco, California 94117.
26. "Select Indian Committee Seen," *Gallup Independent* (31 January 1977).
27. Department of the Interior News Release, 12 July 1977.
28. "Andrus Firm on Top Indian Nominee," *The Daily Oklahoman*, 10 August 1977.

...lackfeet Tribe of
...d briefly in the In-
... the late 1960s. His
...ad the support of the
N... ...al Chairmen's Association.

The new BIA head faces many complex problems, among them the internal personnel situation. Not only must he strive for more harmonious working relationships between Indian and non-Indian employees, but he must be alert to prevent conflict of interest problems with Indian employees who, in working for the Bureau, have, in essence, become their own trustees![30]

The whole concept of BIA trusteeship is extremely complex, and when combined with the self-determination thrust, creates new dilemmas for the Bureau. Because of the many recent Indian victories in the courts, the BIA is probably more

conscious of its trust responsibilities now than at any other time in its history; yet, the new legislation obliges the agency to transfer as much of its authority as possible to the tribes while retaining all or most of the responsibility for the consequences.

One course of action the new Bureau head might follow is to go to Congress for a more precise definition of the trust responsibility. But, to do so now would be unpopular with the Indians who fear that the growing white backlash is converting Congress into a hostile or indifferent body. The Indian leadership prefers to leave unanswered questions to the friendlier courts.

Another area of potential difficulty, also related to the trust, is that of energy resource development on the reservations. High percentages of the nation's remaining deposits of uranium and low sulfur coal are on Indian lands, and tribes with these resources are joining forces to obtain the best possible prices for their development. In discharging its responsibility to help them in this endeavor, the Bureau may find itself again in the old frontier situation where it stood between the Indians and the combine of settlers and soldiers who wished to exterminate them.

29. National Tribal Chairmen's Association, *Highlights*, 14 July 1977.

30. The Indian Reorganization Act provides for preferential treatment of Indians in employment with the BIA. In the mid-1970s, the federal courts held that this preference extends to promotions and lateral transfers, as well as initial hiring. This is the source of the present conflict between Indian and non-Indian employees. The latter are frozen in grade and in place with no prospects for promotions or transfers to more compatible jobs.

ANNALS, AAPSS, **436**, Mar. 1978

Identity, Militancy, and Cultural Congruence:
The Menominee and Kainai

By George D. Spindler and Louise S. Spindler

ABSTRACT: Recent movements of varying degrees of militancy on the part of American Indians can be better understood if we have a grasp of the kinds of adaptations Indians have made to the long-term and continuing confrontation with white culture, white power, and white world views. Native Americans do not constitute a single group. The Menominee are taken as an example of an Indian tribe with a hitherto unaggressive record that has recently engaged in militant activity. The diversity within the Menominee population is described in terms of four major types of long-standing adaptation that were observed as dominant in the 1950s and 1960s and that emerged some time before that. Recent militancy is regarded as a fifth type of adaptive response to the continuing confrontation between Menominee and white culture. Militancy is interpreted, in part, as an assertion of identity.

The responses of the Kainai, the Blood Indians of Alberta, Canada, to white culture and power are contrasted briefly at certain critical points to demonstrate the fact of diversity among American Indians in regard to current actions and to reinforce the interpretation that the degree of difference in cultures and world views between Indian cultures and white culture is a significant factor in the kinds of adaptive response to confrontation native American groups have made and will make.

George D. Spindler is Professor of Anthropology and Education at Stanford University, where he has been since 1950. Louise S. Spindler is Lecturer and Research Associate in the Department of Anthropology at Stanford, where, in 1956, she was the first person to receive the Ph.D. in anthropology. George Spindler received *his doctorate at the University of California at Los Angeles in 1952. They have done much of their field work together, in three American Indian communities, and most recently, in Germany, where over the past decade they have studied the influence of elementary schools on the adaptations children make to an urbanizing environment. Together they have published a number of books and articles, including one on the Menominee published in 1971, Dreamers Without Power. The Spindlers were editors of the AMERICAN ANTHROPOLOGIST from 1963 to 1967.*

RESIDENTS of a wooded resort country area near Big Moose, New York, awoke one morning to find that in the predawn hours a band of American Indians[1] had taken over a 612-acre former girls' camp, now a forest preserve in New York's Adirondack State Park. The occupiers not only claimed this piece for their independent Indian nation, *Ganienkeh*, The Land of the Flint, but also an additional nine million acres in New York and Vermont. This militant action is in the pattern of the occupation of Alcatraz, a former prison island in San Francisco Bay, in 1969, and the area around Wounded Knee, South Dakota, in 1973, though each of these instances had its special features.

On New Year's Day, January 1975, 45 armed "warriors" from the usually peaceful Menominee of Wisconsin occupied the novitiate of the Alexian Brothers, (a Catholic order) near Gresham, Wisconsin, directly adjacent to their reservation boundaries. They claimed the unused 64-room novitiate building, an adjoining 20-room mansion, and 237 acres of land in the name of the Menominee, and for the declared purpose of developing a hospital and drug and alcoholism treatment center there. Though the Menominee had no direct legal claim to the property, the warriors (from the newly organ-

ized Warriors Society) occupying it said they took the vacated property because the land once belonged to the Menominee and should be returned to them for much needed health care facilities—they had lost their own hospital when the Menominee reservation was terminated by federal action in May, 1961. They pledged to fight and die, if need be. The occupation lasted for 34 days. More than 200 officers of the law and 250 national guardsmen patrolled the area during this period—as much to protect the Indian occupiers of the building from irate Whites as to constrain the Indians themselves. The affair ended with the Alexian Brothers pledging the property to the Menominee. Thirty-nine occupiers were taken to jail on charges ranging from armed robbery to criminal trespass. The legal spokesman for the warriors and their sympathizers said that it was not the Indians who would be on trial, but the United States government.

Militant actions of this kind are increasing among native American tribes and communities, and they have met with some success. The responsible leadership of the Menominee was not, in fact, in favor of the occupation and refused to accept the novitiate after the Alexian Brothers offered it. This was both a symptom and a cause of bitter dissension that has afflicted the Menominee since then, though internal

---

1. Our terminology will vacillate between American Indians and "Native Americans," as it does in the current literature.

dissension and factionalism are not new to them.

What lies behind the militancy and the apparent divisiveness? There are many different kinds of answers to this question. Our anthropological research among the Menominee and other native American communities provides useful background, if not an answer, to understanding how these people are reacting to the continuing confrontation with white society—a confrontation that began when the first Europeans landed on the shores of North America to establish permanent settlements in the seventeenth century.

We have been privileged to do field research in three native American communities: the Menominee of Wisconsin, the Blood, or Kainai of Alberta, Canada, and the Cree of Mistassini, Quebec, Canada. In this article we shall focus on the adaptive responses of the Menominee to the continuing impact of North American-European (white) culture upon them and attempt to relate recent militancy and identity-seeking to the longer-standing responses our research has revealed.[2] We will also relate certain dramatic differences in culture and world view, between the Menominee and Whites, to the kinds of adaptations the Menominee made. We will mention the Kainai now and then to provide a contrast to the Menominee situation, but we do not have space to discuss them in depth.

In discussing the Menominee we will use an "ethnographic present" (a time period for which the present tense is used that may, in some ethnographies, be decades in the past) of the year 1975. The last two years have been a period of great trial and tribulation for the Menominee and of great internal divisiveness. We prefer to keep at least the minimal perspective that can be gained by largely ignoring these two years until we understand better what happened during that time.

We started our research with the Menominee in 1948 and have continued it intermittently to the present. We began with the Kainai in 1958 and have also continued to make observations up to the present. In our field work we live close to or with the people we are trying to understand and participate with them in as many customary activities as possible. We also do systematic interviewing and administer various psychological tests, some of them created by us for the particular situation in which we are working. We have built up a sample of individuals in both the Kainai and the Menominee communities of over 100 persons in each case. We have remained in contact with some of these individuals over the years.[3] Our research falls into the subdiscipline of anthropology called today psychological anthropology, formerly culture and personality, and is concerned with long-term psychological adaptations to culture change, urbanization, and modernization.[4]

2. The term "Whites" or "Whiteman" is used by many Indians to refer to all non-Indians in a general way meaning people who live in the United States in a mainstream, Anglo manner. We will use the term "white" as an adjective and "White" as a noun, as a convenience, to avoid cumbersome alternative terminology.

3. See George D. Spindler and Louise S. Spindler, "Fieldwork among the Menomini," in *Being an Anthropologist: Field work in Eleven Cultures*, ed. George D. Spindler (New York: Holt, Rinehart and Winston, 1970), pp. 267–302.

4. See George D. Spindler, ed., *The Making of Psychological Anthropology* (Berkeley: University of California Press, 1978) for an analysis of the history of the field and a chapter by Louise S. Spindler on the research with the Menominee and Blood.

The Menominee and Kainai are particularly useful examples to study because they are relatively small tribes (4,000 to 6,000, as compared to the Navajo or Sioux) but have rich resources—the Menominee their forest and lumber industry, the Kainai their prairie, cattle, wheat, and some oil—which they have battled to keep intact. But they have responded very differently to the white-dominated world about them. There is great diversity among American Indians. There was when the Europeans first came to the new world and there is now, though it is of a different kind.

The Menominee are deeply divided among themselves; culturally, socially, psychologically, and politically. The Kainai are more unified in these same dimensions. This basic difference is reflected in nearly everything that happens as these two tribes try to get along in today's world and improve their lot.

The Menominee

When the early explorers and missionaries first contacted the Menominee they ranged over a vast area of about 9.5 million acres that included their present reservation of 325,000 acres in east central Wisconsin. They were hunters of deer, moose, elk, and smaller animals, gatherers of wild fruits and roots, and fishers of the great sturgeon as well as the trout and lesser fish of the numerous lakes and streams. They also had gardens, though they were marginal horticulturalists. Of particular importance is the fact that they were harvesters of wild rice. The wild rice, from which they take their name, *Omehnomehneuw*, is extraordinarily nutritious, rich in vitamins, and stores well. These varied food resources meant that the Menominee could settle down in semipermanent villages for much of each year and develop relatively complex social institutions and ceremonial organizations.

When the fur trade began shortly after 1667 they shifted to a more nomadic way of life, depending less on their native resources and more upon what they could get for their furs. This shift required a reorganization of social structure and leadership. This was the first major adaptation by the Menominee to the impact of the Europeans on their way of life. The fur trade lasted until the 1830s, when it collapsed, leaving the Menominee destitute. They entered their present reservation area in 1848 and were settled in by 1852.[5] Some attempted to carry on a seminomadic hunting and fishing existence, but the majority began to plant gardens and look for work in the lumber industry which was getting underway in Wisconsin by the 1860s.

The traditional culture continues into the present, however, in forms we shall briefly describe later. The cultural differences between Whites and the Menominee were profound. Especially important for understanding the relations between Whites and Menominee are the seemingly irreconcilable differences between the two world views. The differences between these views of social relations, use of technology, the nature of power, relations with the "supernatural," decisionmaking, and desirable personality traits have influenced every relationship between Whites and Menominee,

5. See Louise S. Spindler, "The Menominee," in *Handbook of North American Indians* (Washington, D.C.: Smithsonian Institution, forthcoming) for a synopsis of the history and ethnohistory of the Menominee.

usually to the disadvantage of the latter, for they were only a handful against a multitude.

The confrontation

We must state the critical differences between white (Western) and Menominee world views in very broad terms, given limitations on space.[6] These differences appear to be the following: 1) In Western culture material power through use of technology is regarded as the way to achieve desired goals. In traditional Menominee culture material power was regarded as useless without spiritual power; 2) In Western culture people must be aggressive in interpersonal relationships to obtain recognition or success. In traditional Menominee culture aggressive people are suspected of being witches; 3) In Western culture extroverted emotional expressiveness is valued as personal salesmanship. People should be friendly, evocative, and lively. In traditional Menominee culture emotions are rarely allowed to surface and the pervasive attitude is "latescent," an expectant and almost passive waiting for action to occur; 4) In Western culture humans are supposed to determine their fate by energetic action and planning. In traditional Menominee culture humans are able to influence events only through living properly in relation to others and in relation to what Whites would regard as supernatural power; 5) In Western culture social interaction is fast and matched by a torrent of words. In Menominee culture social interaction is slow and words are paced and few; 6) In

6. Our understanding of the traditional Menominee culture and the confrontation with Western culture is developed in *Dreamers Without Power: The Menomini Indians* (New York: Holt, Rinehart and Winston, 1971).

Western culture people are supposed to make decisions on the basis of rational and practical considerations. Among the traditional Menominee most important decisions were made on the basis of dreams.

The differences between the two world views were not easily resolved. A person acting in true Menominee style was usually seriously disadvantaged in the white world. The emerging culture of the United States of America was in theory egalitarian, pluralistic, and assimilative. For immigrants of Anglo Saxon and European descent, and to a lesser degree for the Japanese and Chinese who stemmed from complex civilizations, the system worked. It did not work for most other non-Westerners, and particularly not for people like the Menominee, who were both non-Western and dramatically divergent from Western norms in their way of life and particularly in their world views.

It is not possible to explain all the consequences of the prolonged confrontation between white and Menominee cultures on the basis of differences in world view or culture. Economic, political, and social realities set the stage for the interaction in which psychological and cultural differences play decisive roles. The relative prosperity when the fur trade era was at its height, followed by its decline, the loss of lands, the final confinement to a reservation which was only a fraction of the former area, and the attitudes of Whites towards all non-white minorities—these were crucial conditions affecting the continuing Menominee existence and the kinds of adaptations they had to make. But the differences in world view, in outlook, in personality, between the Whites and the Menominee (and other tribes in various ways) were continuing, pervasive influences on the way in which the Menominee were treated by Whites, and the ways in which the Menominee could respond to this treatment.

This interpretation is reinforced by an examination of the Kainai world view, which is oriented toward aggressive action, acquisition of goods, manipulation, and expressiveness, and much more like that of the Whites. It seems significant that the adaptive responses of the Kainai were also quite different from those of the Menominee.[7]

The response

The Menominee responded to the confrontation between their culture and Western culture, and their respective world views, in different ways in different times. When the fur trade began the Whites were few and the rewards to be gained were great. The Menominee saw the advantages in iron tools and utensils, woven cloth, blankets and rifles, and they could only obtain them through trading furs. They lost much of their old sociopolitical organization and residence pattern by accepting the demands of the fur trade, but retained most of their religion, their language, their arts, and their world view. When the fur trade ended they had nothing to turn to but a very small section of wilderness the Whites did not want, and a dependent relationship with the white society and economy. Some

individuals adjusted to the new conditions by adopting white ways as quickly as possible, even to the extent of forbidding their children to speak their native language in the home. Others withdrew further into the forest and attempted to carry on the old existence. Others turned to alcohol and the charity of relatives and white officials. Most just got along from day to day, without long-range goals or purposes.

Out of these varying responses emerged over time four major adaptations. During the period we have known the Menominee these four kinds of adaptations have been apparent, though their distinctiveness has blurred in the most recent generation. They affect the ways in which the Menominee continue to respond to the problem of getting along in a white world. We will consider them as background for a deeper understanding of current behaviors.

These four adaptations are: 1) the native-oriented, which consists of an attempt to revitalize and maintain as much as possible of the traditional way of life in a self-conscious manner; 2) the Peyote or Native American Church, which functions as a synthesis of beliefs and practices from both the traditional Indian and the white culture; 3) the transitional, which is in between the traditional Indian and the white world like the Peyote Cult, but where there is no systematic synthesis of cultural elements; 4) and the acculturated, which consists of individuals who compete with Whites on their terms and who are almost entirely culturally white (though we have some reservations about this last phrase, for we find that cultures almost never die in people). We will describe each of these briefly as adaptive responses to the continuing con-

7. See George D. Spindler and Louise S. Spindler, "The Instrumental Activities Inventory: A Technique for the Study of the Psychology of Acculturation," *Southwestern Journal of Anthropology*, vol. 21 (1965), pp. 1–23 for a synopsis of Blood cognitive orientations.

frontation with Whites and white culture.

The Kainai are not divided by such different adaptive responses. It has been possible for a large number, perhaps a majority of Kainai, to retain significant traditional cultural features, including membership in traditional organizations such as the Horn Society and the speaking of the native language, and at the same time make a viable adaptation to white culture and society.

The native-oriented

Menominee culture has never remained static. It was changing before the Whites came and continued to change after their arrival, though probably more quickly. It was a culture of great sophistication, with a strong cosmological and philosophical orientation, quite different than that of the more activistic and less cogitative Kainai. It was never understood by Whites, including those, such as agents, priests, and teachers who were trying to "civilize" the Menominee.

The 35 or so adults and their children who constituted the native-oriented group during our period of most intense field work with the Menominee (1948–56) tried their best to keep the old culture alive. It seemed very much alive to us; during our field work we attended literally hundreds of ritual meetings, including those few held of the Mitäwin, or Medicine Lodge.

The intent of the Mitäwin is to prolong human life and to see to the final settlement of the souls of the dead in their future abode. The meetings, held infrequently—only once every few years during recent times—center around the funeral ceremony, held some time after the death of a member, the laying away

of the ghost of the deceased forever, and the reinstatement or renewal ceremony that initiates a new member to take the place of the deceased.

Certain other ceremonies were and are today very important, including the Nemeheetwin, or Dream Dance (literally, "dancing rite") diffused from the western plains. The origin story of the Nemeheetwin centers on a young Sioux woman whose people had been killed by white soldiers. She hid for four days in the reeds by the river bank to escape, then a spirit (awe·tok) came to her and said "Arise! I will take care of you." The spirit then took her to the white camp where all were eating. He showed her a plate heaped with food and told her to eat, that she would not be seen by the white soldiers—to eat as much as she desired. Then he gave her the drum and the drumsticks and instructed her in their use and how people who belonged to the drum should act: to help oneself but also to be good to one another; that they should not kill one another; they should live clean and honorable lives and not fear the Whites. Peace and friendship are main themes, as is access to power, for the spirit told the Sioux girl that when the people hit the drum and sang, their voices would reach the Great Spirit making known their needs.

The symbolism is apparent. The Sioux had reached the end of their free life. They were militarily powerless, completely at the mercy of the Whites. The Nemeheetwin ideology rationalized for them a way of getting along in this sad new world. Eating from the table of the white soldiers, but invisible to them, is particularly poignant. The rite and its ideology spread over most of the west and middle west within a few years, and the Menominee, along with the Ojibwa, Potowatomi, Winnebago, and other middle western tribes, adopted it, modifying it to suit their own tribal cultures.

These kinds of movements have often been termed "nativistic" by anthropologists. They are ways of making it possible to cope with altered conditions on native terms. The Mitäwin was probably something of the same kind at one time, though it began much earlier, perhaps only 50 years or so after the fur trade and its radical impact on native life had begun in the seventeenth century. But both the Mitäwin and Nemeheetwin had become so incorporated into the Menominee way of life that the people thought of them as ancient Indian religions.

Not only are these organizations nativistic movements, but the whole of the native-oriented group is a form of nativistic movement, or better, a revitalization movement. The members of it were not unaware of the changes that had taken place around them. Quite to the contrary, they self-consciously battled to keep the more destructive of these changes from destroying their culture and fought to keep the Nemehetween, Mitäwin, Chief's Dance (or War Dance), and a multitude of other traditional customs and beliefs alive. As one woman said, speaking of her children, "We've got to keep them on our side!"

It was a self-conscious choice. They wanted to stay Indian, in recognizable, explicit, ways. They held ceremonies, used medicine bags, spoke Menominee, raised their children to think as they did, brought them into positions on the Drum as soon as possible, and lived well off the main roads in substandard housing without electricity, built of tarpaper and bent saplings in the shape of the old wigwam. This was an adaptive strategy, a way of coping with the overwhelming impact of the Whites and their culture. It was not, as one priest said to us, commenting on the "people at Zoar" (the name for the general area), that they "liked to play Indian." It was a self-conscious exclusion of as much of the Whiteman's culture as possible, and an equally self-conscious attempt to maintain, even to revive, the old culture.

We believe that the native-oriented response is particularly significant as we look at current attempts by the Menominee and other native Americans to reestablish an Indian identity. Of course most attempts do not involve as complete a return to native ways, but even the wearing of plastic ornaments and dyed feathers ("polyethylene Indianism," as one Menominee phrased it) at a weekend of dancing at a political rally in San Francisco or Chicago is a kind of revitalization movement. It is an assertion of Indian identity. And the occupation of the novitiate, Alcatraz, the struggle at Wounded Knee, and the claiming of land for Ganienkeh have strong nativistic, revitalizing overtones. Many of the costumes worn by the participants in these actions show Indian, sometimes even specific tribal symbolism, and the spokesmen for the movements invariably assert that their aim is to restore the Indian to a place of dignity as well as to reclaim the lands that were stolen or forcibly taken by Whites during the settlement of the country. It is also noteworthy that membership in the Nemeheetwin has recently increased and more Menominee have taken to dancing at the "Pow-wows" (their term) than at any time during the fifties or early sixties.

There is no comparable movement among the Kainai. Many dance, and traditional societies sponsor social dances that nearly everyone attends as a part of community life, but not as a movement.

The Peyotists

Most of the members of the Peyote, or Native American Church were brought up by parents who were traditional Menominee. All members had experienced doubts about the validity of native beliefs and practices in young adulthood, and had had considerable experience with the white world. All had some direct contact with Catholicism and a few had been baptized as Catholics. They felt themselves to be suspended between two ways of life.[8]

As one man said "I had been looking for something, somehow, somewhere. This Medicine Lodge was nothing for me. I danced, sung, and had a good time, that's all. I was in school. I looked over this Catholic religion. It didn't satisfy me. People go to church, they say prayers, they cross themselves. But it wasn't in here (taps chest). They didn't feel it in the heart. So I go to some Peyote meeting. I learn more. I listen to them sing songs. I watch people pray. Finally I see this is where we Indians belong. This is our church!"

What was it that satisfied him? The Peyote meetings would seem very "Indian" to an outsider. They are held in a Plains Indian-type tepee,

around a carefully laid fire, the ashes of which are eventually formed into the shape of a thunderbird or a dove. People take peyote, the bud of the cactus lophophora williamsii, that grows in the American southwest and in Mexico (where the ritual originally came from), sing a special kind of song, quite high-pitched, with the traditional tight throat, and pound a small drum with water inside, with a very fast beat. Eventually people begin to pray, each in his or her own way, in their own tongues, and during this time one is likely to have vision experiences, since the cactus is hallucinogenic. This all seems very traditional American Indian. But the thirteen poles holding up the tepee represent Jesus Christ and the twelve disciples, and Christ appears in many of the songs and in many visions. God is often seen as a bearded Whiteman in long flowing robes, though Master Peyote is seen as a powerful Indian sometimes dressed in a policeman's uniform. Kese·manito·w is also there, and power concepts of a traditional kind operate. Whatever the combination of elements, there are Indian and white cultural symbols synthesized together into a synchronous whole and carried through the long night in a most solemn and sacred manner.

The Peyote Church helps resolve personal and cultural conflicts created by the divergence between Menominee and white world views. It is a way station between the traditional world and the new one. Many Menominee left the native-oriented way, entered into peyotism, and eventually went on to a more acculturated state; others remained in the Peyote Church; some did both.

The Peyote Church is another kind of adaptive response to the impact of Whites and their culture upon the Menominee. It is very widespread

8. The chapter on the peyote road in *Dreamers Without Power* combines the observations of the Spindlers and of J. Sidney Slotkin, who made a special study of the Native American Church (*The Peyote Religion: A Study in Indian-White Relations* [Glencoe, Ill.: The Free Press, 1956] and *Menomini Peyotism* [Philadelphia, Pa.: American Philosophical Society, 1952]).

among Native Americans. The Kainai, however, never accepted it. They were not as conflicted as the Menominee; not as suspended between two worlds.

Peyotism appears to be dying out now among the Menominee. They seem to have passed beyond the need for this particular kind of conflict resolution. Peyotism does not aim at social or political change. Its ideology is accommodative. It accepts the deficits of the Indian situation and tries to provide the individual with a way of getting along with it. Native Americans seem to feel that the time for accommodation is past, and are taking more militant stands in the hope of causing changes in their favor.

The transitionals and militant identity seekers

Our analysis has consistently called attention to the transitional character of all groups so far discussed. The transitionals, as an adaptive category, are unlike the native-oriented or peyotists in that their conflicts and cultural losses are not resolved by either a revitalistic movement or by synthesis. The transitionals had early childhood experience with the traditional way of life but moved away from it, or were taken from it by the school and church. Few speak their own language or know anything specific about the old rituals. All have had formal schooling, still mainly in the hands of white teachers, but did not really receive the significant benefits of an education because the schools and teachers were not oriented to Indian needs. Some have tried to move further into the white-dominated society, but have been rebuffed by racist Whites, or have been unable to compete with better-

trained white labor. Unlike the peyotists or the members of the Dream Dance, they have no primary group of their own and no stable social identity. They constitute a large part, probably a majority, of the generation now in its fifties and sixties.

Many of the young people in the Menominee community today are the offspring of transitionals. Nearly all are in the more general sense of the term. In varying degrees these young people have grown up with uncertainty about who they were, a vague sense of inferiority for what they were presumed to be by Whites, and few consistent cultural guides for behavior. There was little satisfaction in school for them, for their teachers could only communicate to them that they should give up being Indian and become like Whites, but that even if they did, it would not guarantee their acceptance. There was little satisfaction within the reservation community, where excessive drinking, family fights, and a generally disordered life resulting from the cultural losses of the transitional situation, were the only environments with which they were intimately familiar. Not all transitional households were like this, but the many of them that were produced a life experience marked by despair and smoldering resentment.

Smoldering resentment coupled with tenuous identities can supply energy for radical social and political movements. However one judges the occupation of the novitiate or the events that have followed, some of them more damaging to life and property within the community than outside, it seems reasonable to interpret them as a kind of striking out that is expressive of pervasive resentment and conflicted identities. (This interpretation does not deny the validity of political aims or the sincerity of participants.) These are people who are ready to occupy buildings, fight police, and "die if need be." They are a conducive base for power movements, and every revolutionary movement in history has used this energy. When the opportunity for militant behavior and identity assertion appeared, they took it. They occupied the novitiate and left only when they had won. Their victory was pointless in that the novitiate was refused by the duly constituted Menominee authorities as a white elephant, too expensive to keep up and too remote to serve as a hospital. Spokesmen for the Menominee Restoration Committee, the interim ruling body, called the occupation "anarchy" and "unethical." But as one acute observer from within the community said, "The whole situation is just a cause to give life a momentary meaning."

The native-oriented group gave their lives meaning by revitalizing the traditional culture. The peyotists did so by creating a ritual and ideology that brought together otherwise unresolvable differences. The transitionals we knew best often dissolved their problems in alcohol or retreated into apathy. The offspring of transitionals find meaning by asserting their Indianness militantly and demanding redress of grievances. Militant behaviors are an adaptive response for them, just as these other behaviors are, to the continuing confrontation with Whites, white power, and white culture.

The Kainai, in contrast, have not engaged in militant actions and have a reputation for moderation that has not made them too popular in some sectors dedicated to radical militancy. The Kainai have striven to separate their resources and facilities from white interference, even to the extent of rebuilding a community center and an industrial development within the heart of their reservation, both geographically and symbolically. But they are not hostile to Whites or to white help, when it is offered in an acceptable manner. The Kainai do not need to assert identity through militancy for it was never as seriously threatened as was the Menominee's, and they have fewer grievances to redress. Nor is there the same reservoir of transitionals to draw the energy from for extreme forms of militancy.

The acculturated and cycles of leadership

A number of Menominee started moving toward full acculturation as soon as they arrived on the reservation. They were quickly joined by others, but they always remained in the minority. Our sample of acculturated men and women from the 1950s includes entrepreneurs, lumber mill supervisors, office managers, trained technicians, and skilled laborers. Their incomes were substantial and in their homes, dress, speech, and habits they appeared to be white. It is from this group that the effective leadership of the Menominee has been drawn in recent decades. They struggled with the problems of partial self-government in the 1940s and 1950s, but always under the watchful eye of the Bureau of Indian Affairs. They struggled with the disastrous consequences of termination, which in May 1961 withdrew apparently forever all federal control and support from the Menominee. Their struggle with the disastrous aftermath of termination went on for more than a decade, with rising costs, lowered profits from the

Menominee lumber industry, which was the sole industry for the new county created out of the reservation, and a tax load that could not be met. Finally they engineered the sale of several thousand acres of Menominee land, in cooperation with a corporation that creates lakes and vacation lands, in order to provide a better tax base for the poorest county in the state of Wisconsin.

This was the trigger that set off a movement that had been smoldering ever since termination became a fact—the Restoration Movement. At first it seemed like a wild pipe dream, but after a long struggle, marked by superb political maneuvering and considerable militant but not unlawful or violent action, the Menominee won their case, and the United States Senate and the House of Representatives voted the Menominee back to semireservation status in December 1973. The old leadership, drawn from the fully acculturated, largely male contingent, was replaced by another leadership that was equally acculturated, but younger, and female rather than male, and uncontaminated by the taint of a "sellout" to Whites. This leadership, in turn, has recently been challenged by a combination of young militants, particularly the Warriors, some of whom occupied the novitiate, and a few old hands who were deposed from power. The revolt is ostensibly against a "dictatorship of women" and what they regard as its arbitrary and authoritarian behaviors.

Whether old or new, male or female, the responsible leadership of the Menominee in the long run will be more interested in stable progress within a recognizable framework of established law than in militancy for the sake of militancy, or militancy for the undeclared purpose of pro-

jecting or forming identities. They will be interested in the maintenance of a Menominee community but will recognize the necessity of getting along with the dominant society. Some of the younger militants, closer to a kind of transitional status and responding with militancy as a means of asserting identity as well as redressing grievances, want to create an Indian retreat where the Whiteman's law does not prevail.[9]

CONCLUSION

It is important for us to keep militancy in the perspective of adaptive response that is an integrating theme in this article. Militancy, for the younger Menominee, is a contemporary adaptive response to the deprivation inherent in the minority position of the Menominee, exacerbated, as it was, through time by the extreme differences in culture and world view that always influenced the interactions of Menominee and Whites. Whereas their parents chose to revitalize tradition, synthesize opposing beliefs with peyote, dis-

9. Others have done research with the Menominee during the past two decades, and we cannot catalogue their influence upon our thinking except to acknowledge that of William H. Hodge, in private conversations. Our interpretations differ, in part due to the different time periods in which we have worked, in part due to his focus on urban Menominee, and our focus on the native-oriented and peyote groups, and in part due to differences in our world views. His "Ethnicity as a Factor in Modern American Indian Migration: A Winnebago Case Study with References to Other Indian Situations," in *Migration and Development*, eds. H. I. Safa and B. M. Dutoit (The Hague, Mouton, 1975) has proven useful. Neils W. Braroe, *Indian and White: Self-Image and Interaction in a Canadian Plains Community* (Stanford, Calif.: Stanford University Press, 1975) has also influenced our thinking about Indian-white relations.

solve the pain of life in alcohol or sink into apathy, or acculturate to white norms to the virtual exclusion of Indian or Menominee values, many of this generation have chosen militancy. However unproductive some of their behaviors may be, they should receive due credit for a fighting stance that has some promise for an improved self-image as well as an improvement in the conditions of their existence. One hopes that they will be able to capitalize on recent gains made and will not destroy or seriously degrade the chances for yet further improvements by thoughtless excesses and random, purposeless expressions of hostility toward all duly constituted authority, including their own.

Legislation and Litigation Concerning American Indians

By VINE DELORIA, JR.

ABSTRACT: The period 1957–77 witnessed an increasing tendency to include Indians in programs and legislation that affected all Americans, particularly in the field of social welfare and development. Indians, as a whole, made good use of their eligibility for these new opportunities, and entered the mainstream of public social concern. Legislation dealing specifically with Indian rights and legal status was generally trivial because no administration made more than a perfunctory effort to define the larger philosophical issues that might have clarified and modernized the Indian legal status. In litigation Indians were unusually successful in some of their efforts, although, again, truly definitive cases that might have proved a fertile ground for long-term gains in the development of contemporary understanding were sparse. Generally, those cases which might have produced landmark theories or doctrines, the Supreme Court refused to take and the decisions, remaining on the federal circuit level, are not sufficiently strong or clear to provide a basis for further development. The era ended with a state of benign confusion, in which Indians seemed more concerned with funding programs than sketching out in broader and more comprehensive terms the ideologies and theories that are necessary for sustained growth. It was, basically, an undistinguished era, but one of maturing and awareness.

Vine Deloria, Jr., is an enrolled member of the Standing Rock Sioux Tribe of North Dakota. A former executive director of the National Congress of American Indians and former chairman of the Institute for the Development of Indian Law, he is an attorney, lecturer, and writer. He served as expert witness and legal counsel in several of the Wounded Knee trials. A member of the American Bar Association, Authors' Guild, and other organizations, he holds degrees in science, theology, and law. He is the author of Custer Died For Your Sins, God is Red and the forthcoming book, The Metaphysics of Modern Existence, as well as numerous articles. He is presently engaged in a book on the theories of Indian law.

AMERICAN Indians occupy a unique legal position within the political structure of our country. Individually Indians are citizens entitled to all benefits of federal and state programs. But in a corporate sense Indian tribes are alternately wards of the federal government, subject to severe and complete administrative supervision, and quasi-independent nations with customary laws originating long before the Constitution and modified only slightly by the relationship with the federal government. Legislation and litigation reflect this confused state of affairs. As Indians are able to clarify their goals the legal apparatus accommodates itself to support the demand for independence and sovereignty. But a profile too high generally invokes the traditional American belief in the equality of the races and produces a demand that treaty rights be abrogated, reservations dissolved, and Indians thrust into the urban slums like other minority groups. The legislation and litigation of the past two decades is representative of this polarization at work in the daily and practical events of American politics.

Beginning with the Hoover Commission Report of 1948 Indians were subjected to an era of forced assimilation and termination of special legal rights. Seeking justification of this program under a number of ideological banners, senators such as Arthur V. Watkins of Utah, Frank Church of Idaho, and Henry Jackson of Washington promoted rapid and forced termination of federal services until the late 1960s, when it became apparent that the trend of social thought prohibited such a policy. From 1961 until 1970, however, the Colvilles of Washington were under the constant threat of termination because of a rider at-

tached to an earlier law which required them to prepare a plan of dissolution. Senator Henry Jackson, using the division of the Colvilles as an excuse, kept the waters of fear and discontent stirred by introducing numerous versions of terminal legislation during this period.

The Senecas, losing the best part of their reservation to the Kinzua Dam, were forced to agree to prepare a plan for termination in order to get compensation for the loss of their lands. When the time to submit the plan arrived the issue of termination was very deftly turned aside by Indian Commissioner Robert Bennett, who made it clear that such a move would prove counterproductive to the programs then being initiated by the government.

By the end of the 1960s it was clear that termination was no longer a feasible alternative to federal services. Under the leadership of Senator Fred Harris the Choctaw Termination Act of 1959 was repealed (P.L. 91–386). The Menominees of Wisconsin, one of the first tribes to be terminated in the 1950s, were successful in a number of efforts to demonstrate the futility of their situation, and in December 1973 the policy was officially reversed as The Menominee Restoration Act (P.L. 93–197) became law, ending the most traumatic period of Indian existence.

Although some senators supported termination during the 1960s, the trend in national legislation beginning with the New Frontier and continuing with the War on Poverty of the Great Society indicated that the mood of the American people was one of helping, not hindering, racial minorities. In 1961 under the Kennedy administration the Area Redevelopment Administration was created to support economic development in chronically depressed regions of the country. Indian reservations were made eligible for this program and many tribes took advantage of the opportunity, building new tribal headquarters, community buildings, and making major capital improvements which had never been conceived in nearly a century of reservation existence. When the program was renewed and expanded in 1964 as the Economic Development Administration, all federal tribes were made eligible for the full scope of programs of this agency and tribes enthusiastically embarked on major economic development projects.

The social programs of the Great Society proved useful to reservation development, but it was not without a degree of irony that Indians were included. An American Indian Capitol Conference on Poverty was held in May 1964 as the Economic Opportunity Act was being considered by the Congress, and Indian poverty was highlighted by a thousand tribal delegates who covered the nation's capitol with visits to their congressional delegations. Being an election year, few politicians could avoid making some statement on the inclusion of Indians in the proposed programs, and the result was that when the Office of Economic Opportunity was authorized, Indians received a special desk.

With this victory under their belts, Indians became sensitive to opportunities that could be created by skillful lobbying efforts, and the favorite tactic was to insist that within the eligibility sections of new legislation the phrase "and/or Indian tribes," be added along with the states and local governments. As a result of this low-profile work, Indians became eligible for nearly every new program authorized during the onrush of social legislation. Thus when the Elementary and Secondary Education Act of 1965 (P.L. 89–19) was passed Indians were made eligible for its provisions. And the renewal of Teacher Corps (P.L. 90–35), Headstart (P.L. 89–794), and VISTA (P.L. 88–452) saw Indians included as regular recipients of the programs. Tribal governments were also included in the Law Enforcement Assistance Act of 1972, and a number of programs designed to upgrade tribal courts and police forces were initiated under the programs funded by this agency.

Education became the focal point of legislative concerns in the late 1960s and early 1970s. Edward Kennedy assumed chairmanship of a minor subcommittee of Public Works following the assassination of his brother Robert, and began extensive hearings on Indian education. Although the investigations were premised upon traditional liberal assumptions which did not exactly fit Indian conditions, the high profile which Kennedy was able to give to Indian education soon made it a major item of congressional interest. A report entitled "Indian Education —A National Tragedy," exploited the wave of sentimental feeling invoked by Dee Brown's best selling book, "Bury My Heart at Wounded Knee," and became the chief item of evidence cited by Indians interested in educational reform.

The Kennedy Report on Indian Education recommended that the Indians take charge of their own education and soon local school boards were being organized to take advantage of this sudden and favorable shift in emphasis. In the Indian Education Act of 1972 a National Indian Education Advisory Council was created, with its members appointed by the president. Political maneuvering, by both the Nixon administration and the Indian political organizations, blunted the impact of this committee because the appointments became more political than educational. Nevertheless it was a major step forward in addressing the subject of Indian education.

Senator Henry Jackson reversed his political position in the early 1970s, as the opportunity for the Democratic nomination seemed within his reach, and this shift in viewpoint created another important piece of legislation for Indians. The rallying cry of the tribes during the 1960s had been "Self-Determination, not Termination." Jackson used this slogan as the basis of new legislation which would enable tribal governments to contract with the federal government to perform some administrative functions which had formerly been the province of the Bureau of Indian Affairs. In 1975, under Jackson's leadership, the Indian Self-Determination Act (P.L. 93–638) was passed. Although it is too early to evaluate the impact of this piece of legislation, indications are that it could only become fully operative with the cooperation of reforms initiated by the Indians themselves in the manner of conducting tribal governments.

Looking at specifically Indian legislation during this two-decade period one is struck with the triviality of the legislation that was considered by the Senate and House Interior Committees. Much of it dealt with simple housekeeping and bookkeeping matters of restoring very small tracts of land, often under ten acres in area, to the respective tribes which had seen lands taken decades earlier for schools, roads, fire stations, and other government projects of the New Deal era. The Secretary of the Interior had been given ample authority to return these tracts to the different reservations in the Indian Reorganization Act. However this period saw a series of men occupy the position of Secretary of the Interior who were frightened at the thought of congressional criticism. They unanimously refused to make land restorations by administrative act and insisted on introducing pieces of legislation to perform this function, thus reducing the constructive activity of the Interior Department to an absolute minimum for Indians.

In order to highlight the legislation of this period, which specifically dealt with Indian matters, one must be selective and willing to view Indian matters in a broad perspective. P.L. 90–280, for example, repealed an old prohibition against the use of federal scholarship funds in sectarian schools. This law released funds for Indian education and broadened the scope of opportunity available in education for Indian youth, but was really something that could and should have been done a generation earlier. P.L. 90–287 recognized the Tiguas of El Paso as a federal tribe and gave responsibility for them to the state of Texas. A welcome respite, to be sure, but the law was needed because of the failure of the Bureau of Indian Affairs a generation earlier to cover all tribes who had federal rights and wished to organize under the Indian Reorganization Act. P.L. 90–597 enabled the Secretary of the Interior to intervene in the administration of Indian trust lands and estates on the Agua Caliente reservation in California, where there had been a notorious scandal in the handling of Indian moneys. Again, this law was welcome, but a couple of decades too late to be of any use to the Indians.

The early years of the Nixon administration saw the use of executive powers to restore lands to tribes. Where this restoration could not be effected, legislation was introduced and received the support of the White House. Such a law was the restoration of the sacred Blue Lake to the people of Taos Pueblo (P.L. 91–550). In the passage of this legislation the White House had to fight very senior senators of the opposite party, such as Henry Jackson and Clinton Anderson, its own Bureau of the Budget, and the reluctant and treacherous Interior Department, which worked behind the scenes against its Indian charges. A great deal of credit must be given to the Nixon administration for keeping this type of promise to the Indians.

Legislation often revolved about personalities rather than legal issues. Thus the Apostle Islands National Lakeshore Act (P.L. 91–424), which confiscated some of the best shoreline lands of the Red Cliff Chippewas of Wisconsin, was regarded by many Indians as a personal bill of Senator Gaylord Nelson rather than a necessary development in the field of Indian policy. At least one congressional career was lost through support of important Indian bills. Senator Fred Harris of Oklahoma opposed the Indian-oil company combination in his native state in order to get P.L. 91–495 passed. This law enabled the people of the Five Civilized Tribes to elect their principal officers for the first time since 1906 when, as part of the dissolution of their tribal governments, the offices were made appointive by the president. The oil companies then worked against Harris in combination with a group of Indian politicians who had been receiving these appointments. By the time of the next election it was apparent that Harris could not win his senate seat and he embarked on an ill-fated effort to win the Democratic nomination for the presidency instead.

Oil companies figured prominently in another piece of major legislation during this period—the Alaska Native Claims Settlement Act (P.L. 91–925). The energy crisis had not yet become important, but it was apparent that the discovery of large oil reserves on Alaska's north slope and the need for transporting the oil to the lower 48 states would produce a settlement to the longstanding claims of the Alaska natives. The bill provided them with 40 million acres, nearly a billion dollars in cash over a decade, and the creation of regional corporations to administer the resources of the natives. A number of native spokesmen who helped get the bill through Congress were later discovered to have been also employees of some major oil companies, raising questions of whether the real natives understood the terms of the settlement. On the whole, however, the settlement has been regarded as more realistic than any of those proposed for Indians in the continental United States, and a minimum of criticism has been directed at the principals of the situation.

Two very pressing problems received legislative attention in this period—Indian civil rights and the federal relationship. For nearly a decade after the passage of P.L. 83–280, which gave jurisdiction to the states in all civil and criminal matters concerning Indians, the tribes had protested that the states purported to take jurisdiction but, in fact, did not provide sufficient law enforcement services to warrant the transfer. In the Pacific Northwest the law was used to justify state intervention in fishing rights and zoning of the reservations without providing any corresponding services to the Indians. By the mid-sixties Indians were totally opposed to the law and sought its repeal but lacked the political strength to make themselves heard. The Senate and House Interior Subcommittees on Indian Affairs absolutely refused to hold hearings on repeal.

In 1968 as the black civil rights bill of that year was being debated in the Senate, Sam Ervin of North Carolina cleverly attached several provisions for Indians derived from extensive hearings that his Constitutional Rights Subcommittee of the Judiciary Committee had held, to the pending legislation. Acting at the close of business, Ervin was able to get the Indian amendments passed and the bill was sent to the House for consideration. Wayne Aspinall, then Chairman of the House Interior Committee demanded that the bill be directed to his Committee because of its Indian provisions. Apparently he intended to bury the bill there. But the liberal forces in the House denied his ploy and the House accepted the Senate's amendments. The repeal of P.L. 83–280 was accomplished without the assistance, and against the wishes, of the western congressional delegations who had Indian constituents and who wished to keep the Indians in this no man's land of jurisdictional turmoil.

The haste with which the Indian amendments were added had some inherent difficulties. Tribes were not prepared to upgrade their tribal courts to courts of record and perform many of the other functions which Anglo-Saxon courts must do as a matter of routine. The amendments appeared to conflict with traditional areas in which the federal government had been reluctant to intrude, such as the application of the Bill of Rights to the relationship of Indians and their tribal governments. Thus the years since the passage of the Indian Civil Rights Bill have been filled with a flood of minor litigation as lawyers and tribes seek to clarify exactly how this new relationship must be conceived.

The occupation of Wounded Knee sparked the nation's conscience and congressional delegations sought to appease the outpouring of concern and anger that followed in its wake. The result was the creation of the American Indian Policy Review Commission Act (P.L. 93–580) introduced by Senator James Abourezk of South Dakota in the summer following the occupation. Originally, the Commission was conceived to encourage extensive field visitations to reservations by members of Congress to observe the conditions which had been responsible for the era of discontent culminating at Wounded Knee. But the Nixon administration, now in the throes of Watergate, did not want an explosive investigation of the treatment of Indians to coincide with the investigations it was already confronting.

When the bill was heard in the Senate, Dewey Bartlett of Oklahoma suggested that the investigation be limited to a management study of the Bureau of Indian Affairs. When this suggestion was finally discussed in the House, the Commission was reduced to impotence by the addition of a number of Task Forces, to be manned by Indians, which would do the actual field work, members of Congress simply serving as sounding boards for reform proposals. The Commission was in existence two years and churned out an incredible amount of material, most of it miscellaneous background papers, and concluded its deliberations without much fanfare and vir-

tually no reforms. The original legislation gave the Commission sub-
poena powers but these were never
used, the Commission staff being
fearful that any aggressive activity
on its part would jeopardize chances
of future employment with the
Interior Department.

The period can best be summarized by a line from a popular
song, "Night Rider's Lament,"—
"they must have gone crazy out
there." Unlike other periods of
Indian history, the last two decades
lacked a strong congressional figure
ablaze with ideological motivation,
seeking reforms and final solutions.
Legislation more often reflected personalities and the movements inside
the Democratic party than it did
issues. The only adequate way to
characterize this period is as one of
generally benign expediency.

In the corresponding field of litigation, Indian Affairs saw the dawn
of a new, aggressive, and exciting
era. A number of private legal
service groups were organized which
began to seek redress for the multitude of wrongs committed by the
federal government in previous
eras. Foremost among these new
groups was the Native American
Rights Fund which, although it
handled few important cases, did
inspire a generation of Indian attorneys. But the field of litigation
made few advances in clarifying Indian rights because of the tendency
of the Supreme Court to avoid controversial Indian cases or to deal
with difficult Indian subjects. It
became almost a rule of thumb that
if a case had little precedent possibilities, it would be taken by the
Supreme Court; if it involved difficult and unresolved ideas, it would
be rejected without comment.

A number of major cases were decided that proved to be important

to Indians. An early case, critical
to the aspirations of the Arizona
tribes, was *Arizona* v. *California*[1]
which established water rights of the
Arizona tribes living along the
Colorado River. The federal reservation of sufficient water for the reservations was affirmed and allowed
economic development of the Colorado River Indian Reservation as a
three-crop-a-year agricultural region.
A lesser case, but nearly as important
to the tribe concerned, was *Pyramid
Lake Paiute Tribe* v. *Morton*[2] which
required the Secretary of the Interior
to justify any diversion of water
away from the reservation, thus clear-
ing the way for the tribe to affirm its
rights to water for its lake.

Two cases decided the matter of
Indian preference in employment
in the Bureau of Indian Affairs.
Both cases decided in favor of Indians. *Morton* v. *Mancari*[3] held
that the Indian preference provisions of the Indian Reorganization
Act were not discriminatory and
Freeman v. *Morton*[4] held that this
right extended to all vacancies in
the Bureau, not simply to the initial
openings which an Indian might accept. Following the *Mancari* victory
the National Tribal Chairmen's Association petitioned Congress to
cancel the decision by legislation,
an ill-fated proposition suggested
by Bureau employees to the pliable
Indian group.

Fishing rights cases in Washington, Oregon, Wisconsin, and Michigan gave indication that this area
of conflict would remain difficult.
The state of Washington and the
Indians had a running battle over
the provisions of the Treaty of Medi-

1. 83 S. Ct. 269.
2. 354 F. Supp. 252.
3. 94 S. Ct. 2474.
4. 499 F. 2d. 494.

cine Creek of 1854. The Indians won a partial victory in *Puyallup Tribe* v. *Department of Game of Washington*[5] when the Supreme Court ruled that the state must not create discriminatory regulations for fishing. A ludicrous example of juridical nonsense was *State* v. *Moses*,[6] wherein a tribe, having changed its name to correspond with the name of its reservation, was found not to be a signatory of the treaty. But the climax of the struggle in Washington was *United States* v. *Washington*,[7] the famous "Boldt" decision, which awarded half of the fish in the state to the Indians. Interior Secretary Morton, allegedly the Indians' trustee, when told that the Indians had won, wanted to appeal the decision until informed that Interior had been supporting the tribes.

An earlier decision with a less satisfactory holding, but one that might have warmed Morton's heart was *Organized Village of Kake* v. *Egan*,[8] in which the fishing rights of the little village were declared to have been lost with the admission of Alaska into the union. In general Indians did fairly well with fishing rights cases at the higher federal court level. *Sohappy* v. *State of Oregon*[9] decided that the state was severely restricted in the manner in which it would attempt to regulate Indian fishing. Even more important was the decision in *Menominee Tribe* v. *United States*[10] in which the Supreme Court ruled that the termination of the Menominees had not affected their rights to hunt and fish within their former reserva-

tion. This holding led directly to the reversal of Menominee termination.

Struggles over the interpretation of state taxing authority on Indian reservations were prevalent throughout Indian country, but Minnesota and Arizona seem to produce the most important conflicts and decisions. In *Commissioner of Taxation* v. *Brun*,[11] the Minnesota Supreme Court ruled that the state could not interfere with tribal self-government by taxing tribal members for income earned on the reservation in tribal programs. *Warren Trading Post Co.* v. *Arizona State Tax Commission*,[12] decided by the Supreme Court, ruled that the federal government had already totally preempted the area of trading with Indians and eliminated the state from entering this field. The state came back by attempting to tax Navajo employees, but in *McClanahan* v. *Arizona State Tax Commission*,[13] another Supreme Court case, the decision was that such an income tax would intrude into a field occupied by the tribal government and therefore that Arizona lacked jurisdiction to tax the Navajos.

The Indian conflict with federal taxing authorities produced successful decisions also. In an early case in the 1950s, *Squire* v. *Capoeman*,[14] income from federal trust allotments was ruled exempt from income taxes but the Internal Revenue Service continued to seek a means of levying against this type of income. A 20-year battle ensued over the income from allotments purchased by the Secretary of the Interior for Indians under the provisions of the Indian Reorganization Act. In

5. 88 S. Ct. 1725.
6. 422 P. 2d. 775.
7. 520 F. 2d. 676.
8. 174 F. Supp. 500.
9. 302 F. Suppl. 899.
10. 88 S. Ct. 1064.

11. 174 N.W. 2d. 120.
12. 85 S. Ct. 1242.
13. 93 S. Ct. 1257.
14. 351 U.S. 1.

Commissioner of Internal Revenue Service v. *Stevens*,[15] such income was also held to be exempt from federal taxation.

The confusion resulting from the uneven application of P.L. 83–280, which gave states permission to extend their civil and criminal jurisdiction over reservations, produced a large number of minor cases. With the passage of the 1968 Indian Civil Rights Bill, the issue of jurisdiction became even more complicated and a number of important suits arose in an effort to clarify the questions of exclusive, joint, and concurrent jurisdiction of states and tribes in regard to tribal members and reservation areas. The first major case in this area was *Williams* v. *Lee*,[16] in which the Supreme Court found no right of jurisdiction inherent in the state of Arizona for cases arising on the reservation. A step toward resolution of this question was probably *Colliflower* v. *Garland*,[17] in which the tribal court of the Fort Belknap reservation was described as a federal instrumentality for some purposes. The doctrine was not extended universally, however, and *Kennerly* v. *District Court of the Ninth Judicial District of Montana*,[18] heard following the passage of the Indian Civil Rights Act, seemed to indicate that tribal consent was requisite to any assumption or sharing of jurisdiction by tribal courts, undercutting to some extent both the *Colliflower* decision and the Indian Civil Rights Act.

City of New Town, North Dakota v. *United States*,[19] another effort to clarify the geographical area in which tribal jurisdiction could be exercised, produced the doctrine that unless and until the Congress specifically reduces the boundaries of reservations they are presumed to include all lands whether held by Indians or not. This doctrine was expanded by the Supreme Court in *United States* v. *Mazurie*,[20] in which the Shoshone-Arapaho tribes of the Wind River Reservation were supported in their effort to police white landowners on the reservation, the controversy in question being the regulation of a reservation liquor store.

A number of cases served to clarify specific points of law dealing with federal regulations and treaties. *Choctaw Nation* v. *Oklahoma*,[21] a Supreme Court case, affirmed the title to the bed of the Arkansas River and the minerals beneath to the Five Civilized Tribes whose boundaries by treaty included the river. In *Ruiz* v. *Morton*,[22] another Supreme Court finding, the Snyder Act of 1924 was given national application rather than the narrow administrative interpretation which had been promulgated by the Interior Department for nearly a half century. *Northern Cheyenne Tribe* v. *Hollowbreast*[23] held that the all-important mineral rights of this reservation should be held in common, thus preserving a semblance of tribal control over the incredibly rich coal lands of the Cheyenne. And *Running Horse* v. *Udall*[24] forever barred the activities of the Secretary of the Interior in allowing states to levy against the estates of deceased

15. 452 F. 2d. 741.
16. 79 S. Ct. 269.
17. 342 F. 2d. 369.
18. 91 S. Ct. 480.
19. 454 F. 2d. 121.
20. 95 S. Ct. 710.
21. 90 S. Ct. 1328.
22. 94 S. Ct. 1055.
23. 349 F. Supp. 1302.
24. 211 F. Supp. 586.

Indians who had received old age benefits.

The inconsistency of the federal courts toward Indian rights during this two-decade period can be illustrated by reference to a number of cases involving the application of general statutes to Indians. In *Simmons* v. *Eagle Seelatsee*,[25] a federal court held that the plenary power of Congress extends over Indians even though they have received citizenship. *Seneca Nation* v. *Brucker*,[26] a case arising in connection with the construction of Kinzua Dam in Pennsylvania, brought forth the doctrine of implied consent of Congress in general statutes to override treaty provisions. Yet in *Crow Tribe* v. *United States*,[27] a case in the Indian Claims Commission, the 1851 treaty was held to be a recognition of internal sovereignty of the tribes, a doctrine that appeared to bolster the contentions of activists that Indian tribes were quasi-independent and that treaties could not be lightly abrogated or changed by implication. Even more strange was *Harjo* v. *Kleppe*,[28] in which the ruling resuscitated a Creek government thought to have been extinguished in 1906.

The Supreme Court avoided the question of tribal legal status when it refused to hear several cases involving a determination of the treaties of different tribes, leaving everyone puzzled at such holdings as the *Native American Church of North America* v. *Navajo Tribal Council*,[29] in which a federal court characterized tribal governments as "higher than states," and *Iron*

Crow v. *Oglala Sioux Tribe*,[30] which seemed to bolster this ideology. *Gila River Pima-Maricopa Community* v. *United States*,[31] another case from the Indian Claims Commission, relied upon the peculiar doctrine that wardship, and the corresponding trustee responsibilities of the United States depend upon the particular statute or treaty under which the United States establishes a legal relationship with the tribe. But even a meeting of the minds involving Indians and the United States can be changed by Congress and when it is, according to *United States* v. *Kiowa, Comanche and Apache Tribes of Indians*,[32] the United States is held to the highest standards of trusteeship. To compound the confusion, one needed only to refer to the *Tuscarora Nation of Indians* v. *Power Authority of the State of New York*[33] to hear a federal court declare that the interest of the United States is in the general, not the specific, welfare of Indians.

As the period ended a potentially explosive situation was in process as eastern Indian tribes sought redress for several centuries of neglect. In *Joint Tribal Council of Passamaquoddy Tribe* v. *Morton*,[34] the Indians of Maine successfully contended that they were a federal tribe under the Nonintercourse Act of the 1790s and therefore entitled to pursue land claims against the state of Maine—with the assistance of the Justice Department. In *Narragansett Tribe of Indians* v. *Southern Rhode Island Development Corporation*,[35] the doctrine of federal responsibility

25. 244 F. Supp. 808.
26. 162 F. Supp. 580.
27. 284 F.2d. 361.
28. 420 F. Supp. 1110.
29. 272 F.2d. 131.

30. 231 F.2d. 89.
31. 140 F. Supp. 776.
32. 163 F. Supp. 603.
33. 164 F. Supp. 107.
34. 528 F.2d. 370.
35. 418 F. Supp. 798.

for eastern Indians was expanded with the holding that even studied neglect by the federal government was not sufficient to break the trust responsibility owed the Indians. The incoming Carter administration sought to prevent these cases from going forward to their logical— and inevitable—conclusion that Indians owned most of the Atlantic seaboard.

The litigation process is most difficult to control and the emergence of any sustained theoretical development must be accidental at best. Indian cases traditionally are subject to the whims of the courts in the sense that not all judges have sufficient familiarity with American history, the complexities of treaty negotiations, or traditional doctrines of Indian law to write comprehensive and comprehensible decisions which will bind the various strands of theory into a coherent whole. That federal court decisions bear little resemblance to corresponding contemporary developments in legislation is well-known and capable of documentation in any period of Indian history. But during this particular period, unless a case was politicized and obviously had the capability of resolving the ancient schizophrenia of ward-domestic dependent nation ideology, judges did not pay much attention to events and movements in the public arena.

Summarizing the two decades in the fields of legislation and litigation one could best describe them as years of confusion, in which a strong leadership by executive, legislative, or judicial branches of the government would have been welcomed but was absent. Indians made substantial progress in a tangible sense with the plethora of new social programs. They successfully defended themselves in the courtroom against intrusions on their self-government and reservation jurisdiction. And they made some progress in reasserting ancient treaty claims respecting land and hunting and fishing rights.

The missing ingredient in the formula for constructive change was a unified Indian community capable of articulating and interpreting future goals. No theoretical conception of the contemporary status of Indians emerged from the Indian community and without the ideological guidelines to act as boundaries for change, there was simply continuous movement to and fro between the twin poles of sovereignty and wardship. No single period of time can be expected to yield a rich harvest of leadership and constructive activity, and it may be that the seeds so carelessly planted during these tumultuous decades will bear positive fruit in the decades ahead. One thing was certain: Indians had broken the back of the termination mentality and had emerged from the shadows of social neglect into a better day. How much better the future would be was the unanswered question as the Indian community faced the last two decades of this century.

ANNALS, AAPSS, **436**, Mar. 1978

The Indian Claims Commission

By NANCY OESTREICH LURIE

ABSTRACT: In 1946, when the Indian Claims Commission Act was passed, it was expected that the Commission would complete its work in ten years. The volume of dockets, about 650, and the time consuming methods of litigation required repeated extensions of the Commission's tenure, with the present cut-off date set for 1978. The Commission's work has been expedited somewhat by procedural reforms introduced in the 1960s, including expansion of the number of Commissioners from three to five. Generally, the Commission has been a disappointment to Indian claimants. Despite exceptionally broad grounds for suit stated in the 1946 Act, the Commission has favored narrow construals and parsimonious settlements. Tribes must obtain congressional approval of plans for the use of their awards. The Indians' usual preference has been for per capita distributions rather than for programmed use which the government prefers, such as investment in securities or tribal enterprises. Since 1974, except for unusual circumstances warranting otherwise, tribes must program 20 percent of their awards.

Nancy Oestreich Lurie is head Curator of Anthropology at the Milwaukee Public Museum. She holds an adjunct professorship in Anthropology at the University of Wisconsin-Milwaukee where she previously served on the full-time faculty. She received her Ph.D. in 1952 from Northwestern University. Her field studies have included work with the Winnebago people of Wisconsin and Nebraska and the Dogrib people of northern Canada. She has testified in a number of cases before the Indian Claims Commission and has published extensively on contemporary Indian affairs as well as on general anthropological topics.

RETROSPECT[1]

THE INDIAN Claims Commission Act of August 13, 1946 (P.L. 79-726) was intended to overcome procedural and financial obstacles in the way of Indian tribes seeking restitution for grievances against the United States. Heretofore, a tribe had to obtain a special jurisdictional act from Congress to bring suit in the U.S. Court of Claims, where the grounds for suit tended to be construed so narrowly that more than two out of three claims were disallowed, and it was not unusual for several decades to elapse from the time attorneys were retained until a decision was rendered.

During the 1930s and 1940s, Congress repeatedly considered the creation of a special tribunal to deal fairly and expeditiously with Indian claims and assure that even poor tribes could have their day in court. The legislation of 1946, in effect a general jurisdictional act, permitted tribes five years to register claims with the Commission, which was expected to hear and adjudicate all cases by 1957. The act also eased the way financially for tribal claimants. Attorneys could enter into total contingency contracts with Indian clients and attorneys' fees were limited to no more than 10 percent of a judgment besides the costs of preparing cases. The Bureau of Indian Affairs had the responsibility of informing tribes of their right to bring suit.[2]

Claims could be brought by any "tribe, band or identifiable group" of American Indians through their governing councils or, if lacking a formal organization, by any member acting in behalf of the tribe, band, or group. The Attorney General was designated to defend the government and a special Indian claims staff was set up in the Justice Department to handle the increase in Indian cases. Hearings were to be conducted according to ordinary federal court procedures with either party having the right of appeal, first to the Court of Claims and then to the Supreme Court.

While operating much like a court, a commission, in theory, has more flexibility to deal with unusual and unprecedented circumstances. In practice, commissions frequently are reluctant to break new ground. The Indian Claims Commission was no startling exception in this regard. In some respects, the procedural provisions of the act itself encouraged conservatism. However, the act also incorporated two features which could have given the Commission the necessary latitude to develop new approaches to old problems. These were the grounds for suit (section 2) and the Commission's power to create an Investigation Division (section 12). In the actual promulgation of suits, neither of these provisions figured importantly.

A remarkable range of complaints was anticipated in the grounds for

1. Unless otherwise cited, material in this section is from Nancy Oestreich Lurie, "The Indian Claims Commission Act," *The Annals of the American Academy of Political and Social Science*, vol. 311 (May 1957) pp. 56-70.

2. The Bureau contacted only federally recognized tribes. Thus, many groups on the eastern seaboard were overlooked. Long

unresolved claims are now being presented through the courts by Indian groups such as the Penobscot and Passamaquoddy of Maine. For a discussion of wider legal issues regarding Indian affairs up to 1957, see the article by Theodore H. Haas, "The Legal Aspects of Indian Affairs from 1887 to 1957," *The Annals of the American Academy of Political and Social Science*, vol. 311 (May 1957) pp. 12-22. On litigation, see Vine Deloria's article in this issue of THE ANNALS.

suit, including elaborately specified claims in law or equity arising in regard to the Constitution, treaties and Executive Orders of the President, as well as claims sounding in tort or involving fraud, duress, mutual or unilateral mistake, and, finally, "claims based on fair and honorable dealings not recognized by any existing rule of law or equity." The door appeared to be open to almost anything, but once cases began to be heard it was shut, quickly and firmly, against any claims which did not deal with a limited number of highly quantifiable issues. In the vast majority of cases this has meant proving that the claimants had been paid less for their land than its fair market price at the time of taking. Awards consist of the difference between these figures minus offsets. Exceptions to this pattern are accounting claims, about 50 out of more than 600 dockets, and concern allegations of mismanagement of tribal funds, lands, and resources. Many of these cases have been transferred to the Court of Claims and are still in litigation. The emphasis in this article will be on land cases.

If employed at all, "fair and honorable dealings" has been mainly "color" in arguments based on unconscionable payments for land or uncompensated takings.[3] Attorneys

for the Indians and the Justice Department assessed the sentiment of the Commission as expressed in the earliest cases, 26 dismissals and only two awards by 1951, and settled for legal theories based on acreage and cold cash. Even the grounds of fraud and duress, traditional sources of Indian grievance, seemed to strike many attorneys as more rhetorical than substantive issues. In fairness, it should be noted that the hazards of contingency contracts and 10 percent fees designed to benefit the Indians also tended to discourage lawyers from striking out in innovative directions.

Presentation of land cases soon followed a routine format. First, there is the need to prove the petitioners' identity as the rightful descendants of those who used and occupied the land in question. The concepts of use and occupancy frequently became matters at issue until a kind of formula evolved out of the Commission's decisions. The Commission chose to honor tribal claims where any kind of aboriginal title to exclusive use and occupancy was shown, if only ritualistic or seasonal, but to disallow compensation for intertribally shared lands although an important portion of several tribes' sustenance might have come from such areas. Where the government moved several tribes into an area and then moved them on, the Commission has recognized such shared interests as a form of legal title to given lands.[4]

If it is decided that a petitioner has a proper claim, a second round of hearings considers the petitioners'

---

3. "Fair and honorable dealings" cannot be used in accounting claims transferred to the Court of Claims, but it has figured in the Commission's decisions in not allowing offsets where administrative procedures worked hardships on tribes. The difficulties of bringing suit on grounds of fair and honorable dealings per se are discussed by James Michael Kelly in a review of *Gila River Pima-Maricopa Community* v. *United States*. His discussion appears in "Recent Developments", *Saint Louis University Law Journal*, vol. 15, no. 3 (1971) pp. 491–507. Kelly concludes, "The holdings . . . did serve to solidify an historical American tradition and belief: Indians never win."

4. Imre Sutton, *Indian Land Tenure* (New York: Clearwater Publishing Co., 1975), provides valuable analyses of Indian land holding, both aboriginal and under federal trust, and extensive discussion of Indian Claims Commission cases.

and government's evaluations of the fair market price of the land at the time it was relinquished. Finally, if the government is proved liable, the question of offsets must be argued. Hearings require extensive testimony by various kinds of expert witnesses, the introduction of hundreds of pages of documentation, and all the customary legal paper generated by opposing attorneys. By 1976, the Commission's records comprised 39 volumes, each averaging well over 500 pages.[5]

In effect, the Commission required the litigants to undertake and pay for much of the work intended for the Investigation Division and sought no major appropriation from Congress to make it an effective source of knowledge to illuminate their deliberations.

TWENTY YEARS LATER

When the Indian Claims Commission was first reviewed in THE ANNALS in 1957, it was observed that it had already become necessary for Congress to extend its tenure for five years and that the claims would "simply not be settled when the Commission expires in 1962." The life of the Commission has had to be extended four more times, most recently to September 30, 1978, when any remaining litigation will be completed in the Court of Claims.

The extended tenure of the Commission is due in part to the volume of cases greatly exceeding congressional expectations in 1946. By the 1951 deadline, 370 petitions were filed but because many included more than one cause of action, by September 1976, the Commission

had gradually separated them into 615 dockets. Dockets are sometimes further subdivided into several issues so that the number of actual claims has been estimated in the neighborhood of 850.[6] The Commission could not possibly have wrapped up its work by 1957. The situation would have been even worse if some procedural changes had not been instituted.

Initially, for example, both the land area and its evaluation had to be decided by the Commission before either party could appeal to the Court of Claims. In 1960, an amendment to the original act allowed for interlocutory appeal when the extent of title alone had been ruled on, with evaluation argued only once, after acreage was determined.[7] With the slow settlement of claims, Indians' attorneys with a number of pending suits were often hard put to finance the preparation of their cases. In 1963, a revolving loan fund administered through the Indian Bureau helped attorneys pay for expert assistance of a nonlegal nature.

The most sweeping efforts to expedite the Commission's work occurred in 1967. The number of Commissioners (appointed by the President with the advice and consent of

5. Indian Claims Commission, *Annual Report* (Washington, D.C., 1976) p. 1.

6. Thomas Le Duc, "The Work of the Indian Claims Commission under the Act of 1946," *Pacific Historical Review*, vol. 26, no. 1 (1957) pp. 1–16.

7. In discussing the legislative history of the Claims Commission Act since 1946, I have relied heavily on "The Indian Claims Commission Act as Amended," a pamphlet edited and printed by the firm of Wilkinson, Cragun and Barker, Washington, D.C., May 1972. I am grateful to Frances Horn, a partner in this firm, for bringing this publication to my attention and for her patient kindness in answering, in personal correspondence and phone calls, my many questions regarding various developments in the work of the Commission incorporated in this article.

the Senate) was increased from three to five. By this time, Chief Commissioner Edgar Witt and Commissioner Louis J. O'Marr had retired and had been replaced respectively by Arthur V. Watkins (1960)[8] and T. Harold Scott (1959). The 1967 legislation called for new presidential appointments. Neither William M. Holt, the last original Commissioner, nor Scott was reappointed, and Watkins chose to retire. Thus, a completely new panel took office with the life title of Chief Commissioner abolished in favor of a changing chairmanship.

Since 1967, procedural streamlining has included prehearing conferences to get technical matters cleared away and regularizing a practice, employed occasionally after 1960, of farming hearings out to smaller panels rather than having the entire Commission hear each case. The most significant saving of time concerned expert testimony. Customarily, both sets of witnesses had presented extensive oral testimony. Since 1967, both parties to the suits have been required to present their experts' direct testimony in written form 30 days before trial so that hearings can begin immediately with cross examination based on the reports.

Appendix 1 of the Commission's 1976 *Annual Report* reveals that in the 18 years from 1949 to 1967, the Commission disposed of 232 dockets, 132 by dismissals and 100 by awards. In the next eight years, 68 dockets were dismissed and 180 resulted in awards, a total of 248 dockets. Despite an enormously accelerated pace of work, the first Chairman, John T. Vance, noted in 1969 that it was unrealistic to expect the Commission to complete, in the three years then remaining to it, more work than had been accomplished in the preceding two decades.[9] Vance called for activation of the Investigation Division to employ experts, assemble evidence and present proposed findings of fact to the Commission which would then hear further arguments from the interested parties to arrive at final opinions. Apparently, the enormous shifting of bureaucratic and legal gears and the necessary appropriation to institute a real Investigation Division met with less enthusiasm than the, by now, familiar technique of extending the life of the Commission to complete its work.

Size of awards

Although complete statistics are not yet available, it is possible to make some general observations as the work of the Commission finally draws to a close. By June 3, 1977, there had been certified to Indian claimants in 285 dockets a total of $657,151,090.33 before deduction of attorneys' fees. This amount must have been equalled, if not greatly exceeded, by the cumulative costs

8. The original Commissioners' lack of prior experience in Indian affairs was deemed an asset of open mindedness. However, when Watkins was appointed, arguments in his favor were that he was already an expert in Indian matters, having been the foremost proponent of the termination policy while he was a Senator (R. Utah)—hardly a qualification to inspire Indian confidence in the Commission. Greater sensitivity has characterized appointments since 1967, including Margaret Hunter Pierce, experienced in Indian claims in her previous positions as Clerk, Chief Clerk and Reporter for the Court of Claims, and Brantley Blue, a Lumbee Indian and formerly a judge.

9. John T. Vance, "The Congressional Mandate and the Indian Claims Commission," *North Dakota Law Review*, vol. 45, no. 3 (Spring 1969) pp. 325–36.

since 1946 for personnel and related expenses of the Commission itself, the Indian Claims Section of the Justice Department, the Court of Claims in appeals from Commission decisions, and the Congress and Bureau of Indian Affairs in regard to various continuing concerns with the course of Indian Claims.

Awards, to date, range from less than $2,500 (Ponca, Doc. 324) to over $29,000,000 in the eight combined dockets of the Indians of California (Docs. 31, 37, 176, 215, 333, 80, 80–D, 347). Some tribes' claims are presented in several dockets and in some cases several tribal groups share in a single docket. The average amount per docket which resulted in an award is under $3,000,000. On a per capita basis Indian people for the most part will realize only a few thousand dollars each from their tribes' awards. From their point of view, it must appear that the federal mountain labored long and mightily to bring forth a pretty paltry mouse, if any mouse was forthcoming at all. With few exceptions, interest is not allowed.[10] Land evaluations are low, offsets cut down the size of claims awards, and the costs of preparing Indians' cases are deducted from their awards.

Fair market value

While it would appear a simple matter to deduct the sum paid for land from the fair market value at the

time of taking, historic land values are subject to many interpretive alternatives. Where cessions were small and surrounded by private land for which there was an active market, comparative appraisal is relatively easy. However, many cases involve large aboriginal holdings more or less remote from white settlement. Even appraisals based on contemporary sales of similar, unimproved lands raise technically, if not ethically, uncomfortable issues. As pointed out by historian Thomas Le Duc:

. . . the United States, by virtue of its vast operations in the land market in the nineteenth century, held a monopolistic power over land prices throughout the country . . . the price of private land was substantially a function of public policy. After 1840, certainly, federal policy affected adversely the value of private land in the United States. . . . The appraiser must, therefore, calculate values as they prevailed within the orbit of prices determined by government dumping of land at low prices.[11]

A number of ingenious formulas were brought forth by the Justice Department in the early hearings to arrive at land values, such as the attempt to set an average dollar amount per acre according to the price the government eventually got from sale of the land. However, included in this "average" were huge sections conveyed under other forms of entry than cash sales, veterans' land paper, and agricultural college scrip, for example. While such flagrant financial fudging was disallowed, demolishing such arguments entailed time and expense for Indian claimants.[12] The inexactitude of restrospective appraisal has

---

10. The Commissioners note a current state of uncertainty about accounting claims and ". . . the Government's duty or lack of duty to pay interest on tribal moneys it withholds from Indians." (*Annual Report*, 1976). In claims arising out of the Fifth Amendment of the Constitution (due process), interest is automatically included from the time of taking. Sale of "surplus" Indian land has figured in a number of Fifth Amendment claims.

11. Le Duc, "The Work of the Indian Claims Commission," p. 12.
12. Ibid., pp. 10–11.

been resolved increasingly over the last decade by stipulations in which both parties to the suits agree to a compromise between their respective experts' appraisals.[13]

Offsets

Offsets also have helped to reduce the size of awards, a few to the point of nullifying them. The following discussion of offsets draws heavily on a detailed study of the subject by John R. White.[14] The Act of 1946 probably would not have been passed without the inclusion of the offset provision. Figures as high as $3,000,000,000 were bruited about as the bill the government might have to pay on Indian claims. Although this sum was patently inflated, apparently it served to frighten legislators into allowing offsets. As White observes of the final form of the Indian Claims Commission Act, "It's as if the government was expressing a willingness to correct the error of its ways—providing the effort wasn't too costly."

Neither the Commission nor Court of Claims has been entirely consistent in determining what constitutes a proper offset. Generally, "money or property given to or funds expended gratuitously for the benefit of the claimant," is understood to mean expenses for group rather than individual welfare. Special considerations to chiefs have been disallowed as offsets but, as White shows, it is then difficult to understand why the government was

allowed to offset the cost of funerals for indigent Indians in the Quapaw judgment of 1954.

The major justification for offsets is that if Indians had received proper compensation for their lands initially they would not have needed subsequent gratuities. Offsets are therefore part of the price paid for the land. However, offsets often turn out to be the price of things that Indian people neither wanted nor would have purchased if given a choice. Also, had tribes not been forced to relinquish the lands and resources which had supported them, they would not have required government gratuities to survive.[15]

As a general point of law, a defendant may not plead against a judgment a gratuity given a plaintiff. Monroe Price notes the questionable legality of Indian claims offsets in observing that "a person defending against a tort claim of rape cannot offset the award by the value of the incidental pleasure his victim enjoyed as a result of the attack."[16]

The Investigation Division

When the Commissioners decided to give the task of generating information to the litigants, they made the hearings unnecessarily time consuming and costly for all concerned, including the tax paying public. The expense of the cases would have been no greater if the Investigation Division had been properly

13. Indians' attorneys tend to feel that stimulations generally work to the tribes' benefit. At least, they hasten proceedings in cutting down the number of appeals by either side.

14. John R. White, "Barmecide Revisited: The Gratuitous Offset in Indian Claims Cases," Ethnohistory, in press.

15. The "Sioux Amendment" to the original Act, approved October 27, 1974 (88 Stat. 1499) states that "expenditures for food, rations, or provisions shall not be deemed payments on the claim" which, in effect, recognized that otherwise the Sioux Black Hills claim would have been virtually wiped out.

16. Monroe Price, Law and the American Indian: Readings, Notes and Cases (New York: Bobbs Merrill, 1973), pp. 497–98.

staffed and funded; it might have been considerably less. The number of researchers and experts hired by the Justice Department are paid for with public moneys which could have been shunted just as easily through the Commission itself, thereby also saving much duplicating of effort by opposing experts.

Not only are Indian claimants' awards reduced by the cost of experts, but there is the incalculable cost of the lack of experts. Indians' attorneys were not equally able to assume what turned out to be extremely long-term risks. There is the nagging possibility that when final analyses are made some of the early dismissals and very small awards will be shown to be the result of differential access to experts, especially before the revolving loan fund was established.

Disposition of awards

Until Indian groups present plans for the distribution of their judgments, their awards draw 4 percent interest in the federal treasury or, with tribal approval, the Indian Bureau invests their money at the highest rates obtainable. Until recently, Congress spent a great deal of time detailing exactly how the money was to be used in the disposition of each award. A general disposition act for Indian claims judgments, passed October 19, 1973, now delegates primary responsibility for review and approval of plans to the Secretary of the Interior. The lengthy rules governing the Secretary's work include the directive that "not less than twenty (20) per centum of judgment funds, including investment income thereon, is to be used for tribal programs unless the Secretary determines that particular circumstances of the af-

fected tribe clearly warrant otherwise."[17]

The fact is that the majority of tribes have argued for complete and immediate distribution of their awards on a per capita basis despite urging by Congress, the Indian Bureau and some of their own members to husband their awards with investment programs or programs to serve the general interest.[18] If ill-advised, as some believe, the widespread clamor for per capitas is understandable.

In the first place, the implementation of the Indian Claims Commission Act coincided with the period of gathering congressional sentiment for termination of federal responsibility to protect Indian land and resources. As Indian people saw it, termination was likely to be the penalty for attempting to program their money. The Menominee tribe, the first to be terminated, was singled out largely because of its apparent "wealth." In 1951, after 17 years of litigation, the Menominee had won a net judgment of $7,600,000 in the Court of Claims. Added to working capital from their tribal

17. "Use or Distribution of Indian Judgment Funds," *Federal Register*, vol. 39, no. 10 (15 January 1974) pp. 1835–36.
18. A Bureau of Indian Affairs statement taken from a memo from the division of Tribal Government Services, Aug. 26, 1974, lists 109 judgment dispositions by special acts prior to the act of 1973. Of 100 plans with complete data, 49 (involving 36 tribes) are total per capita distributions and two more tribes have modified, "family plan" per capita distributions; 11 plans (involving 10 tribes) divide awards between per capita distribution and programming with the largest share in most cases going into per capitas; the remaining 38 plans are totally programmed awards, but 11 of these are accounted for by three tribes each with several awards. In one case a tribe with two programmed awards distributed a third and by far the largest in per capitas.

lumbering industry, they had some $10,000,000 in cash assets besides their substantial, tribally held estate in timbered land. The tribe voted $1,500 per capita payments from their judgment (since individual income had suffered over the years because of government mismanagement of their lumbering, the basis of their suit), setting the rest aside for community purposes, including the actual expenditure of about $250,000 for improving the hospital they maintained with tribal enterprise earnings.

By 1961 when termination became final, with the Menominee still protesting against it, the remainder of their judgment and money they had accumulated previously had gone down the drain in the process of getting them terminated. Virtually bankrupt, they even had to close their hospital and lost a sizeable piece of their land before they succeeded in getting their termination repealed in 1973. While the per capitas made no appreciable difference in individuals' lives, it was the only satisfaction the Menominee got out of their judgment. Had it not been distributed, it would have gone with the rest of their funds.[19]

Besides widespread Indian awareness of the Menominee story, practically every tribe has had its own historical experiences of money managed for their benefit, and when it was gone they were no better off than before. Problems with federal administration and tribal

19. For more information on Menominee, see Debbie Shames, ed., *Freedom with Reservation* (Madison, Wisconsin: National Committee to Save the Menominee People and Forests, 1972); Nancy Oestreich Lurie, "Menominee Termination: From Reservation to Colony," *Human Organization*, vol. 31, no. 3 (Fall 1972) pp. 257–69.

governments have created schisms in Indian communities and, for many tribes, arguments about disposition of claims awards have added to internal political dissent. Although delays of several years between certification of awards and approval of plans have increased judgments through accumulated interest, this fact fails to convince many Indian people of the advantages of investment programs. Explanations of how the equivalent of immediate per capita amounts could accrue from interest over a period of a few years, while leaving the award intact and still producing income, are not enough to overcome an abiding Indian suspicion that the two birds will fly out of the bush before they hatch any eggs.

Tribal business ventures or community improvements are considered at least as risky as investments. Furthermore, while "home" remains the reservation, many people spend much time away at jobs in urban areas and do not see locally-based programs as serving the general interest. Finally, Indian people are inclined to consider community development a federal financial responsibility, part of the promise they relate to treaties, which has never been fulfilled to their satisfaction.

It is less easy to understand why some tribes have chosen to program all or a large portion of their judgments. There is no discernible pattern of tribal programming of judgment funds in terms of geographical location, cultural similarities, or a particular period when Indian people might have felt more confident about programming. As far as my limited observations suggest, one of the persuasive arguments for programming is that future generations of the tribe have an equity in the award. The people deciding on disposition plans just happen to be alive now to collect on debts owed since their ancestors' time. There is also an element of respect for the memory of recently deceased elders, who initiated tribal claims proceedings in the 1940s knowing they might not live long enough to benefit personally, but worked for the on-going interests of the tribe.

The philosophical beauty of all this will be readily admitted by those who insist on per capitas, but they are convinced that inevitably Indian people will be bilked out of their money. Their reasoning is that if the present generation does not cash in, no one will. Moreover, philosophical considerations often are not very meaningful because the source of awards is not clearly understood. Few tribal representatives were able to attend their claims hearings; fewer still were called upon to testify to promote a sense of direct tribal effort in forwarding their claims; and often lawyers and ethnohistorians uncovered causes for suit of which the tribes had been unaware. Not only are many of the Indian people dead whose names appear on the original petitions, but many original attorneys of record have died or retired, their practices passed on to others who may not have maintained their predecessors' close contacts and frequent communications with their clients. There are now simply a lot of Indian people who, as long as they can remember, have heard about money the government owes them and who tend to perceive the awards as a kind of token compensation for personal hardships and grievances they identify generally with the fact of being Indian. Even where there is understanding that awards are based on lost lands,

there is bitterness because often it is not understood that compensation is based on the appraised value of land at the time it was ceded and not on the wealth the land generated for the white man since then.

When per capita distributions have been approved, payments still can be held up for several years by the enormous amount of work entailed in arriving at a complete and accurate enrollment of everyone eligible to share in an award. Tribal membership usually is based on quantum of Indian "blood," a quarter for most tribes. Among the many complications to be dealt with are locating highly mobile Indian people who have lived away from their communities for many years and Indian children who have been adopted by white families. There are people who may be as much as "4/4" Indian but of such mixed tribal descent that they may have trouble proving that a full quarter of their ancestry derives from the tribe with which they may have a life-long sense of identification. Then there are individuals everyone in the tribe recognizes as members, but whose ancestors, through some historical oversight, did not get listed on an early roll used as a basis for checking genealogical credentials of present claimants.

It is too soon to tell whether tribes which programmed all or a large part of their awards will fare better in the future than those which disposed of all or most of their money in per capita distributions. However awards are disposed of, the fact of mounting inflation over the long period of time required to settle most of the claims has made the judgments less significant to the Indian interest than they would have been ten or twenty years ago. If justice delayed has not been justice denied, it has been materially diminished through time.

INDIAN GRIEVANCES

Justice also may have been diminished because, prior to taking office, none of the original Commissioners whose work set the course for all the cases had any significant acquaintance with Indian affairs. Their early decisions limited severely the kind of information subsequently considered. The very first decision certainly had wide reaching effects. This concerned the Fort Sill Apache (Doc. 137) who alleged unfair imprisonment. All of them had been held in federal custody for many years because of depredations committed by the relatively small group led by Geronimo. The Commission dismissed the claim (1949) not for lack of possible merit but on jurisdictional grounds that it concerned a mere aggregate of individual grievances, albeit all derived from the same source, and not a collective grievance of a "tribe, band or identifiable group" specified in the Indian Claims Commission Act. It is possible that faced with hundreds of claims, the Commission simply panicked at the prospect of trying to put a price on mental anguish and similar intangibles and beat an expeditious retreat to high, legalistic ground to avoid the quagmire of moral questions.

Whatever their reason, the Commissioners automatically excluded claims from the start which on careful examination might have been both valid and reasonably manageable. Whether the distinction between an aggregate of grievances and a group grievance was inherent

in the act or only an artifact of construal which attorneys were willing to live with, the difference apparently accounts for the absence of cases concerning allotment as unjust in effect, whatever its benevolent intent, in having reduced enormously the tribes' capital in land and fragmented what remained beyond use by the communities. It helped to further entrench an already repressive bureaucracy to confound the course of satisfying community life on allotted and unallotted reservations alike, right up to the present day.

Allotment meant that after the government granted land collectively to a group, it then aggrieved the group by imposing a policy without the group's informed consent to divide the land in severalty. This interfered with developing the land in the collective interest. It also conveniently reduced any future tribal grievance about the consequences of allotment to an aggregate of individual grievances outside the jurisdiction of the Commission which was created to settle Indian grievances. The only complaints which can be heard concerning allotment involve accounting cases claiming the government did not get the best price it could have in the sale of "surplus," unallotted land or that allocation of allotments was mismanaged in terms of the regulations concerning those qualified to receive them.[20]

Because there was no Investigation Division, there is no way of knowing whether it would have viewed claims in the broad perspective of the whole fabric of Indian

20. For a discussion of allotment and sale of "surplus" Indian land, see Price, *Law and the American Indian,* pp. 483–87.

policy, or whether the Commission would have heeded the Division in making different construals. The fact that the first Commissioners saw no need for an Investigation Division suggests that they reposed their faith in the workings of the law rather than evidence.

The Commission was further isolated from the full scope and nature of Indian grievances by the lack of meaningful Indian involvement in the cases, a point noted by Commissioner Vance, who suggests that there was nothing to prevent Indians from presenting their own cases. It was the Indian Bureau, according to Vance, which erred in interpreting its charge to inform tribes about the Commission as a directive to get competent counsel under contract.[21] Granted the old saw that anyone who tries to represent himself in court has a fool for a lawyer, there could have been Indian input if, at least as a first step, tribes had drawn up their own complaints. The Investigation Division, had there been one, could have systematized the patterns of complaint which would have emerged, researched tribal histories for further bases of claims, and recommended formal handling by attorneys as needed. Even attorneys have complained that most of their research had to follow upon submission of petitions they could only hope covered all likely issues.

No one really listened very carefully to the Indians. It should be remembered that the Commission was the direct result of recommendations in the Meriam Report of 1928:

The benevolent desire of the United States government to educate and civilize the Indian cannot be realized with a tribe which has any considerable unsatisfied bona fide claim against the

government . . . the conviction in the Indian mind that justice is being denied, renders extremely difficult any cooperation between the government and its Indian wards.[22]

It is my opinion that the Meriam staff, upon encountering a pervasive expression of grievance among Indian people across the land, drew an oversimplified conclusion about the nature of that grievance, a conclusion which continued to dominate the Commission's work more than 40 years later. That is, that Indians were complaining mainly about having been shortchanged in the treaty period. This was far from the only issue about which Indian people were becoming increasingly exercised by the 1920s. Inbued with the idea of educating and civilizing Indian "wards" out of their Indianness, the Meriam staff simply could not comprehend the Indians' meaning that it was this very philosophy underlying federal policy and programs, including allotment, about which Indian people were aggrieved.

In other contexts, the Report showed commendable insight in noting the socially damaging effects of the Indian Bureau's efforts to stamp out entirely all trace of Indian custom. However, the Meriam staff did not grasp the connection Indian people made to their current hardships when they talked about land and treaties. As an ethnologist, I submit that in the course of my field work going back to 1944, and of colleagues I have talked with who worked with a variety of tribes even earlier, and right up to Wounded Knee II and the occupation of the Indian Bureau building in the 1970s,

21. Vance, *The Congressional Mandate.*

22. Lewis Meriam, *The Problem of Indian Administration* (Baltimore, Md.: Johns Hopkins Press, 1928), p. 805.

the universal and persisting Indian complaint has not been bad treaties or cheap treaties or even fraudulent treaties. It has been BROKEN treaties. Never mind that it was not a treaty but rather an agreement or Executive Order that set aside land for Indians to occupy. A promise is a promise and governmental "bad faith," another favorite Indian rallying cry, is still bad faith.

The point is that whatever chicanery was practiced in the period when most reservations were established and however meager the consideration Indians received for their lands, they were dealt with as tribes, even "nations," as peoples with common interests and destinies. Certainly, tribes have resented and lamented having had to relinquish their territories for a pittance, but their ancestors negotiated as best they could, insisting that permanent homelands be guaranteed to them by the federal government as part of the low price for their vast domains. The deepest grievance has been with the government's unwillingness to uphold even these sorry bargains in failing to protect the remaining Indian estate and keep it intact.[23]

As Imre Sutton has observed, in this country ". . . only the Indians represent a truly 'territorial' minority, and their constant quest for equity in American society stands alone in being founded on a recognized body of treaties and laws . . . in a society that has openly promised to preserve historical guarantees. . . ."[24]

BEYOND THE INDIAN CLAIMS COMMISSION

If Indian people did not benefit as anticipated from the Indian Claims Commission, both they and scholars derived indirect benefits. Anthropological interest was reawakened in documentary research. The Justice Department's arrangements with Indiana University to study midwest claims led to the creation of a large depository of source materials and the journal, *Ethnohistory*. The greatly increased call for data concerning Indian claims prompted major efforts at the National Archives, making available on microfilm whole runs of Indian Bureau records of general scholarly value. Two commerical publishing houses have deemed claims testimony and supporting documentation of sufficient importance to publish much of this information.

The Indian Claims Commission at least provided an unprecedented opportunity for tribes across the country to become acquainted with the potential of the courts and the operation of law in forwarding Indian interests.[25] The Commission, as well as the civil rights ferment of the 1960s, helped to inspire increasing numbers of young Indian people to enter law careers. A special legal program for Indians has been founded at the University of New Mexico, while law schools across the country are adding courses on Indian law. Two national organizations, founded and administered by Indians, have emerged within the last decade to assist tribes

23. Cf. Kirke Kickingbird and Karen Duchenaux, *One Hundred Million Acres* (New York: Macmillan, 1973); also Edgar S. Cahn, ed., *Our Brother's Keeper: The Indian in White America* (Washington, D.C.: New Community Press, 1969), especially part III, pp. 68–112.
24. Sutton, *Indian Land Tenure*, p. ix.

25. Henry F. Dobyns, "Therapeutic Experience of Responsible Democracy," in *The American Indian Today*, eds. Stuart Levine and Nancy Oestreich Lurie (Baltimore, Md.: Penguin Books, 1970), pp. 268–93.

in legal matters: the Native American Rights fund in Boulder, Colorado, and the Institute for the Development of Indian Law in Washington, D.C.[26] In this connection, there has been important feedback from the Commission. The new Indian litigation has been able to draw upon both the enormous amount of source material now assembled[27] and a cadre of trained researchers familiar with Indian legal history.

An astounding number of cases are being heard on Indian issues from county courts to the Supreme Court, but since tribes must file in such a variety of jurisdictions, Vine Deloria, Jr., an Indian and a lawyer, sees the need for a Court of Indian Affairs. Recognizing the Commission's shortcomings, he still feels it holds potential as a model, especially with the current panel of commissioners, "because they had to deal with one subject matter—Indian law—[they]

have become more knowledgeable than most judges in the federal system about Indian history."[28]

Finally, a justification for going into what went wrong and what might have been. The Commission has stimulated world wide interest. People in Hawaii and the United States trust territories, as well as in Sweden, Canada, Australia, New Zealand and other nations, are in communication with people involved in Indian claims cases. The United States Commission dealing with Indian claims offers a precedent to be studied closely, improved upon and adapted to deal with grievances raised by other "territorial minorities."[29]

26. Cf. Robert McLaughlin, "Who Owns the Land? A Native American Challenge," *Juris Doctor*, vol. 6, no. 8 (September 1976) pp. 17–25; "The Native American Challenge: In Pursuit of Tribal Sovereignty," *Juris Doctor*, vol. 6, no. 9 (October 1976) pp. 51–58.

27. Margaret Hunter Pierce, "The Work of the Indian Claims Commission," *American Bar Association Journal*, vol. 16, no. 2 (February 1977) pp. 227–32.

28. Vine Deloria, Jr., *A Better Day for Indians* (New York: The Field Foundation, 1977), pp. 26–29. Deloria notes that in accepting an award, the claimant Indians sign off forever any residual rights they might have to the land involved, an agreement they may regret.

29. I would like to express my special thanks for reviewing an initial draft of this article and for providing valuable data, comment, and criticism to Stephen E. Feraca, Division of Government Services, Bureau of Indian Affairs, Washington, D.C., Frances Horn (see footnote 7), and John R. White, Anthropology Department, Youngstown State University, Youngstown, Ohio. Any errors and interpretive shortcomings are, of course, my responsibility.

ANNALS, AAPSS, 436, Mar. 1978

Current Demographic and Social Trends Among North American Indians

By SAM STANLEY AND ROBERT K. THOMAS

ABSTRACT: The American Indian population has continued to increase at a rate greater than other identifiable populations in the United States. The 1970 census returns indicate that 45 percent of the Indian population resides in urban areas. Indians have moved to urban centers and urban life has moved to Indians since many communities are surrounded by urban and surburban sprawl. The total Indian population has experienced cultural and language loss. At the same time more Indians are being educated up to and beyond the college level. Young Indians with institutional experience, whether in schools or prisons, are becoming either militant or bureaucratic. We infer that the turmoil which has characterized American Indian life since 1950 is a function of Indians' determination to maintain their identity and values in the face of overwhelming pressures to change. The future will feature more of the same unless Indians feel free to make their own adjustment.

Robert K. Thomas is Professor of Social Science, Weekend College, Wayne State University, Detroit, Michigan. He is a Cherokee Indian and has conducted anthropological research on reservations and in the city. He was co-director of the Carnegie Cross-Cultural Education Project from 1961 to 1966. He has taught at Wayne State since 1960.

Sam Stanley is Research Anthropologist at the Smithsonian Institution. He has a doctorate from the University of Chicago (1958) and has carried out research in Indonesia and with North American Indians. He has been at the Smithsonian Institution since 1966.

TWENTY years have passed since "American Indians and American Life" was published by THE ANNALS. Included in the volume was an article by the late J. Nixon Hadley on the "Demography of the American Indians."[1] It contained a short discussion of the aboriginal population, the history of population fluctuation, a short description of the modern population, and a few suggestions about future trends. In this article we propose to give some basic facts about American Indian population, but in particular we want to discuss trends since 1950.

In 1956, under the stimulus and leadership of Sol Tax, we compiled a population estimate for American Indians. The original estimate was confined to the continental United States and our data were mainly derived from congressional reports and ethnographic investigations. Later, with the help of Bruce B. McLaughlin, we expanded that estimate to include Alaska natives and all of Canada.[2] In the case of the lower 48 states, we counted only those who were listed as Indians by the B.I.A. and/or those who lived in Indian communities and were identified as Indians. Our total was 572,024, which was considerably more than the Bureau of Census total of 343,410 or the official B.I.A. total of 368,401. Most of the "extra" Indians were in Oklahoma, California, and the Dakotas. Presumably they were In-

dians who identified as such but might not have been living in Indian communities at that time. Our research showed that most American Indian communities had been slowly increasing since 1900, with a minority of the community's population moving into the general society. At the same time it was true that a few tribes like the Navajo were having a spectacular increase in situ.

But the research at the University of Chicago in the 1950s focused on more than simple population fluctuation.[3] There was an assumption, best articulated by Tax, that enduring strong relationships in an ongoing community are the corollary of a strong, continuous cultural tradition. We discovered that American Indian groups were slightly increasing cohesive wholes, conservative in their life patterns, and wholly continuous with their past. This was the case even though individuals often opted to join the mainstream. Length of exposure to non-Indians had not necessarily shattered Indian communities. Some groups, such as the Pueblos, with a long and enduring contact with Europeans, were among the most conservative and traditional. Except for Michigan and the West Coast, we found that the native language was the home and community language of most American Indian settlements in 1950. In addition we noted that life in most communities involved such pre-Columbian institutions as food habits, kinship behavior, and religious ceremonies. These overt characteristics of culture seemed to

1. J. Nixon Hadley, "The Demography of the American Indians," The Annals of the American Academy of Political and Social Science, vol. 311 (May, 1957) pp. 23–30.

2. Expanded and published in 1960 as The North American Indians, 1950 Distribution of Descendants of the Aboriginal Population of Alaska, Canada, and the United States. It is available for $1.00 at the Center for the Study of Man, Smithsonian Institution, Washington, D.C.

3. See, for example, Robert K. Thomas, "Population Trends in American Indian Communities," in Reference Materials Compiled for the American Indians Chicago Conference (The University of Chicago June 13–20, 1961), pp. 70–78.

be sustained and complemented by more covert levels (in those days called personality, values, and world view) which remained intact in most of the small cohesive communities. We also confirmed that, as a whole, American Indians were the worst educated, had the lowest income, and the poorest health of any group of people in North America.

Finally, we observed that excessive drinking was a problem in a great many Indian communities, although other social ills, such as juvenile delinquency and family breakdown, were evident in only a few localities. But excessive drinking is an old problem for North American Indians and has been since the arrival of Europeans in the New World. As of 1950, then, American Indian communities were relatively cohesive socially and very conservatively "Indian" despite their lack of formal education, their low income, and their poor physical health.

The data for our research at the University of Chicago utilized a variety of resources. We strove most of all to identify as Indian those individuals and communities which identified themselves as Indian. Our resources included tribal roll figures, census figures, and anthropological estimates—but only where those figures met our criterion of self-identity as Indians.

1970 CENSUS RETURNS

In 1970, the Census counted as Indians those who identified themselves as Indians. Despite the difference in criteria there is a consistent finding of continuing increase in the American Indian population, a population explosion which started in 1910. (See table 1.) In 1950, the Census reported 357,499 Indians; in 1960, 523,591; and 792,730 in 1970.

The figures for 1970, however, show many new facets of American Indian life. In fact there seems almost to have been a revolution during the 20 years after 1950. No longer is the stable, rural community of 1950 slowly increasing and sending out individuals into the mainstream. Rather, we find that a surprising 45 percent of those people who call themselves Indian live in the towns and cities of the United States. (See table 2.) Many tribal groups had more members living in towns and cities, away from their rural communities and reservations, than at "home." Clearly some rural Indian communities lost population in the great migration to the cities that took place in the 1950s and 1960s. On the whole these migrants appeared to be culturally more marginal than those who remained. They were younger, more competent in English, better educated, and possessed more trained skills. The rural community remained a core of older and more culturally conservative people who cared for an almost equal number of young people under age 20. Almost half of the migrants to the city live in the large metropolitan areas. At the same time most of these metropolitan areas are close to Indian "country." Tulsa, Oklahoma City, Phoenix, Minneapolis, Seattle, Tacoma, Tucson, Albuquerque, and Buffalo are cases in point.[4]

We imagine that the people living in the above cities are still in close contact with their home communities, so that no appreciable separate city Indian life is forming in these centers. At the same time there are a

4. See footnotes 7 and 8 in the article by Sol Tax "The Impact of Urbanization on American Indians" in this volume. They contain references to the sources for our data for the 1970 Census.

TABLE 1

GROWTH OF THE AMERICAN INDIAN POPULATION SINCE 1900, BY STATE

	1900	1910	1920	1930	1940	1950	1960	1970
Alaska*	(NA)	11,244	(NA)	10,955	11,283	14,089	14,444	16,276
Alabama	177	909	405	465	464	928	1,276	2,443
Arizona	26,480	29,201	32,989	43,726	55,076	65,761	83,387	95,812
Arkansas	66	460	106	408	278	533	580	2,014
California	15,377	16,371	17,360	19,212	18,675	19,947	39,014	91,018
Colorado	1,437	1,482	1,383	1,395	1,360	1,567	4,288	8,836
Connecticut	153	152	159	162	201	333	923	2,222
Delaware	9	5	2	5	14	—	597	656
Dist. of Columbia	22	68	37	40	190	330	587	956
Florida	358	74	518	587	690	1,011	2,504	6,677
Georgia	19	95	125	43	106	333	749	2,347
Hawaii	(NA)	(NA)	(NA)	(NA)	(NA)	(NA)	472	1,126
Idaho	4,226	3,488	3,098	3,638	3,537	3,800	5,231	6,687
Illinois	16	188	194	469	624	1,443	4,704	11,413
Indiana	243	279	125	285	223	438	948	3,887
Iowa	382	471	529	660	733	1,084	1,708	2,992
Kansas	2,130	2,444	2,276	2,454	1,165	2,381	5,069	8,672
Kentucky	102	234	57	22	44	234	391	1,531
Louisiana	593	780	1,066	1,536	1,801	409	3,587	5,294
Maine	798	892	839	1,012	1,251	1,522	1,879	2,195
Maryland	3	55	32	50	73	314	1,538	4,239
Massachusetts	587	688	555	874	769	1,201	2,118	4,475
Michigan	6,354	7,519	5,614	7,080	6,282	7,000	9,701	16,854
Minnesota	9,182	9,053	8,761	11,077	12,528	12,533	15,496	23,128
Mississippi	2,203	1,253	1,105	1,458	2,134	2,502	3,442	4,113
Missouri	130	313	171	578	330	547	1,723	5,405
Montana	11,343	10,745	10,956	14,798	16,841	16,606	21,181	27,130
Nebraska	3,322	3,502	2,888	3,256	3,401	3,954	5,545	6,624
Nevada	5,216	5,240	4,907	4,871	4,747	5,025	6,681	7,933
New Hampshire	22	34	28	64	50	74	135	361
New Jersey	63	168	100	213	211	621	1,699	4,706
New Mexico	13,144	20,573	19,512	28,941	34,510	41,901	56,255	72,788
New York	5,257	6,046	5,503	6,973	8,651	10,640	16,491	28,355
North Carolina	5,687	7,851	11,824	16,579	22,546	3,742	38,129	44,406
North Dakota	6,968	6,486	6,254	8,387	10,114	10,766	11,736	14,369
Ohio	42	127	151	435	338	1,146	1,910	6,654
Oklahoma	64,445	74,825	57,337	92,725	63,125	53,769	64,689	98,468
Oregon	4,951	5,090	4,590	4,776	4,594	5,820	8,026	13,510
Pennsylvania	1,639	1,503	337	523	441	1,141	2,122	5,533
Rhode Island	35	284	110	318	196	385	932	1,390
South Carolina	121	331	304	959	1,234	554	1,098	2,241
South Dakota	20,225	19,137	16,384	21,833	23,347	23,344	25,794	32,365
Tennessee	108	216	56	161	114	339	638	2,276
Texas	470	702	2,109	1,001	1,103	2,736	5,750	17,957
Utah	2,623	3,123	2,711	2,869	3,611	4,201	6,961	11,273
Vermont	5	26	24	36	16	30	57	229
Virginia	354	539	824	779	198	1,056	2,155	4,853
Washington	10,039	10,997	9,061	11,253	11,394	13,816	21,076	33,386
West Virginia	12	36	7	18	25	160	181	751
Wisconsin	8,372	10,142	9,611	11,548	12,265	12,196	14,297	18,924
Wyoming	1,686	1,486	1,343	1,845	2,349	3,237	4,020	4,980

SOURCE: U.S. Bureau of the Census, vols. 2–52, *1970 Census*, table 17: Race by Sex: 1900–1970.
* Does not include Eskimo and Aleut population figures.

TABLE 2

RURAL-URBAN DISTRIBUTION OF THE AMERICAN INDIAN POPULATION 1970, BY STATE

	1970 (URBAN) CENTRAL CITIES	1970 (URBAN) URBAN FRINGE	1970 (URBAN) 10,000 OR MORE	1970 (URBAN) 2,500 TO 10,000	1970 (RURAL) 1,000 TO 2,500	1970 (RURAL) OTHER RURAL
Alaska*	—	—	1,698	3,219	2,035	9,324
Alabama	501	250	222	234	72	1,164
Arizona	7,819	2,772	2,032	5,560	2,377	75,261
Arkansas	468	64	366	254	79	783
California	27,867	30,780	6,053	5,102	1,671	19,545
Colorado	3,249	1,636	394	438	130	2,989
Connecticut	982	517	156	134	54	379
Delaware	73	107	35	20	22	399
Dist. of Columbia	956	—	—	—	—	—
Florida	1,824	1,641	451	538	108	2,115
Georgia	618	607	234	157	63	668
Hawaii	421	197	235	132	36	105
Idaho	160	27	784	927	222	4,567
Illinois	7,222	2,307	482	328	204	870
Indiana	1,484	470	618	269	125	921
Iowa	1,211	216	278	257	95	935
Kansas	2,415	742	2,470	669	486	1,890
Kentucky	306	249	242	134	64	536
Louisiana	763	423	533	258	83	3,234
Maine	95	30	246	531	132	1,161
Maryland	1,740	1,576	128	156	54	585
Massachusetts	1,879	1,272	179	200	116	829
Michigan	5,175	3,505	1,231	1,298	662	4,983
Minnesota	8,454	1,861	667	860	985	10,301
Mississippi	230	22	189	182	48	3,442
Missouri	2,093	981	458	411	212	1,250
Montana	1,993	206	1,331	1,921	3,258	18,421
Nebraska	1,619	271	521	602	449	3,162
Nevada	1,013	592	610	742	575	4,401
New Hampshire	69	10	68	36	25	153
New Jersey	1,248	2,558	131	153	50	566
New Mexico	3,351	361	5,099	4,520	6,407	53,050
New York	14,545	3,469	669	839	398	8,435
North Carolina	2,174	2,344	2,060	814	1,475	35,539
North Dakota	174	3	1,257	457	1,888	10,595
Ohio	3,311	1,466	481	234	129	1,033
Oklahoma	17,618	5,176	11,462	13,427	7,470	43,315
Oregon	2,609	1,486	1,516	900	561	6,438
Pennsylvania	2,676	1,307	264	230	158	931
Rhode Island	541	241	115	217	45	231
South Carolina	175	341	175	179	83	1,288
South Dakota	480	49	3,048	4,950	2,301	21,537
Tennessee	783	67	316	172	45	893
Texas	10,041	2,742	1,413	1,068	421	2,272
Utah	1,509	1,241	589	443	771	6,720
Vermont	—	—	27	42	28	132
Virginia	1,249	1,492	116	165	60	1,771
Washington	7,766	4,755	2,814	2,375	1,245	14,431
West Virginia	131	43	79	37	52	409
Wisconsin	5,035	1,112	661	1,003	1,514	9,599
Wyoming	—	—	411	645	97	3,827

SOURCE: U.S. Bureau of the Census, vols. 2–52, *1970 Census*, table 17: Race by Sex: 1900–1970.
* Does not include Eskimo and Aleut population figures.

number of cities far removed from Indian country which boast large Indian populations. The Los Angeles area contains at least 30,000; San Francisco some 20,000; Chicago at least 8,000; Detroit 5,000; and Dallas-Fort Worth 7,000. In these cities we find a concerted attempt to form a separate Indian social group and separate Indian life.

TYPES OF INDIAN URBAN MIGRANTS

We hypothesize that in these large cities far from Indian country there seem to be three types of Indian migrants. The first, a very large group in the inner city, is still oriented to its home reservations, rural communities, and relatives in the city. Most move back and forth from rural area to metropolitan area in California, Illinois, Michigan, Texas or elsewhere.

The second category of Indian migrants is those who live in the outer city or working class suburbs, being skilled laborers or having steady laboring jobs. They seem to be most committed to city life and generally dedicated to some form of Indian community in the city. They are the people who are the core of Indian centers in California and the lower midwest.

Finally, there is a small group of professional, middle class Indians in the city. Some are divorced from their fellow Indians, but many provide "leadership" in Indian organizations and developing institutions in the city.

American city institutional structure

The most prevalent institution in American cities, the Indian Center, has been plagued with factional fighting and manipulation by out-

side forces. The real core of Indian social life in most cities today consists of networks of friends, kin networks, local bars, and alcoholics anonymous organizations. Parenthetically, we might observe that recent migrants to American cities— southern whites, Puerto Ricans, blacks, and American Indians— have not had the option of building their own institutions as did earlier migrants. This may be because the large American city is already complete institutionally, and new immigrants must find interstices in the existing institutional structure in which to build formal or informal organizations of their own. American Indians in cities are trying very hard to build together some kind of community life, or ethnic group perhaps, but against tremendous odds. They are a small minority, scattered throughout the metropolitan area, and struggling desperately to avoid becoming a part of the anonymous mass. Not only is the institutional structure already built and in the hands of others, but integrated schooling, urban redevelopment, and other such forces work against what remaining community life there is in the American city. Paradoxically, while many ethnic groups have been fighting to hold on to some kind of community life, American Indians have been struggling to develop some kind of community life. In the process a whole generation of Indians has been born and socialized in large metropolitan areas.

Urban and suburban sprawl

Not only were Indians moving to the city between 1950 and 1970, but the city was moving to them. Urban sprawl touched almost every Iroquois reservation in New York state. The Florida Seminoles found themselves in the midst of the country's most rapidly growing region. Southern California's urban growth was encircling almost every reservation in that part of the state. Areas of the Southwest, in particular Tucson, Phoenix, and Albuquerque, were developing rapidly, and Indian communities not only experienced the influence of this expansion but found themselves being pressed to give up land and water to the growing society. This trend has been accelerating since 1970.

The 1970 census indicated that about 25 percent of all American Indians lived in small cities and towns. We do not, as yet, know how to assess this figure in social terms, but we have some guesses. Our hunch is that many are simply living in the small city or town closest to their rural home community. But for others, who are living in such locales far from home, it must be an extreme acculturative experience. Further field research would doubtless clarify the situation.

Language and culture loss

Another major shift since 1950 has been the tendency for American Indian groups to be much less conservative. In a score of years there has been extensive language loss in many areas. The vast majority of young Indians raised in the city do not know a tribal language. On the other hand tribal languages still thrive in eastern Oklahoma, the Southwest, some Rocky Mountain tribes, and some communities of the Northern Plains. Opposed to this as a phenomenon has been the loss of native language in the Great Lakes area (New York, Wisconsin, Minnesota), in western Oklahoma and in some areas of the Northern Plains. The language loss can be partially explained by the fact that marriage

between members of different tribes has increased since 1950. Intertribal intermarriage is so prevalent in western Oklahoma that, of necessity, English has become the common language. A similar situation exists in the cities. Another factor in language loss has been the large number of marriages with non-Indians, with the accompanying need to use English to communicate.

However, the really spectacular loss has been in the rural communities of the Great Lakes area and those of the Northern Plains. We can only conclude that in these rural communities Indians have come to see themselves differently in the past 20 or 30 years and, as a result, have simply abandoned their tribal languages. Together with language loss in most of these communities there has also been loss of unique cultural traits. Since in many communities these particular traits have been replaced by Pan-Indian cultural items, many American Indian cultures are coming to look more and more alike. We could describe this process as a generalization of culture in many areas.

Education, economic development, and bureaucracy

Another area of spectacular change has been in the American Indians' level of education. Numerous American Indian children are attending integrated public schools and many Indians are now attending college. As late as 1956 it was very difficult to recruit even 30 Indian college students from all over the country to attend a summer workshop in Colorado. Now one could draw from a very large pool. On the whole, the educational level has risen markedly, especially in the cities, though there has been much less increase in the rural areas. The rise in level of education has not been accompanied by a corresponding rise in Indian health or income.

Since 1970 there has been a proliferation of economic development programs on the reservation. This has been accompanied by the creation of large tribal, state, and federal bureaucracies dealing with Indians to insure that the "development" is accountable. Most of these bureaucracies are now staffed by educated Indians to the extent that one might suspect that American Indians have a larger percentage of their people in bureaucratic service niches than any other distinguishable population.

During the period of 1950–70 and extending to the present, there appears to have been a staggering increase in crime and other social ills. The number of Indians in prison has risen much faster than the increase in the general Indian population.[5] This can be inferred from the dramatic appearance in the late sixties and up to the present writing of numerous American Indian organizations within penitentiaries from coast to coast. Their publications list sizable memberships and the organizations feature consciousness sessions together with organized sports activities. Every issue of "Akwesasne Notes" contains numerous letters from inmates

of Indian ancestry.[6] The fact that accidents are the leading cause of death among Indians and Alaska natives and that one out of five deaths results from this cause (compared with a national ratio of one out of sixteen) signifies in part that Indian social life is in some degree of trouble. The increase since 1955 of crude death rates from cirrhosis of the liver, suicides, and homicides points to the same conclusion. One cannot escape the impression that a great many Indian communities, both rural and urban, are in dire social trouble.

INTERPRETATION

In trying to understand the changes which American Indians have experienced over the last 20 years or so, we are reminded of some important points stressed by Sol Tax. He has emphasized that internal cultural change occurs only when a human group, a community, is undergoing a new experience which rearranges relationships and creates new cultural meaning within the group. A prime example of this process was the impact of the horse on some American Indian cultures and the revolutionary development of Plains Indian culture. He also emphasized that significant acculturation only came about when there was close association on an individual basis between members of different cultures—so close that there was communication of cultural meaning and new cultural experience. But these two processes only take place in the context of what is already there; that is, if the meanings that are already in the heads of

5. The Native American Rights Fund has instituted a new program for Indian inmates in five states (Montana, South Dakota, North Dakota, Nebraska, and Minnesota) and federal inmates within the same area. They estimate that there are 800 Indian inmates in these state penitentiaries and another 500 in federal penitentiaries for the same area. With a population of approximately 100,000 in these five states, this means that more than one out of 100 are in prison.

6. *Akwasasne Notes* (Mohawk Nation, Rooseveltown, N.Y.). See especially the issues from 1971 to 1976 which contain numerous letters from inmates and inmate clubs.

At the Smithsonian Institution we have also received requests from inmates and inmate clubs for assistance in supplying books, pamphlets, bibliographies, and other resources.

the culture bearers. New experience is meaningful only in the context of old, and new meanings are built on old. And finally from Tax's and our own experience, we have learned that for North American Indian tribal members, their most precious possession is their identity as members of a tribe and the special and unique character of that group identity—their culture if you will.

When we look at the changes in American Indian life since 1950 in light of the above we can begin to see what the facts mean in terms of general social and cultural process. In the first place there has doubtless been a great deal of significant acculturation taking place during the last 25 years. Clearly American Indian individuals are now having very close ties with representatives of the general society. In particular, those born and raised in the American city have associated intimately with blacks and whites in great institutional complexes such as schools and factories. At the same time rural American Indian children, many of them now adults, have had close association with whites in public schools. The extensive language loss in some rural communities must reflect some intimate association with whites and new conceptions of the good and the right in such communities. Indeed it is our impression that American Indian young people, particularly in the cities, but in rural areas as well, now have a great deal in common with their white and black counterparts of the same generation—their mode of thinking, categories of thought, and rhetoric have much in common. At the same time it is important to recognize the range of individual acculturation in the city and to observe that many new social types have emerged in the process.

Miraculously a few young Indians manage to learn their native language in the home, though they reside in the city. Many maintain close associations only within their families; others spend their summers at "home" in their ancestral rural communities. All this happens in the face of pressures which make it so easy for an Indian child in the city or suburbs to acculturate and assimilate to the larger society.

The combination of acculturative pressures and language and culture loss has produced a growing sense of identity loss for many American Indians, especially the young, in both urban and rural areas. This appears, however, to have generated a drive for cultural and language revival. Larger institutional complexes such as schools, tribal bureaucracies, Indian institutes in colleges, language and cultural courses in schools have tried to respond, and in many cases preempt, the new mood. Despite pressures toward acculturation, many grass roots Indian communities are continuing to control and bolster their own unique development. In many cases ceremonies have been revived and some young people are becoming apprentice Indian doctors and ceremonialists.

The increase in education and sophistication of American Indian groups, first evidenced in the middle sixties, has been accompanied by a rising nationalism. American Indians no longer hide their desire for social and cultural continuity from the larger society; they no longer hope to be overlooked. To use a current expression, they have come out of the closet. The educational experience, with exposure to middle class values, can supply people with the view that they are members of a legitimate minority. The new Indian nationalism is contributing to the drive to create an "Indian" ethnic group in the cities and a pan-Indian movement generally, although, for the vast majority, the focus of nationalism is on the local tribe and only secondarily on American Indians as a whole.

Life in the cities for American Indians, particularly those born and raised in them, has been an urbanizing experience in the sense that as people become more aware of themselves and their situations, they become more analytic, more impersonal, and more aware of the existence of alternative life styles. For many young Indians, both rural and city, immersion in total institutions like schools and prisons seems to be an especially important urbanizing experience. They develop objectivity and analytic skills as a result of such a total institutional experience and many become very ideological and heavily committed to the Indian cause. Prisons and colleges are seedbeds for militant cultural nationalism and an antiestablishment stance. Some of these young people get recruited into the burgeoning Indian bureaucracy, while others have become the core of the militant movement. The latter have clashed with the Indian bureaucratic establishment at several places in the United States, most notably at Wounded Knee on the Pine Ridge Reservation in South Dakota.

The trends which we have discussed—acculturation, cultural revivalism, nationalism, and militancy—are not separate from one another. Rather, they are aspects of the American Indian's experience in grappling with life in modern America. Indians have become more educated, have had significant relationships with whites, blacks, and members of other tribes, and have looked reflectively at their own situation. Most of their efforts can be characterized as a cry for life— a search for identity, an attempt to preserve uniqueness and to bolster community. Some social scientists see these trends in American Indian life as third generation ethnic phenomena or as the last step before assimilation into the American mainstream. However, to us this is only the latest chapter in the struggle of North American Indians to maintain their identity and their culture, their peoplehood and their uniqueness in the presence of an overpowering, but not irresistible, civilization.

THE FUTURE

No one knows for sure how Indians will fare in the future. Their population appears to be increasing more rapidly (3 percent per annum) than any other definable group in the United States.[7] They should number close to a million by 1980. Their recent successes in federal courts have created a noticeable backlash. The recent report of the American Indian Policy Commission contains recommendations for sweeping changes in the Bureau of Indian Affairs and other agencies relating to Indians.[8] The only clear fact of the coming years is that Indians will continue to experience excruciating pressures to change, and they will continue to resist unless they perceive such changes to be consonant with their ageless values.

7. Conversation with Mr. Spector of the Indian Health Service. He estimates that the IHS population will be 627,000 in 1978. On the whole the IHS does not minister to terminated tribes, nonfederally recognized eastern tribes, and most urban Indians.

8. American Indian Policy Review Commission, *Final Report*, vol. I (Washington, D.C.: USGPO, 1977).

ANNALS, AAPSS, 436, Mar. 1978

The Impact of Urbanization on American Indians

By SOL TAX

ABSTRACT: Native Americans are among the few peoples who maintain kinship and sharing cultures which contrast greatly with our large, economically oriented, individualized, impersonal, urbanizing society. Purely material requirements lead to rapidly increasing involvements. The question is "with what effect?" This paper suggests that Indians somehow frustrate attempts even to research the question by methods which suit the impersonal society. Answers will come from them when Indian people are given the means to find their own ways in the new environment.

Sol Tax is Professor of Anthropology at the University of Chicago.

121

WHAT IS the question implied in this title? By common agreement North America becomes with each passing decade more and more urbanized. Are we asking what effect this changing environment has on our Indian population? It is also evident that with each decennial census an increasing proportion of Indians are counted off-reservation and in or near urban areas. Do these two sets of data together imply that Indians are becoming more urbanized? In what sense: only in that they live more and more in urban areas, or also in that they behave more like urbanites?

Being or becoming urbanized; behaving like urbanites: with respect to North American Indians, these phrases imply a deep difference going far beyond the place of residence or the number of people per square mile. Until a few thousand years ago, humans lived in small, independent, cooperating groups of kith-and-kin, within which the position of each person was understood by all (which is a definition of the word "person"), and outside of which individuals were strangers. In recent millennia, and increasingly more rapidly, almost all of humankind has come to live instead in very large societies of strangers. Of the billions, only a few million have successfully resisted; and among these notably are native North Americans who maintain still their independent kin-based communities within a society which has gone as far as any in the world in the process of individualization. Drops in a bucket. The question is, how are they doing?

One answer is that they survive and grow in numbers. From one decade to the next it appears that there are more ill-fed, ill-clothed, ill-housed, and ill native people. It is not as clear who and where these increased numbers are; whether proportions are up or down from group to group among them; what happens to the ratios of needs and expectations to their fulfillment; how native Americans compare with other minorities. Whether or not their frustrated and angry leaders need more statistics to know whether their kinfolk are drowning not in 400 feet of water but only in 40, their friends and/or those responsible for fulfilling trust responsibilities surely need what facts there are. But all the figures may be less than useless if they are isolated from a clear understanding—preferably acceptance—of the native Americans' perception of their situation. One remembers the case of Helen Hunt Jackson's famous 1881 book, *A Century of Dishonor*, which was to do for Indians what *Uncle Tom's Cabin* had done for slaves; the author not only provided copies to every member of Congress but she personally engaged leaders, including Carl Schurz, the famous liberal who was Secretary of the Interior. The result was the 1887 Dawes (Allotment) Act arising from white misperceptions of Indian culture (as well as from avarice) which led immediately to the second century of dishonor.

I begin therefore with the basic sociology of the Indian situation taking into account what I understand to be their own perception.

GEOGRAPHY OF NATIVE AMERICA, 1977

In 1956 I presented at the American Anthropological Association a map of the distribution of Indians, in the then 48 states, showing why government policy was based on a patently false assumption that the problem of Indians would end as Indians inevitably became absorbed into the general population. On this map, Sam Stanley and Robert K. Thomas had located Indians county by county and community by community. They counted only those people who were listed as Indians by the Bureau of Indian Affairs and/or those individuals who resided in Indian communities and identified with Indians. A variety of doubtful cases were rather excluded than included; nevertheless, their conservative estimates mapped 572,024 persons, as compared with the Bureau of the Census total of 343,410 or the Bureau of Indian Affairs total of 368,401. The largest numbers of "extra" Indians found were, in round numbers, 133,000 in Oklahoma (50,000 of them Cherokees), 28,000 in California, and 14,500 in the Dakotas. The map showed that many more people than supposed identified with virile societies of Indians which, from Maine to California and from Puget Sound to the Everglades, were largely in situ, except for those who had been removed to Oklahoma. In every part of our country Indians had simply been pushed off of their better lands to what had been their less desirable lands, and there they remained and increased.

In revised form[1] this map has been much appreciated by thousands of Indians who found on it the names of their own and other tribes and communities, and who occasionally supplied corrections. The map provided systematic information of what we vaguely knew. To most people, its implications were a revelation; but not to the Indian people, who

not only know that they were there, but also are conscious of where they have been in the unbroken line from their first ancestors. They know their losses, and hint that their sorrow and anger are often brushed with hope for recovery of their lost lands.

The map also represents for many of them redefined social boundaries. Almost all native Americans originally lived in small bands. These now find themselves grouped together as tribes on reservations, sometimes two or three tribes or parts of tribes on a single reservation, often a tribe divided, whether or not along old lines of its own, on more than one. The Indians have long lived with, and have not themselves been confused by, such changes. Perhaps these years of occupation may not have made as much difference in their perception as we think. Mobile bands of Indians were once spaced out from sea to sea among virgin forests, mountains, prairies, and deserts, in most of which now also live strangers with machinery and cities. From whence the hunters brought in game, now there are jobs to be had, money to be earned to buy meat. Where once there were spirits, some of them evil, now there are strangers and din and bitter air, and also talk of great, insoluble problems in a world without wise elders or ways to listen. The strangers and the bad air and the bad news also penetrate some reservations. The defense, as always, is prayer and right living, and patience. But it is doubly hard to wait it out when living requires money which —to earn—requires wrong behavior. It is not surprising that some individuals are both tempted and able to change their ways and their values. Before Europeans came, similar alternatives were offered by Mexican civilizations. Apparently, then as

1. Expanded and published in 1960 as *The North American Indians, 1950 Distribution of Descendents of the Aboriginal Population of Alaska, Canada, and the United States.* It is available for $1.00 at the Center for the Study of Man, Smithsonian Institution, Washington, D.C.

now, most native North Americans rejected them, presumably happy in the ways of life they had themselves developed. Many of us, products of technologically advanced civilizations, may wonder at this. I turn therefore to the kind of life native Americans see as their own.

"A SCHEME OF LIFE"

I first lived with native American people in the summer of 1931, and have learned from them, in North and Central America, most of the little I know about human beings and the different ways we are taught to think and to behave. Among the lessons learned is that we cannot escape our own up-bringing. Like the proverbial Chinese philosopher, who once dreamed he was a butterfly, and could never thereafter feel sure that he wasn't really a butterfly only dreaming he was a man, I am confident I know the difference, but do not know when I describe the cultures of Indian people how much I may be overreacting to my own. Like many anthropologists, I am also increasingly sensitive to the rights of others not to be talked about— surely not wrongly or in stereotypes —and seek ways to let Indian friends speak for themselves. Thus, rather than citing one of the recent non-Indian descriptions of how a kinship society works, I quote sentences from a small book published in 1944 by the late Ella Deloria,[2] a Teton Dakota who was also an anthropologist, and which seeks precisely such understanding from church people imbued with the values of our civilization, the idea of progress, and the middle class work ethic.

The first sampling comes from a section (pp. 24–38) called "A Scheme

2. Ella Deloria, *Speaking of Indians* (New York: Friendship Press, 1944).

of Life that Worked," describing the culture of her own people as it was "something more than a hundred years ago":

Kinship was the all-important matter. . . . By kinship all Dakota people were held together in a great relationship. . . . Everyone who was born a Dakota belonged to it. . . . Camp-circles were no haphazard assemblages. . . . The most solitary member was sure to have at least one blood relative . . . through whose marriage connection he was automatically the relative of a host of people. The ultimate aim of Dakota life . . . was [that] one must be a good relative. . . . Every other consideration was secondary—property, personal ambition, glory, good times, life itself. To be civilized was to keep the rules. . . . Thus only was it possible to live communally . . . with a minimum of frictions and a maximum of good will.

[There follows a description of the kinship system in which one has as blood relatives very many mothers, fathers, sisters, brothers, uncles, aunts, sons, daughters, grandparents, and grandchildren and in which] "when your blood relatives marry, all their new relatives are yours too. . . .

A proper mental attitude and a proper conventional behavior prescribed by kinship must accompany the speaking of each term. As you said "Uncle" . . . you must . . . assume the correct mental attitude in its fitting outward behavior and mien. . . . This exacting . . . obedience to kinship demands . . . made [the Dakotas] a kind, unselfish people, always acutely aware of those about them. . . . A socially responsible Dakota might not thoughtlessly indulge his moods lest there be within range . . . a kind of relative before whom his feelings must be suppressed. . . . Everyone had his part to play and played it for the sake of his honor, all . . . obligations and honorings being reciprocal. Kinship had everybody in a fast net of interpersonal responsibility and made everybody like it, because its rewards were pleasant. . . .

The kinship appeal was always a compelling force. . . . Outsiders were deeply concerned over [a quarrel] until it was straightened out. . . . Two . . . influential men would visit the unhappy ones and appeal to them to cool off their hearts—for the sake of their relatives who were unhappy over their plight. Such an appeal . . . placed the responsibility for his relatives' peace of mind squarely on the troubled man, reminding him that no Dakota lived unto himself alone. He might not rightly risk even his very own life needlessly. . . . However slightly he valued himself, he must regard the relatives. . . . The quarreling men smoked the pipe together and were feasted before the council. Friends brought them presents. And thus peace was restored in the camp-circle to the relief of all. . . .

Everyone was related to all the people within his own circle of acquaintances. But all those people had other circles of acquaintance within the large tribe. All such circles overlapped and interlocked. Any Dakota could legitimately find his way to any other. . . . Thus, anyone could go visiting anywhere, and be at home.

The author then describes "Life in Tipi and Camp Circle," "Praying for Power," and "Education—by Precept and Example" and concludes the description with "Economics: Giving to Have":

The best teaching said things were less important than people; that pride lay in honoring relatives rather than in amassing goods for oneself; that a man who failed to participate in the giving customs was . . . something less than a human being. If someone made you a gift . . . he did not mean for it to grow old along with you. He expected you to use it when and as you chose to honor someone else, and, indirectly, yourself. . . . There was little pride in ownership of goods, but much pride in "honorship" of relatives. If you wished to honor me publicly, you did not load

me down personally with presents. You made someone else glad in my name . . . and that is where the honor lay for me. . . .

Disdain for material things as against human considerations was the basis of the people's life and philosophy. But . . . do not imagine that they spent their days . . . ridding themselves of property. . . . The Dakotas could not afford to be shiftless and wasteful. For centuries . . . they had known of a vast variety of wild foods, both vegetable and animal, and the securing of them. . . . They made caches, great underground rooms [where] the stores of several co-operating families were piled around the walls as high as might be . . . each woman's rawhide containers painted with her own overall design. Now and then they had a famine, when snow was too deep for hunting, or when all the animals seemed to organize to keep out of range. As a people they did not dare let themselves drift into an easy, haphazard existence. They were wise in self-preservation, even though they were committed to constant hospitality. . . . The principle of giving-to-have was the very essence of Dakota community life. A man who showed [a] tendency [to use] the giving system . . . for enriching [himself] at the expense of others was suspect, as if he were not quite human. . . . Gifts of unequal value were happily exchanged. . . . A horse for a beautiful pair of moccasins or a blanket . . . the recipient of the lesser gift might be so startled and delighted by the compliment thus unexpectedly paid him that he unhesitatingly gave a horse to indicate his pleasure.

I quote this much to indicate how difficult it must be for people brought up in such a social system with such values and practices to be plunged into our impersonal, materialist, competitive society. The author devotes the next section of her book, "The Reservation Picture" to the coming of "a totally different way of life, far-reaching in its influence, awful in its power, insistent in its demands." The last part of the book, "Indian Life in Wartime," takes the story to 1941 when many went into the armed services and into industries: "Whole families have moved into the cities and are meeting problems they have never faced before. As workers they are valuable. Skillful with their hands at tasks requiring meticulous care, they are extremely accurate, patient, dependable. . . . They will not stop to bargain for themselves; it is not their tradition to think of self first; and they will not grumble."

LIFE IN THE CITY

I have been an Indian-watcher in Chicago since the early fifties, when government "Relocation" began and the American Indian Center was organized; and I was kept involved personally and through a succession of Chicago graduate students including Thomas Segundo (Papago), Robert K. Thomas and John K. White (Cherokees), Leonard Borman, and Robert Rietz. Through other students, and/or visits I also knew something of Rapid City, Los Angeles, San Francisco, and Milwaukee, and others through publications of colleagues.[3] Nevertheless, I do not

3. The Indian Historical Press (1451 Masonic Avenue, San Francisco) publishes an annual *Index to Literature on the American Indian* which includes a classification "Urban." Among recent books that are especially useful are: Howard M. Bahr, Bruce A. Chadwick, and Robert C. Day, *Native Americans Today: Sociological Perspectives* (New York: Harper and Row, 1972); Rudolph O. de la Garza, Z. Anthony Kruszewski, and Tomás A. Arciniega, *Chicanos and Native Americans, The Territorial Minorities* (Englewood Cliffs, N.J.: Prentice-Hall, 1973); Jeanne Guilleman, *Urban Renegades: The Cultural Strategy of American Indians* (New York: Columbia University Press, 1975); J. O. Waddell and O. M. Watson, eds., *The American Indian in Urban Society* (Boston: Little, Brown, 1971).

understand at all what goes on in cities, even Chicago, even after a year-long seminar with students doing volunteer work in Indian organizations, and with some of their Indian friends. I begin to think that the ignorance and confusion with which I am forced to leave questions unanswered is in the reality and not in the minds of participants and observers. Instead of a describable structure, we may be dealing with a tangled web of mobile threads.

Local estimates of the number of Indians in Chicago at any one time range from 12,000 to 20,000. Opinions differ on migration patterns; are Indians in Chicago in summer when it is easier to find jobs in construction or in winter when money, hence food, is harder to come by on the reservation? The problem of how many, moreover, appears to be no great concern to Indians, except when pressed by government agencies or students doing research.[4] Talk about numbers of individuals or families, when and where, depersonalizes and qualifies the freedom Indians have always felt to come and go in pursuit of their own activities. However, talk about the number of tribes represented at any affair, or in any organization, personalizes Indians; for the tribe is the beginning of specification, which goes then to geographical location and family. Thus city organizations are ideally intertribal, whether general or for

4. To get suggestions for the 1980 count, the Chicago office of the Bureau of the Census called a meeting of American Indian leaders which Leonard Borman and I observed. The Indians were told that the Census had grossly undercounted minority groups, including Indians, which cost them federal funds allocated by numbers. Discussion quickly indicated that many Indians are reluctant to be counted in the city because they belong on the reservation. The economic argument backfired.

special skills and interests like dancing, photography, basketball, and the arts; for youth, educational, and recreational activities; or for problems like alcoholism; or welfare programs.

Although like others, Indians require the help of private and public welfare agencies, for whom they are impersonal clients, Indians in cities especially require their own organizations and services because they are not only poor and deprived and new to cities, but unlike any others they come directly from small independent kin communities without having shared several thousands of years in economically-oriented peasant societies. American urbanized culture is perhaps at one extreme of a continuum, and American Indian bands at the other. It is possible to argue that native Americans prone to overcome the difference have, over the years, had incentives and opportunities to do so, and those who have not done so are precisely those "not prone," whatever that may mean. Touchy even in their native social interrelations, they are uncertain and very uncomfortable in their contacts with non-Indians and are quickly put off, withdrawing embarrassedly either physically (if they can escape) or in alcoholism; more so in the strange environment of the city. They are honest and hard working people; but they have special problems on the job as well as in other situations, and so are often jobless. When they need help they especially need to relate to friendly people, and preferably kin or tribesmen. With strangers who are Indians they are in some ways more comfortable than with other strangers; but the differences of tribes can take on significance unimagined by the non-Indian, both when they are defined as historic enemies and when specific features of cultural behavior happen to conflict. Tribal stereotypes and/or antipathies that remain unconscious when they are hundreds of miles apart in their respective communities suddenly come into play when persons become interdependent, or competitors, in city situations. It is little wonder that organizations take much pride in whatever "all-tribal" character their members achieve by rising above not only old prejudices and newer religious differences but also assaults on their notions of good taste and right behavior.

Meanwhile, the most constant complaint continues to be that "we can't get along; if only we would stop pulling one another down, we could do great things." Nancy Lurie[5] suggests that Indian "factionalism" may be exacerbated by guilt feelings and that both might result from historic unfamiliarity with systems that support political parties. In any case, the result in cities is extreme instability of Indian organizations, so that one with a longer history changes its personnel about as frequently as others come and go, continually replaced with equivalent new organizations. In situations where continuing consensus—traditional Indian unanimity—is difficult to achieve, the alternative to stable organizational structure is in fact what Indians have in cities: ad hoc programs which come and go like traditional hunting or war parties. Such a system worries Indians mainly when it bothers non-Indian friends and sources of funding.

These remarks concern that fraction of the Indians in the city who participate actively in organizations.

5. "The Will-O'-The Wisp of Indian Unity," *The Indian Historian* (Summer 1976), pp. 19–24.

These are people who have put down roots in the city and who identify both with their tribes back home and with one another. They are sometimes blue-collar, trade union people, but more usually clerical workers and professional people (teachers, nurses, etc.), some of whom work in offices, institutions, agencies, and organizations inside, and others outside, the Indian community, or both serially. In Chicago and in other cities, around universities and in national meetings, and in Washington, these are virtually the only Indians I know. They include varying combinations of individual orientations thought of as traditional, radical, and professional.

Sam Stanley and Robert K. Thomas distinguish two other kinds of Indians in cities; those who do not participate in city "organization life" but are otherwise like the people I know, including, again, presumably traditional Indians who may participate in ceremonies back on their reservations; young radicals interested in Indian affairs but not in the local organizations; and professional people. The second kind are numerically most important; they are in the city for a few months or a few years, or come and go seasonally or occasionally, but in any case have sunk no roots. If they get into trouble of any kind they either go to Indian Agencies for help—providing the bulk of these agencies' clients—or alternatively return to their reservations. These people include in their number the poorest and the least educated of the Indians in the city, who may also disproportionately fill the bars favored by Indians, and get into difficulties with the police, thus providing statistics for studies about urban problems.

This floating population is like the paradoxical, fast-flowing stream of ever changing drops of water. Passing a point, or traced source to mouth, the stream as a whole is real; and so is each individual drop. It would be as correct to say that there are 10,000 Indians in Chicago (2,000 rooted, 8,000 floating at one time) as to say that there are 18,000 (2,000 plus 16,000 different Indians during the year). Since native Americans are few in numbers, might an experimental census be devised that would associate them with their home communities and indicate the time factor? Indians in 1970 were asked their tribal identifications; and off-reservation Indians could be asked the location of the tribes or bands they give. Indian reservations and other Indian communities might provide names and locations of members who presumably were being censused elsewhere. A sample of those who checked out as identical persons (or families) in both places might then provide additional socioeconomic data which could test William H. Hodge's hypothesis[6] that the urban workforce, favoring healthy people with formal schooling, who can quickly acquire work skills and adjust to a complex and changing environment, is likely to select, for young to middle aged adults, from Indian communities not too isolated from industrial experience.

Numbers

But aside from hypotheses and research it is of practical importance for Indians in their changing situation to get a better handle on their numbers.

Indians in tribes and reservations

6. "Relocation and Urban Experiences," in *Indians in Contemporary Society*, ed. d'Arcy McNickle. (Vol. XI of the *Handbook of North American Indians*, Smithsonian Institution, Washington, D.C., forthcoming).

are traditionally "enrolled" and countable. The whereabouts of those absent from the community, whether or not on official rolls, are locally known; but to identify and locate them where they are, seems peculiarly difficult. When an Indian organization in the city seeks funding for a health center or a training or employment program, for example, its greatest difficulty is to provide data on the "unmet need" which is inferentially and anecdotally well recognized. How many Indian people and of what kinds there are in the city, is simply not known. The decennial census therefore becomes exceedingly important. For local purposes it lacks detail and by the time it is published it is out of date; but it is the only source from which systematic comparisons—and therefore reasoned inferences—can be made. Tables 1, 2, and 3 summarize, in as brief a form as possible, the 1960 and 1970 statistics directly relevant to the question of what is happening to native Americans under increasing urbanization.[7]

7. The published censuses in 1960 and 1970 consist of many-tomed Volume 1 *Characteristics of the Population*, and Volume 2 *Subject Reports*. For each state, Volume 1 includes the population of Indians in central cities; urban fringe; other urban over 10,000 and from 2,500 to 10,000; and rural from 1,000–2,500 and under 1,000. Volume 2, for 1960, includes a report on nonwhite races which includes six tables on American Indians based on the 25 percent sample which was used throughout the Census. Volume 2, for 1970, includes an entire report—PC(2)–1F—on *American Indians*, which includes 18 tables, 17 of them based on a 20 percent and one (on mother tongues spoken) on a 15 percent sample, both used throughout the Census. The sample of households from whom special data were obtained turned out in 1960 to have overcounted Indians by 4.3 percent, and in 1970 to have undercounted them by 3.7 percent. The entire special report, *American Indians*, uses the mistaken lower figures including 763,594 total population instead of 792,730 which the

Table 1 shows for 1970 some characteristics of people who identified themselves and families as Indian *and* who named their tribes *and* who lived in Urban places with at least 3,800 Indians. Table 2 shows, for the 18 states with over 10,000 Indians, the increase in number of urban Indians between 1960 and 1970. It is ordered by the number in 1970. As table 1 provides tribal context, table 2 provides statewide context for table 3, which, in turn, shows changes from 1960 to 1970 in socioeconomic characteristics of Indians in 14 Standard Metropolitan Statistical Areas (SMSAs) and 11 tribes/reservations for which the censuses provide relatively comparable data.

Table 1 orders the tribes by their percent urban, and provides economic and educational data in which differences are often associated with urban life. Moving down the table it is evident that, as expected, the employment and income figures generally decrease and the percentages below the poverty line increase. The changes here supply some control for interpreting the ten-year changes in occupations, income, and com-

Census found. The lost 32,158 people are mentioned only once in the Introduction, and never shown, and tend to get lost in other writings which use this report as "the census"; for example Helen W. Johnson's widely-used *American Indians in Transition* (U.S. Department of Agriculture, Economic Report no. 283, 1975).

In both 1960 and 1970, Aleuts and Eskimos were counted among "other races" so that separate data on them are not published, and hence are not included in my tables.

In addition to the published books, there are "public use samples" on computer tapes of material which can provide new unpublished combinations of data. But for Indians there appears to be nothing that goes beyond what is published. Only the Census Bureau itself could supply additional information, on request, for a charge.

TABLE 1

INDIANS IN 1970 IN TRIBES WITH POPULATIONS OVER 3,800

	TOTAL	URBAN		% OVER 16 EM-PLOYED	MEDIAN FAMILY INCOME	% BELOW POVERTY LINE	MEDIAN SCHOOL YEARS COM-PLETED	% OF HIGH SCHOOL GRAD-UATES
		NUMBER	%					
Census total	792,730	355,738	44.9					
Total from sample	763,594	336,420	44.1					
Tribes not reported	161,543	97,845	60.6					
Tribes under 3,800	92,962	43,357	46.6					
Tribes over 3,800	509,089	195,218	38.3					
Mohawk	6,105	4,551	74.5	79.1	$9,064	17.8	10.3	32.9
Chickasaw	5,616	3,790	67.5	70.0	6,640	20.3	10.9	41.9
Comanche	4,250	2,862	67.3	69.5	6,102	28.7	12.0	49.6
Kiowa	4,337	2,776	64.0	61.0	5,285	38.0	12.1	52.0
Oneida	5,673	3,542	62.4	75.8	8,183	19.2	10.2	33.8
Potawatomie	4,626	2,816	60.9	74.0	6,831	20.4	10.7	38.9
Zuni	7,306	5,871	58.7	54.8	6,401	35.6	10.6	34.9
Seminole	5,055	2,898	57.3	67.1	5,956	29.7	10.5	40.5
Creek, Ala., Coushatta	17,004	9,674	56.9	67.2	6,248	27.6	10.8	41.2
Cherokee	66,150	36,943	55.8	68.7	6,329	26.5	10.4	37.7
Kaw, Omaha, Osage Ponca, Quapaw	6,849	3,676	53.7	60.4	6,752	27.7	12.1	51.9
Choctaw, Huoma	2,356	12,558	53.3	67.3	5,925	30.2	10.1	37.1
Tlingit, Haida	7,543	3,755	49.8	59.1	7,477	26.2	10.6	37.8
Chippewa	41,946	18,738	44.9	66.3	5,928	33.0	9.9	29.6
Cheyenne	6,872	2,995	43.6	60.1	5,567	38.0	10.4	34.7
Onandaga, Tus-carora, Cayuga, Wyandotte	5,051	2,159	42.7	69.3	7,537	20.4	10.6	37.2
Sioux (Dakota)	47,825	19,842	41.5	59.5	4,734	44.2	10.2	33.5
Yuman	7,635	3,158	41.4	66.1	5,870	32.6	10.0	31.7
Seneca	4,644	1,856	40.0	70.3	7,580	18.7	11.1	42.3
Blackfeet	9,921	3,883	39.1	64.9	5,588	33.9	10.9	38.7
Yakima	3,856	1,427	37.0	61.6	6,123	32.4	10.6	35.6
Hopi	7,236	2,641	36.5	57.2	5,644	41.6	11.3	44.0
Shoshone, N. and S. Paiute and Chemehueve	14,248	5,039	35.4	63.5	6,032	26.3	10.3	34.7
Menominee	4,307	1,509	35.0	59.0	6,124	27.9	10.5	33.7
Apache	22,993	7,821	34.0	57.7	5,106	41.4	8.9	23.3
Papago, Pima	16,690	4,468	26.8	51.6	4,095	55.8	8.3	20.7
Ute	3,815	894	23.4	51.6	4,761	43.3	9.2	25.9
Tanoan	6,342	1,408	22.2	55.0	5,009	45.2	10.0	33.8
Kareson	10,087	1,895	18.8	56.8	5,638	35.9	10.4	37.1
Navajo	96,743	16,276	16.8	48.9	3,434	58.2	5.3	18.8
Lumbee	27,520	3,497	12.8	70.8	5,157	37.3	8.2	19.0

pleted school years shown in tables 2 and 3.

To American Indian specialists, the specific data of table 1 are also intrinsically interesting, requiring explanation in terms of particular data. For example, the Lumbee are only few and recently urban, and shown as poorer and less educated than any of the peoples east of the Rocky Mountains; yet one has to go almost to the top of the page to find the three groups who have a larger percentage employed. Or why are the Tlingit 5th in income but 21st in the percent employed? These are questions probably easily answered by those familiar with the cases. A more general and quite striking characteristic of the distributions is the comparatively high position of all of the Iroquois nations (Mohawk, Oneida, Seneca, Onandaga). This may be due to special circumstances

in each case; but their long contact with the White man must also be significant. That the equally urban Southeastern nations (Chickasaw, Creek, Cherokee, Choctaw), which also had early white contacts, are poorer may be associated with the removal of most of them to Oklahoma while most Iroquois remained in situ in New York. Or will it be suggested that the nature of the cultures and the political organizations of these two sets of nations are also important in explaining the difference?

Tables 2 and 3 are geographically based in a way that table 1 is not. To clarify this difference, think for example of the Cherokee entry in table 1. These are all the people who identify as "Cherokee"—that was a free choice—who, by census definition, lived in urban areas, whether in North Carolina, where there is an

TABLE 2

URBAN INDIANS IN STATES WITH OVER 10,000 INDIANS

STATE	1960		1970		% INCREASE	No. SMSA's WITH 2,500+	
	NUMBER	% OF ALL INDIANS	NUMBER	% OF ALL INDIANS		1960	1970
California	22,574	55.8	67,202	76.1	66.4	4	7
Oklahoma	23,257	37.0	47,623	49.2	51.2	2	3
New York	13,257	63.1	17,161	67.1	22.8	2	2
Arizona	8,662	10.4	16,442	17.4	47.3	2	2
Washington	11,882	55.9	16,102	52.2	26.2	1	2
Texas	4,643	69.8	14,567	86.1	68.1	—	2
New Mexico	9,023	16.1	13,405	18.7	32.7	1	1
Minnesota	4,994	31.6	11,703	52.4	57.3	1	1
Michigan	5,064	51.2	10,541	65.8	52.0	—	1
Illinois	5,895	91.5	9,542	92.6	38.2	1	1
South Dakota	4,615	17.9	9,115	24.4	49.4	—	—
Wisconsin	4,062	21.2	7,439	39.6	45.4	—	1
Oregon	2,662	32.3	6,976	52.8	61.8	—	1
North Carolina	1,616	04.2	6,194	14.0	74.0	—	1
Montana	2,804	14.0	5,070	19.2	44.7	—	—
Alaska	3,745	25.3	4,696	29.2	20.3	—	—
Utah	1,990	28.6	3,689	35.0	46.1	—	—
North Dakota	1,193	10.3	1,810	13.3	34.1	—	—

TABLE 3

CHANGES 1960–1970 IN SELECTED PLACES AND CHARACTERISTICS

Standard Metropolitan Statistical Areas	American Indian Population			Occupations %					Median Income of Individuals			Median School Yrs. Completed		
	1960	1970	% Incr.	White Collar		Blue Collar		Change to White Collar	Dollars		% Change	1960	1970	In-crease
				1960	1970	1960	1970		1959	1969				
Albuquerque, N.M.	3,253	5,822	44.1	34.3	47.3	36.9	29.4	20.3	1,698	3,627	53.2	9.9	12.2	2.3
Buffalo, N.Y.	5,567	5,606	50.6	13.0	21.7	63.5	53.3	18.9	2,484	3,471	28.4	8.9	10.0	1.0
Chicago, Ill.	5,329	8,203	35.0	28.9	36.0	52.6	51.5	8.2	2,684	4,230	36.5	9.9	11.1	1.2
L.A.-Long B., Ca.	9,330	23,908	61.0	23.5	36.2	56.2	47.1	21.8	2,459	4,136	40.5	10.3	11.8	1.5
Minn.-St. P., Minn.	3,408	9,911	65.6	20.1	32.0	52.0	48.5	15.4	1,743	3,754	53.6	8.8	11.4	2.6
New York, N.Y.	8,112	9,984	18.1	36.9	48.2	43.4	30.5	24.2	2,902	4,194	30.8	9.4	11.2	1.8
Okla. City, Okla.	6,178	12,951	52.2	26.9	40.6	52.6	44.1	22.2	1,806	3,851	53.1	10.2	12.2	2.0
Phoenix, Ariz.	8,707	10,127	14.0	12.6	26.6	35.5	34.3	15.2	1,245	2,312	46.2	8.3	9.6	1.3
S. Bernardino-Riverside, Ontario, Ca.	3,949	5,941	33.5	15.9	26.2	62.0	49.7	22.6	2,037	3,544	42.5	9.3	11.1	1.2
San Diego, Ca.	3,365	6,007	44.0	21.5	31.7	44.1	45.3	9.0	1,909	2,394	20.3	10.4	11.6	1.2
San Francisco, Ca.	4,422	12,041	63.3	25.7	43.0	51.8	42.4	26.7	2,292	4,424	48.2	10.7	12.1	1.4
Seattle-Everett, Wa.	3,820	8,814	56.7	17.2	30.9	54.6	47.1	21.2	1,640	3,731	56.0	9.4	11.1	1.7
Tucson, Ariz.	7,007	8,704	18.8	07.1	20.1	48.4	48.1	13.3	1,000–	1,526	34.5	6.3	7.0	0.7
Tulsa, Okla.	7,534	15,183	50.4	29.5	36.9	49.3	43.9	12.8	2,099	3,579	41.3	9.9	12.0	2.1
INDIAN RESERVATIONS														
Blackfeet, Mont.	4,959	4,757	-4.1	26.7	34.2	17.6	30.7	18.6	1,000–	1,781	43.6	8.8	9.9	1.1
Cherokee, N.C.	3,223	3,455	6.7	19.4	20.5	49.8	54.4	-3.5	1,000–	1,977	49.4	8.3	9.0	0.7
Cheyenne River, S.D.	3,412	3,440	0.1	24.7	29.2	14.8	16.4	29	1,000–	1,402	28.7+	9.5	9.4	-0.1
Fort Peck, Mont.	3,351	3,182	-5.0	18.6	29.8	29.4	39.4	10.8	1,026	2,031	49.5	8.7	9.6	0.9
Menominee, Wis.	3,145	2,445	-22.3	12.2	24.9	70.2	60.1	23.0	1,000–	2,873	65.2+	8.3	10.2	1.9
Navajo	2,654	56,949		03.3	32.7	64.5	41.6	52.3	1,183	1,606	26.3	0.8	4.1	3.3
Pine Ridge, S.D.	7,476	8,280	9.7	17.5	31.2	29.7	24.3	19.1	1,000–	1,521	34.3+	8.3	9.0	0.7
Red Lake, Minn.	2,908	2,741	-5.7	19.4	26.2	60.2	43.4	23.6	1,419	2,346	39.5	8.9	9.6	0.7
Standing Rock, N. & S. Dak.	3,323	2,925	-12.0	32.8	32.9	20.7	17.8	3.0	1,000–	1,654	39.5+	8.8	9.7	0.9
Wind River, Wyo.	3,486	3,319	-4.8	16.2	29.4	29.1	33.0	9.6	1,000–	1,415	29.3	8.7	10.3	1.6
Yakima, Wash.	3,966	2,508	-36.7	16.6	28.2	30.6	36.8	5.4	1,109	1,772	37.4	9.0	10.0	1.0

official Cherokee reservation, or in Oklahoma, where most "enrolled" Cherokees live, but where reservations have long since been terminated; or in Manhattan, Anchorage, Miami, or anywhere else in the United States. Not all people in any Indian reservation or community are Indians, or Indians of the tribe that gives the community its ?abel. When the Census groups people not only by the tribal identification they give, but also by the place where they live, needless to say they find many largely Indian communities, some of which are also official reservations. This is not the meaning of the "tribes" listed in table 1. The 1970 Census provides data also on "identified reservations" which together include only a minority of Indians. Both because the populations of reservations are, with few exceptions, 100 percent rural, and because they were not chosen in 1970 by the same criteria or frequently with the same names as in 1960, I have not made a general comparative table. But in table 3 I have, as a control, appended to the list of metropolitan areas corresponding data on 11 Indian groups which are probably identical in the two censuses, excepting Navajo which is too much smaller in 1960.

Table 2 shows that at least in all of the states with large Indian populations, except Washington, the number and proportion of urban Indians increased substantially. The last columns of table 2 show the number of Standard Metropolitan Statistical Areas which had at least the minimum number of Indians— 2,500—to be included in the published census report. The number of such SMSAs in these 18 states increased from 1960 to 1970 from 14 to 25. Table 3 includes data only on

the 14 SMSAs for which data are published for both decades.[8]

Table 3 provides the most relevant census material for the question asked. I have tried in vain to learn also from the material on housing and related socioeconomic data, but interpretations here would require comparisons with other minorities, and probably more than my small experience in these matters. I am unable, also, to make much of the material on education in the last column. Apparently, with urban living, the amount of education increases; but rather than a result of urbanization, this may be largely a product of migration to cities by Indians who seek opportunities to use their higher education. The figures on income, comparing either the reservation and metropolitan areas or the two decades, seem obvious until one asks how much noncash income may be included in rural areas; how one can take into account the offsetting increased cost of living in metropolitan areas; and, of course, the inflation factor from 1960 to 1970.

The changes shown in occupations in the ten-year period are the distillation of a laborious process. The census used essentially the same definitions in 1960 and 1970:

White-Collar:
1. Professional, technical and kindred workers
2. Managers and administrators, except farm

8. The "Indian SMSAs" added in 1970 were Anaheim, et al., Sacramento and San Josè, California; Lawton, Oklahoma; Tacoma, Washington; Dallas and Houston, Texas; Detroit, Michigan; Milwaukee, Wisconsin; Portland, Oregon; and Fayetteville, North Carolina. In states with fewer than 10,000 Indians there were three additional "Indian" SMSAs (2,500 or more Indians): Baltimore, Philadelphia, and Washington, D.C.

3. Sales workers
4. Clerical and kindred workers

Blue-Collar:
5. Craftsmen and kindred workers
6. Operative, except transport
7. Laborers, except farm

Farm Workers:
8. Farmers and farm managers
9. Farm laborers and farm foremen

Service Workers:
10. Service workers
11. Private household workers

The order of these items was changed from one census to the next, and males and females were listed separately. The first tabulation suggested the need to combine the items as well as the sexes to get four figures for each community. These were translated into percentages for study.

In 1960 farm workers were a substantial minority in three metropolitan areas: Phoenix 29 percent, Tucson 23 percent, and San Diego 17 percent; in 1970, they fell to 16 percent, 6 percent, and 4 percent respectively. Eight of the 11 reservations had substantial minorities of farm workers: Yakima 43 percent; Cheyenne River and Blackfeet 39 percent; Wind River 37 percent; Pine Ridge and Fort Peck 36 percent; Navajo 26 percent; and Standing Rock 25 percent. These fell in 1970 respectively to 27 percent, 29 percent, 11 percent, 18 percent, 17 percent, 6 percent, 4 percent, and 15 percent.

The proportion in service occupations turned out to vary least, as can be seen in a listing following the order of table 3 (the 1970 figure is in parentheses): 24(22); 17(19); 17(12); 28(19); 20(21); 17(15); 22(23); 12(21); 17(19); 20(14); 22(21); 21(25); and 15(16) for metropolitan areas, and for

the reservation 17(24); 22(24); 21(25); 15(25); 16(15); 6(22); 17(28); 20(26); 21(35); 18(19); and 10(8).

Deciding that these figures might confuse more than inform, I limited table 3 to the shift from blue-collar to white-collar, which appears to be universal, consistent, and substantial, with scarcely any exceptions. Explanations—or at least feasible hypotheses—will emerge for persons with experience in the communities listed. For example, it seems evident that the change in Chicago has different meaning from what seems to be a similar change in San Diego. The apparently similar quantitative small net changes from blue- to white-collar in Chicago and San Diego—or in Tucson and Tulsa—are probably, in fact, quite different. The Census does (for these same localities) provide data also on public versus private employment which might be useful in understanding some of these figures. Probably the largest help comes from understanding similarities and differences in the total contexts. For example, metropolitan areas in Indian country often include rural communities of Indians and even reservations. Some Indians may even come to the city in the sense that Indians come to Chicago; but they would be only a small part of the population of Indians included in table 3 as being part of the SMSA called Tucson, to use an obvious example.

The lesson is an old one. There are no "Indians," but rather different communities of Indians. And that goes for so-called urban Indians, as well. Indian people from time immemorial have explored and found ways to live in new environments without losing their identities or values. They "accepted the horse" fully, but nobody supposes they should have become horses. They are, presumably, fully capable of learning to live with us without becoming like us.

Policy

The historic facts are that Europeans overran North America; that the native people have not assimilated into the larger new population but remain peaceful conscientious resisters and exemplars; that neither the inclinations nor the laws of the majority permit cold-blooded "final solutions"; and that therefore it lives uneasily with an unresolved problem. Yet, the remedy is obvious and at hand, dubious mainly because it asks that we relax our demand that the Indian people assimilate and instead exercise a fraction of the patience that they have so long shown.

Let us understand first that native Americans are as intelligent and adaptable as any people known to history. I would add "perhaps more so," thinking of cultural rather than biological factors, if there were need to do so. Everything anthropology knows about these people shows their remarkable capacity to change, to adapt, and to survive. In recent years few have had satisfactory options, and almost all of them live with adaptations that are far from good, for them or for the larger society. They await the one option that people everywhere desire, but which most are unable to use: to remove obstacles to finding their own ways. Though it is a bad figure of speech, again I mention horses to suggest removing both blinders and reins.

In 1961, in their "Declaration of Indian Purpose," a national assembly told what they wanted:

When Indians speak of the continent they yielded, they are not referring only to the loss of some millions of acres in real estate. They have in mind that the land supported a universe of things they knew, valued, and loved.

With that continent gone, except for the few poor parcels they still retain, the basis of life is precariously held, but they mean to hold the scraps and parcels as earnestly as any small nation or ethnic group was ever determined to hold to identity and survival.

What we ask of America is not charity, not paternalism, even when benevolent. We ask only that the nature of our situation be recognized and made the basis of policy and action.

In short, the Indians ask for assistance, technical and financial, for the time needed, however long that may be, to regain in the America of the space age some measure of the adjustment they enjoyed as the original possessors of their native land.

At that time perhaps there were no practical ways to do what was wanted except to begin ending the threats to Indian rights and identities embodied in the then explicit policy called termination; to continue to provide funds for health, education, and social services; and to transfer their control from outside bureaucracies to the Indian communities. But how individual families would make their living in their poor territories was an unanswered puzzle until more recent years.

Indian families need cash to live while they freely explore the new environment and discover ways, as the Mohawk high steel workers once did, to make their livings which suit their cultures. The answer, now at hand, is the federally-provided, but completely unadministered, minimum family income, perhaps through a negative income tax. If a general system is long delayed, perhaps it could be tried out with American Indians. With cash income assured, no matter where they are, combined with health insurance and perhaps school vouchers, Indians will be free to explore abroad. But, also, more will probably stay in their communities, where living is cheaper. Here their funds could be used to add to their lands, but their cooperative spirit will also suggest ways to develop economic enterprises. If they can ward off the benevolent hearts and greedy hands of outsiders, we should soon learn from them, in our common new environment, how to adjust to externals without sacrificing inner values.

ANNALS, AAPSS, **436**, Mar. 1978

The Integration of Americans of Indian Descent

By J. MILTON YINGER AND GEORGE EATON SIMPSON

ABSTRACT: When the members of two societies come into contact, changes in the direction of assimilation may occur on four different levels—biological, psychological, cultural, and structural, or, in more descriptive terms, amalgamation, identification, acculturation, and integration may take place. At present, most Indians favor integration but resist forced acculturation. The integration and cultural assimilation of Native Americans have been inhibited by a number of fundamental differences between the majority culture and the cultures of Indian peoples. At the same time, other factors have furthered integration and cultural assimilation. Migration, urbanization, education, economic changes, and intermarriage will facilitate structural integration, a shared identity, and cultural assimilation. In time, full assimilation, or the interaction of all persons without reference to ethnic or racial descent, may come about. For the immediate future, however, pluralism, associated with increasing acculturation and structural integration, seems to be the most likely pattern of relationship between most Indians and non-Indians.

J. Milton Yinger is Professor of Sociology and Anthropology at Oberlin College. Among his publications are Toward a Field Theory of Behavior, The Scientific Study of Religion, *and most recently,* Middle Start: An Experiment in the Educational Enrichment of Young Adolescents *(with Kiyoshi Ikeda, Frank Laycock, and Stephen Cutler). With George E. Simpson, he edited an earlier volume of* THE ANNALS *on* American Indians *(May 1957); and together they have written* Racial and Cultural Minorities, *now in its fourth edition. Professor Yinger recently served as President of the American Sociological Association.*

George Eaton Simpson is Emeritus Professor of Sociology and Anthropology at Oberlin College. He is the author of Melville J. Herskovits *(1973);* Religious Cults of the Caribbean *(1970); and* Racial and Cultural Minorities *(with J. Milton Yinger), which won the Anisfield-Wolf Award in Race Relations in 1958.*

DESPITE decades of scholarly work, the concepts of integration, acculturation, assimilation, and related terms are used in a variety of ways. And lacking clear definitions of these basic intergroup processes, we cannot attain reliable measurement of them. In this paper we cannot hope to resolve these problems of definition and measurement; but we would like to suggest a mode of approach that may take us toward a solution and help us to clarify the situation of American Indians.

FOUR BASIC INTERGROUP PROCESSES

When the members of two societies come into contact, changes in the direction of assimilation—the blending of formerly distinguishable sociocultural groups[1]—may occur on four different levels: biological, psychological, cultural, and structural. Or, to use more descriptive terms, amalgamation, identification, acculturation, and integration may take place. These processes are strongly interconnected, but because they can proceed at different speeds and in different mixtures, we need to keep them analytically distinct in our minds. Each is a variable, of course, but lacking clearly specified units and techniques of measurement, we tend to speak of more or less, or in terms of broad categories.

Amalgamation, defined in strictly biological terms, is doubtless the least ambiguous of the concepts. An exclusively biological approach proves to be an inadequate index to assimilation or integration, however, when social factors become involved, as

the following question suggests: What proportion of one's ancestry can be non-Indian and still allow one to retain the designation Indian? This is an issue wherever biological mixture has occurred, and the answer varies widely. Some persons with three Indian grandparents and one white regard themselves, and are regarded by others, as white. Other persons with one Indian grandparent are Indian.

It is also important, in discussing amalgamation, to distinguish between two modes of measurement: the proportion of individuals who have mixed ancestry and the proportion of the gene pool that is derived from the various stocks. Thus it is one thing to say that about 80 percent of black Americans have European ancestors; it is something else to say that about 30 percent of their ancestry—viewing them as a group—is European. Similar figures are more difficult to estimate for Indians, since it is likely that a larger proportion has passed over into the general society, even some persons with very little or no non-Indian ancestry. With respect to some particular group of native Americans, it would be possible to say, for example, that 40 percent of them had some European ancestors and that 30 percent of their gene pool was European (which would be the case if all those of mixed ancestry were one-quarter Indian).

One other aspect of amalgamation deserves comment. It is often stated that amalgamation occurs late in a succession of intergroup processes.[2]

1. George E. Simpson, "Assimilation," in *International Encyclopedia of the Social Sciences* (New York: Macmillan and The Free Press, 1968), vol. I, p. 438.

2. Prodipto Roy, "The Measurement of Assimilation: The Spokane Indians," *American Journal of Sociology* 67 (March 1962), pp. 541–51; Lynn C. White and Bruce A. Chadwick, "Urban Residence, Assimilation, and Identity of the Spokane Indian," in *Native Americans Today: Sociological Perspectives*,

This may or may not be true, and the timing both reflects and affects the nature of intergroup relations. If two groups are quite unequal in power and status, amalgamation, as a result of sexual exploitation, tends to occur in the early period of contact. The rate of amalgamation may decline during a second period, even though acculturation continues. At a still later stage, if inequality and prejudice are reduced, intermarriage may become more common. It is estimated that now about one Indian in three marries a non-Indian.[3]

The psychological process of identification refers to a set of related concepts: the degree to which individuals from groups A and B have come to think of themselves as belonging to the same society—as many immigrants and their descendants think of themselves as Americans; the degree to which members of A identify themselves with society B; and the degree to which members of B identify with society A. All three of these processes may go on at the same time; and the nature of their mixture is a significant aspect of the relationship between A and B. Some Americans of Indian ancestry identify themselves simply as Americans. This is correlated with the degree of acculturation and mixed ancestry, but is analytically separate from them: many substantially acculturated persons of mixed background identify themselves entirely as Indians. Throughout American history, a few white persons have identified themselves as Indians, have lived in tribal villages, married Indian spouses, and have sometimes

become chiefs.[4] And at least a few persons of European and of Indian background (as well as some of Asian and African ancestry) identify themselves with a new society that is neither A nor B, but the product of interaction among persons and cultures of many types.

If we think of acculturation as ". . . the process of cultural change resulting from intercultural contact,"[5] it is clearly a two-way process. It has been difficult to arrive at a widely agreed upon definition in part because of a failure to distinguish between individual and group referents. It is one thing, for example, to say that some individual white persons have absorbed various Indian values, perhaps thinking of themselves, and being thought of, as somewhat deviant as a result. It is something else for the dominant society to absorb various Indian values as part of its normative system, teaching them to its young through normal processes of socialization. And of course the same distinction between individual and group processes can be applied to Indians. If both processes are called acculturation, it is important to distinguish them conceptually, because their causes and effects are quite different.

Acculturation has been difficult to define and analyze also because it is empirically mixed in various ways with the degree of amalgamation, identification, and integration. Undoubtedly these processes are correlated, often highly correlated, but

eds. Howard M. Bahr, Bruce A. Chadwick, and Robert C. Day (New York: Harper & Row, 1972), p. 240.

3. E. J. Kahn, Jr., *The American People* (Baltimore: Penguin Books, 1973), p. 207.

4. A. Irving Hallowell, "American Indians, White and Black: The Phenomenon of Transculturalization, *Current Anthropology* 4 (December 1963), pp. 510–31; J. Norman Heard, *White into Red: A Study of the Assimilation of White Persons Captured by Indians* (Metuchen, N.J.: Scarecrow Press, 1973).

5. Bahr, Chadwick, Day, eds., *Native Americans Today*, p. 193.

one can occur without the others, the pace may be quite different, and the sequence can vary. With regard to the last point, acculturation is often regarded as an early process, leading to integration, identification, and amalgamation. There are exceptions to this common sequence, however, particularly in contact between an overwhelmingly powerful society and one possessing few weapons with which to defend itself. Workers may be brought into the economy of the dominant power before anything more than minimal acculturation has taken place; sexual exploitation, as we have noted, may make amalgamation an early process; some members of a society, unable to defend its way of life, may identify with the dominant society before they are acculturated to its ways. Thus the place of acculturation in the sequence of intergroup processes is a question to be kept open for examination in each situation, as the papers in this volume by Sol Tax, George and Louise Spindler, Robert Havighurst, Murray and Rosalie Wax, and others indicate.

Integration, the term we use to refer to mixture in the social structure of persons from two or more formerly separate societies or status groups, can be associated with different levels of acculturation, identification, and amalgamation; and, like these other processes, it can occur at various points in the sequence of change. As with acculturation, it is important in discussions of integration to distinguish between individual and group aspects. Individual integration exists to the degree that persons from groups A and B belong to the same social groups, including private associations, and interact within those groups on the basis of equality. Group integration, which

we shall call pluralism, exists to the degree that A and B as groups are accorded the same rights and public privileges, the same access to political and economic advantages, and the same responsibilities as citizens and members of the total society, while at the same time they are accepted as legitimate subdivisions of the society, with partially distinctive cultures. Integration into the economy, for example, implies similarity between groups in their occupational distribution and income. Indians have gained significantly in the last generation, particularly those residing in cities, but remain behind the national standard. Group integration, or pluralism, implies the continuing existence of separate groups and a continuing feeling of identification with those groups on the part of many members; but it can exist in the context of extensive acculturation and amalgamation. In fact, strongly acculturated persons of mixed ancestry are often leaders in movements to define the boundaries and win the rights implied by pluralism or structural integration.

Among American Indians, structural integration is occurring, or is being sought, on both tribal and national levels. The movement to secure equality before the law, recognition of group rights, and an equal share of economic and educational opportunities rests upon and implies, not separation from, but pluralistic integration with, the larger society. Aspects of this movement are discussed by Vine Deloria, Jr., Nancy O. Lurie, Sam Stanley and Robert K. Thomas, and other authors in this volume. The pan-Indian or national Indian aspects of pluralism, substantially but not entirely among those living in cities, are indicative of a shift from American Indian to

Indian American.[6] In it we see the search for new ground on which to stand as Indians, a new basis for identity, for pluralism rather than assimilation.[7] Among the tribes, there are significant differences in the extent to which integration has taken place, depending upon the aboriginal culture, the size of the population, the tribal economic picture, and other variables.[8]

We shall think of assimilation as a variable subsuming the biological, psychological, cultural, and structural processes and their interactions. If, in the contact between two groups, amalgamation, shifts in identification, acculturation, and integration have occurred to only a slight degree, we will say that assimilation has been minimal. If these processes have gone so far that the group boundaries have been wiped out, we can speak of maximal assimilation. Since each process is a variable, one might specify any number of values along an assimilation scale, but we are a long way from having the kind of data that would make such refined measurement possible.

INTEGRATION AND ACCULTURATION OF AMERICAN INDIANS

We turn now to a more direct application of some of these concepts to Indian Americans. The focus of our attention will be on the processes of integration, particularly pluralistic integration, and accul-

turation, which seem to us to be the most significant aspects of Indian-white relationships at this stage of American history.[9]

Who Is An Indian? We can scarcely discuss the process of integration without at first examining this difficult question. If one is speaking of "administrative" or "official" Indians, that is, those who are eligible for services from the Bureau of Indian Affairs, the number in September 1968 was 452,000.[10] These persons were members of tribes with federal trust land, who had one-quarter or more Indian blood, and who lived on a federal reservation or nearby. This number included all Indians, Aleuts, and Eskimos living in Alaska, a total of 54,000. Instead of the legal or "heirship" definition followed by the BIA, the Census Bureau employs a cultural definition of Indian. Criticisms of the variations in procedures used by enumerators led the Census in 1960 to make it possible for members of a household to classify themselves. (In the 1970 census, the questions under "Color or Race" included: White, Negro or Black, Indian [American], Japanese, Chinese, Filipino, Hawaiian, Korean, and Other. For Alaska, the racial categories Aleut and Eskimo were substituted for Hawaiian and Korean).

American Indians are currently increasing faster than the general population. The 1950 Census listed ap-

6. John H. Bushnell, "From American Indian to Indian American: The Changing Identity of the Hupa," *American Anthropologist* 70 (December 1968), pp. 1108–16.
7. Bahr, Chadwick, and Day, eds., *Native Americans Today*, pp. 401–4.
8. John A. Price, "The Migration and Adaptation of American Indians to Los Angeles," *Human Organization* 27 (Summer 1968), pp. 168–75.

9. For an account of earlier Indian-white contacts, see the excellent article by D'Arcy McNickle, "Indian and European: Indian-White Relations from Discovery to 1887," *The Annals of the American Academy of Political and Social Science*, 311 (May 1957), pp. 1–11.
10. Murray L. Wax, *Indian Americans: Unity and Diversity* (New York: Prentice-Hall, 1971), p. 215.

proximately 350,000 Indians; the 1960 Census, nearly 525,000; and the 1970 Census, about 792,000. Population increases of Indians in recent decades, however, cannot be attributed solely to natural increase. For example, the 1960 Census included as "Indian" certain groups of mixed white, black, and Indian descent which had been variously classified in previous censuses. Also, after the passage of legislation and the establishment of a special court of claims under which Indian tribes could sue the United States government for taking their land in the past for insufficient compensation, many individuals who were only marginally Indian in ancestry, and not at all Indian in any other way, claimed a share of the awards. Similarly, federal benefits, such as access to the Indian branch of the Public Health Service, are available to individuals who can establish that their ancestry is at least one-quarter Indian. Finally, it has become fashionable in some circles to claim to be "Indian." In recent years, therefore, there has been a "drifting in" process which is comparable to the "drifting out" process of the previous two and one-half centuries and of the present time. It has been estimated that if persons were counted as Indian in the way that residents of the United States are counted as Negro, that is, any degree of Indian ancestry, the Indian population would number several millions.[11] This would surely be the case if the count included those Americans of Mexican background who identify with their mestizo heritage. Some refer to the Southwest as Aztlán—an Aztec term—and express a kinship with American Indians.[12]

11. Ibid., p. 34.
12. Ibid., p. 179.

The definition of American Indian which appears in the Office of Native American Programs' Final Regulations states that:

'American Indian or Indian' means any individual who is a member or a descendant of a member of a North American tribe, band, or organized group of native people who are indigenous to the continental United States or who otherwise have a special relationship with the United States or a State through treaty, agreement, or some other form of recognition. This includes any individual who claims to be an Indian and who is regarded as such by the Indian community of which he or she claims to be a part. This definition also includes Alaskan Natives.[13]

With various rights to land, education, and health care dependent on tribal or racial identity, the question of who is an Indian will continue to be important and controversial. "Instant Indians" will be resented and federally recognized and urban Indians will face some conflict of interest.[14]

Indian-non-Indian acculturation in American society

In their well-known memorandum on acculturation,[15] Redfield, Linton, and Herskovits conceived this phenomenon as a two-way process, but in actual practice American anthropologists and sociologists have usually treated it as a one-way proc-

13. Department of Health, Education, and Welfare, Office of Human Development, "Native American Programs: Final Regulations," *Federal Register* 42 (19 January 1977), p. 3785.
14. *The New York Times*, 21 March 1976, p. 38.
15. Robert Redfield, Ralph Linton, and M. J. Herskovits, "Memorandum for the Study of Acculturation," *American Anthropologist* 38 (January-March 1936), pp. 149–52.

ess.[16] For example, in the May 1957 issue of THE ANNALS entitled "American Indians and American Life," Vogt referred to "our earlier expectations concerning the rate of American Indian acculturation and why full acculturation to white American ways of life is not occurring in the contemporary scene."[17] Using a terminology somewhat different from ours, Gordon distinguishes between cultural or behavioral assimilation (acculturation) and structural assimilation (large-scale primary group relations), but he regards the former process as "change of culture patterns to those of the host society."[18] In our view, acculturation is cultural change occasioned by prolonged contacts, face-to-face or through communications media, between representatives of different societies or between ethnic groups within a society, and overall it is a two-way process. The concept of two-way borrowing does not imply equal borrowing, quantitatively or qualitatively, by the different groups. On specific items, one-way borrowing may occur. Often both one-way and two-way cultural borrowing proceed faster than the spread of structural assimilation.

Among Native Americans, borrowing from whites has been greatest in material culture, where most of the Indian artifacts have been replaced by those of modern industrial

society.[19] The borrowings of whites from the American Indian in the realm of material culture, however, have been numerous. Plants domesticated by American Indians, including "Irish" potatoes, corn, beans, squash, and sweet potatoes, provide almost half of the world's food supply today. Among native American drugs found in modern pharmacology are coca in cocaine and novacaine, curare in anesthetics, cinchona bark (quinine), ephedra in ephedrine, datura in pain relievers, and cascara in laxatives. The woolen poncho, the parka, and moccasins came from Indian cultures, and the commercial cottons of today are derived principally from the species cultivated by American Indians.[20] Another category of borrowing is found in the acquisition and use of Indian-made objects, the most striking examples of which are Navajo rugs, silverwork, and pottery.

In esthetics, many Native Americans have been influenced by contemporary developments in mainstream music, but American Indian music has strongly affected a number of American composers. In 1939, Charles S. Skilton asserted: "Many devices of the ultramodern composers of the present day have long been employed by Indians—unusual intervals, arbitrary scales, changing tune, conflicting rhythm, polychoral effects, hypnotic monotony."[21] In the early 1900s, a number of composers visited reservations in the western United States, borrow-

16. A. Irving Hallowell, "The Impact of the American Indian on American Culture," American Anthropologist 59 (April 1957), pp. 212–13.

17. Evon Z. Vogt, "The Acculturation of American Indians," Annals of the American Academy of Political and Social Science, 311 (May 1957), p. 139.

18. Milton M. Gordon, Assimilation in American Life (New York: Oxford University Press, 1964), p. 71.

19. Kenneth M. Stewart, "Retrospect and Prospect," in The Native Americans, eds. Robert F. Spencer et al. (New York: Harper & Row, 1965), pp. 503–4.

20. Alan R. Beals, with George and Louise Spindler, Culture in Process (New York: Holt, Rinehart, and Winston, 1967), p. 215.

21. Quoted in Hallowell, Impact of the American Indian, p. 207.

ing themes and gathering and arranging melodies. Parts of Euro-American literature have reached numbers of native Americans through the schools, the mass media, and direct contact, but American literature also reflects the influence of American Indians. Among the best-known of these works are James Fenimore Cooper's *Leather Stocking Tales* and Longfellow's *The Song of Hiawatha.*

A fascinating question concerning the "contributions" of Native Americans to American civilization is the possibility of a characterological "gift." In analyzing the historical development of an American national character, the psychological effects of frontier contacts with American Indians may prove to be of considerable importance.[22]

Two aspects of the nonmaterial culture that have persisted within the Indian world are the emphasis placed upon the extended family as the basic social unit and the importance of the role of Indian land. According to Witt, as the economic level of the Indian people rises, the extended family is strengthened despite the loss of some members through relocation. It is the basic element in tribal organization, and these two social units reinforce each other as they have in the past.[23] Tribal peoples who wish to be incorporated into industrial civilization favor partial inclusion while retaining the solidarity of the social group.[24]

Indian land itself constitutes a habitation site and an economic resource, and it provides a focal point for Indian culture and identity both for reservation and many nonreservation Indians.[25] In the past 25 years the movement toward termination and the individualization of tribal assets has been led mainly by factions with higher percentages of off-reservation members than have the opposing factions.[26]

Formal education is desired by Native Americans today, but for many, the purpose of education is to make Indian life better and to support cultural pluralism, as Robert J. Havighurst shows in his article in this volume. The concern is more with levels of living than complete assimilation.[27]

Among modern Indian tribes that have continued a traditional religious life, the Pueblos are outstanding. Although most Pueblos are employed in modern jobs that require a thorough knowledge of the white world, they retain religious beliefs and practices that have served them for many generations. In recent years, the increased interest of younger Indians of numerous tribes in the positive aspects of tribal culture has led to a demand for the restoration of traditional religious ceremonies. In addition, an effort is being made by the Indians of the Joint Strategy and Action Committees of major Protestant denominations to combine traditional Indian

22. Ibid., p. 211.
23. Shirley H. Witt, "Nationalistic Trends Among American Indians," in *The American Indian Today*, eds. Stuart Levine and Nancy Lurie (Baltimore: Penguin Books, 1970), p. 123.
24. Robert K. Thomas, "Pan-Indianism," in *The American Indian Today*, eds. Levine and Lurie, pp. 139–40.

25. Witt, "Nationalistic Trends," p. 123.
26. Deward E. Walker, Jr., "Measures of Nez Perce Outbreeding and the Analysis of Cultural Change," *Southwestern Journal of Anthropology* 23 (Summer 1967), pp. 155–56.
27. Nancy O. Lurie, "The American Indian Renascence," in *The American Indian Today*, eds. Levine and Lurie, p. 313; Harriet H. Kupferer, "The Isolated Eastern Cherokee," in ibid., p. 144.

beliefs and the modern Christian social gospel. A leading part in this movement has been taken by the Cook Christian Training School in Tempe, Arizona.[28]

Cultural pluralism and structural integration

Throughout the world, there are some minorities that do not want to be culturally assimilated, to lose their separate identity. In some countries, dominant groups permit cultural variability within the range they consider consonant with national unity and security. Whether viewed from the perspective of minorities or dominant groups, such positions are called cultural pluralism. The concurrent social process of integration implies full equality in health services, educational, political, and economic opportunity among all groups.[29]

At present, most Indians favor integration but resist forced cultural assimilation. They prefer partial assimilation. They want to adapt to modern life, keeping what they value in Indian cultures and adopting what they admire or need in white culture. In time, of course, full assimilation, or the freedom of all persons to interact free of constraints based on ethnic or racial descent,[30] may come about. Migration, education, economic changes, and intermarriage will facilitate structural integration, a shared identity, and cultural assimilation—in short, a much larger degree of assimilation than now exists or is desired by most persons of Indian descent.

Persistence of American Indian groups

Few Indian tribes have disappeared completely. Since attempts to exterminate whole groups were almost always thwarted, most American Indian groups in existence at the time of initial white contact are still present. The Indian population declined until 1900, but after that date significant and even spectacular population increases are evident for most tribes. The fact that virtually the same groups of Indians encountered by the original settlers are still represented strikes some Americans as surprising, especially in the light of the efforts at integration that occurred after World War II. In terms of the melting pot conception of democracy, namely, the fusion of diverse ethnic and racial groups into a composite American people, the American Indian situation indicates that these people are not being absorbed structurally into American society. Indeed, American Indian groups still retain many aspects of their own distinctive ways of life and have in only rare instances become fully Americanized. It is clear that Indian-white relations in the past have mitigated against both cultural and structural assimilation. One must recognize, however, that despite the relative lack of structural assimilation of Indians as groups, the process of integration has moved forward. There are still ongoing Indian communities, differing from one another and from the dominant American culture, yet forming parts of a complex society.

28. Vine Deloria, Jr., "Religion and the Modern American Indian," *Current History* 67 (December 1974), pp. 250, 253.
29. George E. Simpson and J. Milton Yinger, *Racial and Cultural Minorities*, 4th ed. (New York: Harper & Row, 1972), p. 19; E. P. Dozier, G. E. Simpson, and J. M. Yinger, "The Integration of Americans of Indian Descent," *The Annals of the American Academy of Political and Social Science*, 311 (May 1957), p. 159.
30. Simpson, "Assimilation," p. 438.

Even the melting pot notion of democracy, however, has not been completely negated. Because of historical relationships between American Indians and the majority population, and because Indian groups persist, we have been relatively unaware of another process. This process has rarely been referred to in the literature. The important fact is that through the years many individual Indians have passed into the main American society. Although exact figures are difficult and perhaps impossible to get, there is reason to believe that the number has been large. At least as many Indians as are enrolled as tribal members today have been absorbed into the larger society. Throughout the country there are ordinary "white" American citizens, and "Negroes" as well, with enough Indian admixture to entitle them to be enrolled on a reservation. The reason that such individuals are not enrolled is that often a full-blooded Indian, who left his reservation and married an Indian from another tribe, a Negro, or a white, did not care to enroll his children in his own tribe—or his wife's tribe if she were Indian—or did not want to bother with the technicalities. In the case of a man marrying a white or black woman, his children and his children's children would all have been entitled to tribal enrollment as defined in many reservations because they possessed one-fourth or more "Indian blood." Thus the individual Indian who leaves his group and his descendants, including individuals up to the third degree of kindred, are excluded as Indians. The children growing up in an environment that is not Indian become culturally American and racially either white or black. This "drifting out" process was certainly an important factor in the American Southwest. There was a tremendous increase in the Spanish-American population in this area in the years from 1700 to 1900, from approximately 10,000 to 150,000, an increase which cannot be explained on the basis of natural increase and immigration from Mexico. Indeed, we have conclusive evidence that the population was fed from Peublo, Navaho, and Apache groups.[31]

American Indians appear not to be absorbed socially as groups, unless rewards for doing so are available in their indigenous environments. There are few instances of such successful transitions, although a favorable reservation locale with rich natural resources may bring them about. The Spindlers have described such a case among a group of Menominee who have undergone a psychological reorientation.[32] This example is a rather special case, however. Most Indians are absorbed as individuals, leaving their communities voluntarily to seek a livelihood elsewhere. Once they surmount social and economic barriers, they often remain indefinitely in new occupations and surroundings quite different from those of their reservation communities.

Factors limiting integration and assimilation

The integration and assimilation of Native Americans have been lim-

31. Dozier, Simpson, and Yinger, "The Integration of Americans of Indian Descent," pp. 160–61. The statement concerning the increase in Spanish-American population is based on Frederick Webb Hodge, *Handbook of American Indians, North of Mexico* (Washington, D.C., U.S. Bureau of Ethnology, Smithsonian Institution, 1972), bulletin 30, pt. 2, p. 325.

32. George D. and Louise S. Spindler, "American Indian Personality Types and Their Sociocultural Roots," *Annals of the American Academy of Political and Social Science*, 311 (May 1957), p. 152.

ited by a number of fundamental differences between the majority white culture and the cultures of the Indian peoples.[33] Among these differences are conceptions of time, decisionmaking, and being. In white culture, all activities and institutions are ordered by arbitrarily established units of time, and punctuality is a virtue. In contrast, most Indians have internalized a concept of natural time that is related to an ongoing continuum—sunrise and sunset and the changing of the seasons. Community meetings, for example, are held "this evening" rather than at six o'clock, seven o'clock, or eight thirty, and they continue until everyone who wishes to speak has spoken. Within white culture, decisionmaking is based on a concept of vertical authority. Following discussion or debate, decisions are made, often by a majority vote, and orders are issued that others then act upon. In Indian cultures, authority tends to be of a more horizontal type. The councils of many tribes meet for days because of the necessity of reaching unanimous decisions. Consensual agreements make the issuing of orders unnecessary. A third cultural difference of some importance is found in the identification of self and how one regards self in relation to the world beyond self. In white culture, individuals are brought up to think of themselves in a perpetual state of becoming. They are taught to live for the future, to plan all their lives to improve their situation. In Indian cultures, one is continually in a state of being rather than of becoming. One is what one is, and while one will become other things, the impor-

tant thing is to improve oneself as he is now.[34]

Integration and assimilation (cultural and structural) have been limited also by the Indian's character, value system, and philosophy. The traditional Indian's character is "passive, deferential, and reflective," qualities not in keeping with a capitalist society. These tendencies hinder him in off-reservation competition for jobs, and discourage businessmen who might otherwise provide employment opportunities on the reservation. Among other Indian values, nepotism and factionalism are important. Also, a postulate that is widespread in Indian cultures, the Image of Limited Goods, holds that the world's supply of goods is limited and that if one individual acquires too much, others are deprived of their fair share. Another belief that affects the Indian's relations with non-Indians is his concept of man's harmony with nature. This belief has caused him to reject mechanization, special fertilizers, and improved seeds. His view that sickness is a result of disharmony in spiritual life has discouraged visits to health centers on the reservations, although this is less true today, as Patricia D. Mail makes clear in her paper in this volume. The view that immortality is achieved through the survival of one's descendants contributes to a birth rate that is two and one-half times that of the general population of the United States.[35]

33. Theodore D. Graves, "Urban Indian Personality and the 'Culture of Poverty,' " *American Ethnologist* 1 (February 1974), pp. 65–86; Weston La Barre, *The Ghost Dance: Origins of Religion* (New York: Dell, 1972), chap. 4.

34. Robert Faherty, "The American Indian: An Overview," *Current History* 67 (December 1974), pp. 244–74. For a stimulating discussion of the implications of Indian-white cultural differences for factories located on reservations, see Robert J. Bigart, "Indian Culture and Industrialization," *American Anthropologist* 74 (October 1972), pp. 1180–88.

35. Gerald S. Nagel, "Economics of the Reservation," *Current History* 67 (December 1974), p. 249.

At the same time, a lack of understanding, as well as bungling and prejudice, on the part of whites has hindered the integration of Native Americans. For more than a century after 1820, the reservation policy in particular, and United States policy in general, denied the Indians the experience of managing their own affairs. These policies insured the continued helplessness of the Indians.[36] Of special importance now is the climate of rejection met by migrants to certain urban centers. Towns and cities which are located adjacent to reservations are widely known for the discrimination, including open hostility, that they show toward Indians who move into them. For example, several South Dakota and New Mexico communities are noted for their inhospitality to Sioux and Navajo families who wish to move from a reservation to these towns.[37] Most of the books on American Indians document how prejudice and discrimination on the part of whites have retarded the integration and assimilation of Indians.

In the cities, most Indians prefer to associate socially with other Indians, usually with relatives and members of their own tribal group. In their early years in the San Francisco area, migrants tend to go to Indian centers of interaction; later, the Indian himself makes the choice of association. Ablon refers to the constant psychological and social awareness of Indianness as "a neo-Indian identity."[38] Many individuals have not been aware that Indians have a shared heritage until they leave their reservation, with its limited interests, and meet Indians from other parts of the country. In the urban environment, pan-Indianism often provides a new dimension, and sometimes, a substitute for their tribalism.[39]

Factors furthering integration and assimilation

Despite the tendency of Native Americans to interact mainly with other Indians in towns and cities, the movement to urban areas that began at the middle of the twentieth century may prove to be the most important factor in the continuing integration and the ultimate assimilation of the Indian. The Bureau of Indian Affairs estimates that during the 1960s about 200,000 Indian people migrated to urban areas. By 1970, approximately 45 percent of all Native Americans resided in cities. Even if many of the urban Indian people eventually leave the city, the urban experience will have become a major influence in determining their attitudes and behavior.[40]

Conditions in the urban community lead the Indian away from tribal patterns. The range of occupational, religious, political, and recreational alternatives is vastly increased in the city. The relative social anonymity and high-pressure salesmanship in the city cause the Indian to make

36. Robert Berkhofer, Jr., "Commentary," in Indian-White Relations, eds. Jane F. Smith and Robert Kvasnicka (Washington, D.C.: Howard University Press, 1976), p. 84.

37. Joann Westermann, "The Urban Indian," Current History 67 (December 1974), pp. 259-61.

38. Joan Ablon, "Relocated American Indians in the San Francisco Bay Area: Social Interaction and Indian Identity," Human Organization 23 (Winter 1964), p. 304.

39. Price, "Migration and Adaptation," pp. 174-75.

40. Howard M. Bahr, "An End to Invisibility," in Native Americans Today, eds. Bahr, Chadwick, and Day, pp. 408-9.

choices that he would never make on the reservation.[41] Some Indians who migrated to the cities in earlier years, and their children and grandchildren, are truly urban Indians. Some have never visited their tribal homes, and a fraction of these have abandoned any sense of Indian identity. Intermarried and adapted to industrial culture, these city dwellers are merely Americans of a particular ancestry. It is true, of course, that some urban Indians have remained traditionalists despite years of residence in the urban community.[42]

An increasing intermarriage rate tends to promote integration and assimilation, and a significant proportion of Indian young men and women are marrying outside the tribe and race. In a study of migration of American Indians to Los Angeles, Price found that 64 percent of the marriages within the generation of the respondent's parents were within the tribe, but only 39 percent of the marriages in the respondent's generation were within the tribe. Approximately one-third of the married respondents had married whites.[43] Walker's analysis of the reduction of Nez Perce breeding isolation in the Plateau area showed that interbreeding with other Indian groups and racial minorities of Euro-American society is increasing, but that whites are contributing most to the reduction of Nez Perce blood quanta at present. The predominance of whites in these intermarriages is due in part to the fact that this is the largest non-Nez Perce

group to which the Nez Perces are exposed. Part of the explanation lies, however, in the disapproval of Nez Perces of intermarriage with blacks, Latin Americans, and Shoshonean-speaking peoples to the south in the Great Basin. Walker found marked variations in outbreeding among different segments of the Nez Perce population. The off-reservation segment possesses much less Nez Perce blood quanta than does the on-reservation group. Also, the Lapwai people on the reservation are more outbred than the Kamiah population, largely because of the preference among the latter, almost totally Presbyterianized, group for endogamous marriages.[44]

Wax points out that intermarriage need not lead to a loss of Indian identity, but adds that the heirship definition of Indianness, in terms of blood quanta as written into the law, makes it almost inevitable that the children of Indian-white intermarriage will not be defined by themselves or others as Indian. In theory, absorption into the white group could be avoided if the married couple were to reside within an Indian community and bring up their children among Indian children. Actually, the tendency in intermarriage seems to be consciously toward the adoption of white ways. Among children who are the product of intertribal marriages, as among those who are raised in an urban environment where Indians from a number of tribes live, a generalized sense of Indian identity tends to emerge. The problem for the generalized Indian is that his role and his relationships with other Indians have not been clarified.[45]

41. Price, "Migration and Adaptation," pp. 174–75.
42. Westerman, "The Urban Indian," p. 260.
43. Price, "Migration and Adaptation," p. 172.
44. Walker, "Measures of Nez Perce Outbreeding," pp. 150–52.
45. Wax, *Indian Americans*, pp. 191–92.

CONCLUSION

What can one say in summary about the extent of assimilation, using that concept to include the four intergroup processes we have discussed, between Indians and whites in the United States today? Amalgamation and acculturation are increasing, as we read the evidence, with both Indians and non-Indians being affected. The "gene pool" of the Indian population is slowly acquiring a larger "European" inheritance; but at the same time, the European-descended population is absorbing an unmeasured amount of Indian inheritance. The latter process involves a small proportion of the non-Indians, but it is probably no smaller in absolute terms.

Many Indians are in increasing contact, via the mass media, in school, in jobs, in the army, with the culture of the larger society. With approximately half of the self-identified Indians now living in cities, not to mention those with some Indian background who no longer regard themselves as Indians, the generations-long process of acculturation continues. But this is still a two-way influence. Among other factors, the disenchantment among some white Americans with the dominant culture and many recent public policies has renewed the attraction of Indian cultures. The attraction is doubtless quite superficial in many cases and may often be based on a romanticized picture of Indian life; but there are also sincere and informed choices being made in favor of life styles strongly influenced by Indian cultures.

It seems to us that acculturation may mean the giving up of some elements of one culture, with replacements from another, or it can mean, as well, simply the addition of values and norms and styles, creating a more complex cultural repertoire for those involved. Considering the great mobility many people have today, and the variety of groups within which they interact, it seems reasonable to think of acculturation as addition, not substitution, in some circumstances. This may help to account for the continuing strength of ethnic identities in many parts of the world today, in the face of powerful acculturating forces. It may better describe the situation of some urban Indians and of white Americans who are attracted to many aspects of Indian culture.[46] If acculturation is seen, in part, as additive, we need to begin to explore many questions related to it: What conditions make it most, or least, likely to work in this way? What aspects of culture can be added, which ones almost certainly can only be substituted? What are the consequences for the individuals and groups involved of this form of culture change?

Although Indian-white relationships are probably characterized by continuing amalgamation and acculturation, the situation with regard to identification and structural integration is different. In this day of renewed attention to one's ethnicity, most Native Americans identify themselves more strongly as Indians rather than shifting their identification to the larger society. We shall not here examine the reasons for this surge of ethnicity, but will only note that political and economic factors, cultural forces, and individual needs all play a part.[47] There is a danger

46. Malcolm McFee, "The 150% Man, A Product of Blackfeet Acculturation," *American Anthropologist* 70 (December 1968), pp. 1096–1103.

47. J. Milton Yinger, "Ethnicity in Complex Societies," in *The Uses of Controversy*, eds. Lewis Coser and Otto Larson (New York: The Free Press, 1976), pp. 197–216.

that judgments are based on headlines, on the dramatic stories of Indian claims and reaffirmations, while the quieter process of identify shift goes unnoticed. Nevertheless, in our judgment that aspect of the assimilation process based on individual identification seems at this time in American history to indicate a lesser amount of assimilation.

There are counter currents affecting the process of structural integration of Indian Americans. In the last generation tens of thousands have entered the urban job market, as Alan L. Sorkin shows in his article in this volume, and an active movement for Indian rights has taken many into the political arena. (Several papers in this volume—see especially those by Raymond V. Butler, James E. Officer, Vine Deloria, Jr., and Nancy O. Lurie—document the defeats and victories for this movement: "the trail of broken treaties," but also the land restored, the fishing rights affirmed, the payments made to tribes for past losses.) These are indications of pluralism, of the integration of Indians, primarily on a group basis, into a multicultural society, with more nearly equal rights and opportunities.

Another trend, however, is more toward separation than pluralism. Some Indians now speak of "Indian countries," not reservations. In October 1976, the National Congress of American Indians resolved that "Indian Tribes possess all inherent powers of sovereignty and self-government".[48] We are not arguing for or against such a view (although we should note that this position tends to be matched with an anti-Indian organization, the "Interstate Congress for Equal Rights and Responsibilities"), but we call attention to the fact that structural integration of a society is different from treaties or accommodations between societies. In examining the situation of native Americans, it is important to try to understand the different consequences of these strategies.

If we assume a measure of free choice for individual Indians, no one policy or pattern is adequate in the United States today. Some Indians want to strengthen the tribal pattern (albeit with continual change often being recognized), whether pluralistically or in a more separatist sense. Some want to, or feel compelled to, live in cities, away from tribal communities, while still keeping their Indian identities. Some are more fully acculturated, perhaps married to non-Indians, and prefer a larger national identity.

A major scholarly task is to study the degree to which these several patterns are mutually compatible. A major policy task, if they are all seen as legitimate, is to design the ways by which the different goals can be attained, their contradictions recognized and accommodated, and the full rights of Indian Americans to select their preferred goals protected.

48. *International Herald Tribune*, 13 December 1976, p. 4.

ERRATA

In the January issue of the ANNALS, an error occurred in the article by Robert Parke and David Seidman entitled "Social Indicators and Social Reporting." The mistake occurs in the second paragraph of page 7. The entire paragraph is printed here in its correct form.

Given the view of the social indicators enterprise as the measurement of social conditions and social change, the major tasks can be seen as conceptual and methodological work toward the definition of measures of social conditions and social change; development of the data base; and the development of social indicator models. Social reporting is a fourth major task, implied not by the view of social indicators as the measurement of social change, but rather by the belief that one of the purposes of social indicators is to contribute to public enlightenment.

The ANNALS regrets that the paragraph did not appear in this form in the January issue.

Book Department

INTERNATIONAL RELATIONS AND POLITICS

EDMUND BEARD. *Developing the ICBM: A Study in Bureaucratic Politics.* Pp. viii, 273. New York: Columbia University Press, 1976. $15.00.

Professor Beard poses this question: Why was the United States so slow (compared with the U.S.S.R.) to develop an ICBM? This carefully researched and nicely written study finds that after 1945 the Air Force was driven by two potentially incompatible perceptions of its own and the nation's interests. One was that missiles would someday supplant bombers; thus the Air Force must control those missiles. The other was that bombers would be supreme for years ahead, that the central Air Force mission was flying bombers, and that this should guide defense spending. The first perception led the Air Force to fight vigorously to monopolize long-range missile development. But the second led it to develop such missiles in lackadaisical fashion. The Air Force reconciled its interests via hypothetical missiles for the distant future and its beloved bombers in the present.

Until 1954 little was done to develop an ICBM; then it received top priority. Why the change? Beard points to efforts of people outside the service, in particular to those of a special assistant to the Secretary of the Air Force. This individual, believing strongly in missiles, organized a blue ribbon civilian panel stacked with ICBM proponents. That panel, and a parallel RAND report, concluded that missiles needed much more emphasis—with a separate Air Force command to supervise the program. These findings, plus the special assistant's maneuvers, aroused congressional attention and the support of top Pentagon officials, leading to adoption of the recommendations. The leader of the new command displayed masterful bureaucratic skills in sustaining his program's independence, direct access to the Secretary of Defense, and priority claims on resources. From 1954 on, the ICBM program moved smartly ahead, though too late to avoid the shock of Sputnik. Thus the often-voiced charge that the Eisenhower Administration let missile programs lag out of budgetary considerations is unfair—the fault lay with earlier Air Force foot-dragging, which the Administration managed to circumvent.

Beard's subtitle, *A Study in Bureaucratic Politics*, is misleading, for the book contributes more than the author suggests. In a bureaucratic politics model, issues are decided by struggles among actors whose arguments reflect their organizational interests. While this applies to many participants in the ICBM decisions, the book indicates it does not explain the behavior of all those involved. Beard does not point out, though it is clear from his findings, that a bureaucratic politics approach is fruitful and that there is also more than bureaucratic politics behind government decisions.

PATRICK M. MORGAN
Washington State University
Pullman

DAVID MCCULLOUGH. *The Path Between the Seas: The Creation of the Panama Canal, 1870–1914.* Pp. 698. New York: Simon & Schuster, 1977. $14.95

WAYNE D. BRAY. *The Common Law Zone in Panama: A Case Study in Reception.* Pp. v, 150. San Juan, Puerto Rico: Inter-American University Press, 1977. $20.00.

The historical account of the creation of the transisthmian canal between the Caribbean and the Pacific by David McCullough covers the period of the French effort to the triumph of the United States in opening the Panama Canal to world commerce on the eve of World War I. The author is primarily interested in the human element in the story, and he has written it in accordance with the principle that history is biography. He has produced a living gallery of the men who made the Canal, from Ferdinand de Lesseps to Colonel George W. Goethals.

This eminently readable volume is written with a keen eye to the drama of the story, but never at the expense of scholarship. Though emphasizing personalities the author does not neglect the political, diplomatic, and social phases of the canal project. He is critical of the diplomacy of Secretary of State John Hay and President Theodore Roosevelt with Colombia in 1903, but he conclusively acquits them of any complicity in Panama's independence movement in that year, though he severely scores Roosevelt's later indiscreet and unwarranted explanations of the events of 1903. The author's carefully researched account of those events should go a long way toward correcting the error, shared by the news media and Washington policymakers, that the United States stole the Canal Zone and the Canal from Panama.

His account of the doleful experiences of the canal builders with the mammoth slides should administer a coup de grace to the chimerical project of a sea-level canal across the isthmus. His graphic description of the tremendous achievements of the chief engineer John Frank Stevens in rescuing the canal from chaos, organizing the transportation system to remove spoil from Culebra Cut, securing the "great decision" to build a high-level lake and lock canal, and ensuring the ultimate success of the Canal, makes Stevens a top candidate for election to the Hall of Fame of Great Americans.

Outstanding is the author's account of the triumph of Colonel William Crawford Gorgas, United States Army, in overcoming the dread diseases, cholera, malaria, and yellow fever in the building of the Canal, his unbiased discussion of race relations in the Zone, and his explanation in layman's language of the technical and mechanical problems of canal and lock construction.

This is a fascinating and timely account of the building of one of the world's greatest engineering marvels, which the Carter administration is now seeking to relinquish to Panama.

The McCullough story should have been must reading for Wayne Bray, author of the second book here under review, as a corrective to many of his unsubstantiated charges and false conclusions.

The immediate extension of the United States Bill of Rights to Panama by Executive Order of President Theodore Roosevelt on May 9, 1904, marked a first step in a gradual process of introducing the Anglo-American common law into the Canal Zone. Since the Hay-Bunau Varilla treaty made no specific provision for the exercise of the judicial power in the Zone, this process of gradual transfer of the common law to the Zone, including both common law procedures and equity, was corollary to the right of sovereign control which was granted to the United States in the treaty. This book gives a thorough and much needed descriptive history of the judicial system in the Canal Zone since 1904, including useful analyses of the laws and judicial decisions by which the common law was extended in the Canal Zone.

The volume is, however, basically a political tract, marred by the opinions of the author and expressions of his prejudices. His excursions into political propaganda in the first 50 pages and the last 10 set an emotional framework for the study which largely detracts from the solid scholarship of the intervening chapters. He dismisses the decision of the United States Supreme Court in *Wilson* v. *Shaw* in 1907 as human error and ignores the corollary sustaining opinions in *Luckenbach S.S. Co.* v. *U.S.* (1930) and *U.S.* v. *Husband* (R) (1972).

This book is not worth the price.

DONALD MARQUAND DOZER
University of California
Santa Barbara

ANTHONY SAMPSON. *The Arms Bazaar: From Lebanon to Lockheed.* Pp. 352. New York: Viking Press, 1977. $12.95.

An aphorism of that perspicacious political pundit, Pogo, would aptly convey Anthony Sampson's main message in *The Arms Bazaar*: "I have met the enemy and they is us!" Perhaps we had not quite thought that about the venal shenanigans of the armaments/aerospace industry. Sampson does recount the intricate web of influence buying and peddling; of outright bribery, outrageous commissions, illegal political "contributions" and subordination; of self-aggrandizement and power-tripping; of mendacity, duplicity, naiveté, intrigue, and subterfuge; of crassest lobbying and logrolling; of any number of other heinous activities, all perpetrated upon humanity in the name of "business as usual" by such grand purveyors of weaponry as Krupp, Vickers, Dassault, Northrop and, not to be overlooked, Lockheed. We vaguely remember, or Sampson causes us to recall, extortions by, or bribes of, highest elected officials and of royalty (and not only in those countries where it is "the custom"),

commissions of $106 million to one Saudi for a decade of "facilitating," payments of over $12 million, mostly bribes, in order to sell a few wide-bodied jets to a Japanese airline. We learn, too, of a puppeteer's ping-pong game, in which sophisticated weaponry is the ball and Israel and its Arab enemies the puppets, a game the more perilous after Nixon had sold to the Shah of Iran an arsenal as technologically up-to-date as our own, making Iran the first Third World country to be permitted to overcome the arms-technology gap. We are—according to our particular fancy—furious, appalled, aggrieved, apoplectic, or merely distressed by these recollections. We are also fascinated, but no longer surprised, so jaded have we become.

Still, a good storyteller could have done this for us. Sampson does much more. He demonstrates that these events are inexorable, that these "actors" are inevitable, given (1) that there is a profit-motivated armaments/aerospace business at all; (2) that it is a pawn of both political maneuvering and international diplomacy; and (3) that its economic "structure" is what it has become. True to a well-tested hypothesis, here as elsewhere structure dictates the parameters of behavior and these jointly determine results. Since it is "we"—or rather our elected representatives—who set, or tolerate, the structure, it is "we" who are perpetrating ominous conditions on ourselves.

There is not room to elaborate sufficiently, so let us focus on a few obvious structural characteristics of the armaments/aerospace business. Note that both production and marketing are subject to vast economies of scale and therefore that the case of actors, even on a global scale, is small, and that weapons standardization, not just within a nation but among allies, is urgent, both conferring paramountcy to a single big sale. Observe that governments, certainly for major weaponry, are monopsonistic conduits, if not salesmen outright, for virtually every transaction, spawning a military-political-industrial nexus of awesome scope and power. Recall that, with only one exception among major powers (Japan), a viable and technologically-advancing armaments/aerospace industry is deemed absolutely essential so that the industry and government are truly symbiotic. Among other things this gives rise, on the one hand, to various forms of government paternalism (sometimes allocating orders according to firm-by-firm survival rather than cost-effectiveness, sometimes arranging for production consortia or licensing agreements; financial "bailouts" when these schemes fail; pressures on other sovereign nations so that exports will augment flagging domestic sales) and, on the other, to firms that perennially overrun their own cost estimates and successfully insist on accommodation; that feel rapaciously victimized by their own and foreign governments and demand, and even get, redress; that are probably more cutthroat among themselves than firms in any other major industry; and that all-too-obviously cannot prosper in a truly free market which, perversely, they tout and glorify. When to this structure is added a consequent and all-pervasive secrecy it is easy to understand—but fatal to condone—the bizarre behavior and rationalizations that Northrop and Lockheed officers confessed to Senator Church's Subcommittee. And for those among us who might fear that "all will be forgiven and forgotten"—which does not seem unlikely—a perusal of Sampson's book will provide renewed energy, ammunition, and commitment.

M. O. CLEMENT

Dartmouth College
Hanover
New Hampshire

HERBERT Y. SCHANDLER. *The Unmaking of a President: Lyndon Johnson and Vietnam.* Pp. vii, 419. Princeton, N.J.: Princeton University Press, 1977. $16.50.

A doctoral dissertation provided the foundation for this book. In addition to printed sources, the young author held interviews, used oral historical collections and personal correspondence. His style is lucid, his narrative is easy to follow.

Our taking over for France in French Indo-China in 1954 was the second attempt to replace French failure with American success. The digging of the Panama Canal was the first. Our involvement in Vietnam, the author writes convincingly, was "a major decision made without much fanfare, deliberation or planning" (p. 20). As the world knows America's role in the war in Vietnam was a failure, if not a national disgrace. Quite a contrast to our success in digging the Panama Canal.

General William C. Westmoreland, supported by the General Staff and the Pentagon militants, repeatedly urged that more troops be sent to Vietnam and that they be allowed to do more fighting. The General was opposed by George Ball, Under Secretary of State, who was outvoted by the Secretary of State Dean Rusk and by President Lyndon Johnson.

After the Tet Offensive and over 500,000 American soldiers were unable to produce a victory, Clark Clifford, soon to become Secretary of Defense, persuaded President Johnson to reconsider the request of the military. After much debate and increasingly vocal public opposition, the President ordered a halt to the bombing of North Vietnam. Eventually negotiations began and Johnson announced his decision to retire to private life. According to this young scholar the chief impetus for changing America's course in South Vietnam came from Clark Clifford and not from L.B.J.

Dr. Schandler's conclusion that the Tet Offensive was the turning point in the war is not likely to be disputed. His careful analysis of the critical decisions that finally helped the United States extricate itself from the morass in Southeast Asia will be welcomed by students of the long traumatic involvement in Vietnam.

GEORGE C. OSBORN

Gainesville
Florida

JEREMY TUNSTALL. *The Media Are American: Anglo-American Media in the World.* Pp. 352. New York: Columbia University Press, 1977. $14.95.

The Media Are American is the latest addition to the Communication and Society series edited by Tunstall and initially published by Sage. The book focuses on the role of British and American technology and models of organization in the structuring of communication media around the world.

The organizing locus for this study is the so-called "media imperialism thesis." In its most benevolent interpretation, this holds that through skillful commercial exploitation, superior know how, good timing, and an easily adapted professional ideology (that of "value neutrality"), but not through any purposeful conspiracy, Americans have come, both directly and indirectly, to dominate the style, structure, technology, and content of domestic mass communication in a majority of countries. In its more malevolent interpretation, as, for example, that of Herbert Schiller in *Mass Communications and American Empire*, these same effects are seen as the result of systematic actions by the American military industrial complex directed toward the ultimate subjugation of the world. In the end, Tunstall accepts much of the evidence supporting one or another interpretation of the thesis, but rejects the argument itself. In his view, American media, or more correctly Anglo-American media, have indeed had a disproportionate impact on the patterns of information dissemination, and in turn on the cultures, of many nations, but that impact is increasingly likely to be mitigated by local counterforces.

The style of the book, like that of Tunstall's earlier contribution to this series, is ponderous, and the organization of material within the various chapters, though not the organization of the chapters themselves, detracts from the coherence of the argument. In addition, one wishes for more empirical substantiation of many of the points that are made.

Nevertheless, *The Media Are American* adds a significant new dimension to the study of American and world media history. Of particular value are the discussion of media development in the Third World (especially Africa) and the numerous tables summarizing media import patterns, market penetration, and program costs for various time periods and countries.

The Media Are American is a welcome addition to the growing literature on the international traffic in public information and entertainment. It is similar in style and provides a good complement to another recent contribution to that literature, Julian Hale's *Radio Power.*

JAROL B. MANHEIM
Virginia Polytechnic Institute
and State University
Blacksburg

DANIEL YERGIN. *Shattered Peace: The Origins of the Cold War and the National Security State.* Pp. x, 526. Boston: Houghton Mifflin, 1977. $15.00.

The origins of the cold war continue to be restudied as we seek answers to the big questions of our time: Who was responsible for starting that conflict? How was the "national security state" born in the United States? Was Soviet expansionism an imperative only to be countered by threat of force or were other interpretations plausible? In his detailed study of American policy making between 1945 and 1949 Daniel Yergin mercifully does not offer monochromatic answers to these questions. He does not advance any single cause theory. Instead, his focus is on the ideas and drives individual policymakers brought to international affairs and the decisions they made.

Yergin contrasts the two schools of thought interpreting the Soviet Union on what he calls the "Riga axioms" and the "Yalta axioms." The latter were favored by President Roosevelt but by few others. They included a wish to estimate Soviet power realistically, a willingness to negotiate, and an implied recognition of "spheres of influence." Most of the book narrates how the Riga axioms came to command a consensus, first among the policymaking elite, and then in American public opinion. These axioms flowed from a belief that Soviet policies were coherent and inflexible, dictated by a theology of world revolution and by innate aggressiveness. This simplistic outlook furthered the ambitions of some men and frustrated those of others. It also led to a virtual abandonment of diplomacy as a tool of foreign policy in favor of military confrontation.

Yergin recounts the interplay of personalities and the sequence of events in smooth prose. Among a host of characters he shows us President Truman demanding sharp distinctions between right and wrong in foreign affairs; George Kennan, ideologue in 1946 and diplomat later; Dean Acheson, "selling" evangelical anticommunism and urging expansion of a military industrial establishment. He sketches in the institutional spurs to founding a national security state by describing dogfights for higher budget allocations among the armed services, the drive for power in Navy Secretary James Forrestal, the complementary needs of the Air Force and the aviation industry, and the 1945 Eberstadt Report calling for a realignment of governmental organization to serve an expanded vision of national security.

Yergin, unfortunately, leaves unexplored two very relevant questions: To what extent were American policymakers guided by the domestic economic implications of their decisions? What were, in fact, Soviet intentions in those years? He occasionally hints at possible responses other than his own humane conclusion: "There are no final answers, only the spectacle of men and women moved by ambitions and opportunities, beset by fears and dangers, struggling to find transient certainties midst the onrush of events."

SURJIT MANSINGH
The University of Texas
San Antonio

AFRICA, ASIA, AND LATIN AMERICA

GODWIN C. CHU. *Radical Change Through Communication in Mao's China.* Pp. vi, 340. Honolulu: University Press of Hawaii, 1977. $14.00

BILL BRUGGER. *Contemporary China.* Pp. 451. New York: Barnes & Noble, 1977. $22.50.

Since 1949, the Chinese Communist leaders have transformed their war torn and poverty-stricken country rapidly into a powerful, self-disciplined and developing socialist country. The above two books deal with the developmental process of the Chinese society under Communist rule for the past three decades, but they analyze it from different theoretical angles.

Chu's book avoids the chronological treatment of China's development experience. Its main purpose is to demonstrate, by using both original and secondary sources, that communication (particularly when used in a group setting) is an effective instrument of social change through an examination of six factors specific to development and through showing how communication in Mao's China has been used as a basic social process. In so doing, Chu's primary theoretical interest lies in the functional consequences of the various communication processes, through mass media as well as other channels, to individual members, their groups, and social system in the process of societal change. The author contends that Mao Tse-tung and his colleagues have successfully employed communication on a massive scale as a powerful mechanism to shake off the Chinese people's bondage to old traditions and values and push them on the road to new collective effort and development. Chu concludes that the Chinese developmental case is unique because the drastic and swift societal change has been brought about not by a revolution of technology, nor by the brutal application of force in Stalinist fashion, but rather, primarily by the skillful use of communication.

Based on a mass of material drawn largely from secondary sources, Mr. Brugger's book is intended to be a textbook for undergraduate college students interested in contemporary Chinese politics or history. The book gives a chronological account of events in China from the 1940s, and sociological tools such as models and cycles are employed merely to provide a relatively simple framework for understanding the dynamics of socialist transition and development in China during the mid-twentieth century. The author treats Mao's Communist revolution as a process rather than an art, and the main theme of his book is related to the interaction and the battle ("contradiction" in Maoist lexicon) between "conservatives," "radicals," and "ultra-leftists." All three groups probably agreed to the ultimate goals of building socialism and communism in China, but they emphasized different means to achieve them. The author identifies nine cycles (up to August 1973) of alternating radicalism and consolidation and asserts that these divergencies of political line have profoundly affected a cyclic or spiral pattern of China's revolutionary development.

Any definite consensus as to the best methodology for the study of contemporary China is virtually unknown among Western scholars of Chinese affairs. In this reviewer's opinion, our scholarly efforts on modern China, particularly on its Communist period, must of necessity be multidisciplinary in scope and nature, drawing on theoretical concepts and empirical findings primarily from the social science fields. For this reason, the publication of the above two books in 1977 (the immediate post-Mao era) is a welcome and timely event for our academic world. Chu and Brugger are to be commended for having produced the informative, useful, objective, and well-researched scholarly pieces. Their books deserve careful reading by all those interested in contemporary China, although readers may not accept all of their interpretations and judgments.

The two books are equally good in overall scholarly value, but Chu's work is better in terms of readability. Because of his writing style, readers may find Brugger's book not exactly exciting reading.

TAI SUNG AN
Washington College
Chestertown
Maryland

FREDERICK COOPER. *Plantation Slavery on the East Coast of Africa.* Pp. vii, 314. New Haven, Conn.: Yale University Press, 1977. $18.50.

Rising interest both in the institution of slavery and African history may, in some measure, be stated by this elaborated Ph.D. thesis. The reader, however, need hardly follow the path of this reviewer by reading its chapters in sequence for the conclusions adequately summarize its theme. Much of this diligently researched work consists of footnotes, and unfortunately, much of the text ought to be consigned to them.

Limiting himself to the islands of Zanzibar and Pemba (the world's great clove producing centers and which had most of the slaves) and the coastal cities of Mombasa and Malindi, Cooper traces the rapid growth of slavery in the territories of the Omani Arabs during the nineteenth century until it was outlawed in 1897. Throughout, he makes copious reference to slavery in the Americas.

In his view, East African slavery (as distinct from capture and transportation to the coast—and which he does not discuss) differed from that in the Americas in being less harsh. This was due to a combination of factors. The Omani need for dependents to augment their communal power required that they bring slaves into a more acquiescent, patriarchal arrangement. They knew, too, that there was an absence of any powerful political authority to enforce a rigid, tyrannical structure. East Coast Africans could escape more easily then American slaves. Although some did escape, most did not try. Cooper continually says that in an insecure world, slaves, themselves, felt the desireability of "protection" in a communal group. They were also placated in part by being permitted to own their plots of land and by being given a large measure of social independence. Furthermore, manumission was more frequent. Slaves worked intensively during the clove-picking season, but even including the grain field work at Malindi, he repeats that pressure on slaves was not as great as in the New World. Nor was racialism as extreme on the Coast. Offspring of concubines became free. In fact, "Arab and Swahili slave-owners were willing to arm their slaves. Individuals and communal groups relied on the support of slaves for political and military strength" (p. 255).

Lest one think that East Coast slaves rejoiced in these conditions, he describes the variety of ways that Africans used to beat the system, from occasional rebellion, escape, selling covertly to Indian middlemen and, in an ideological irony, to using Islam to judge the slaveowners' greed and "to assert their own moral equality" (p. 257).

Within its confines, Cooper has amassed a great deal of data and statistics (sometimes minutia), making this a useful reference work.

WALLACE SOKOLSKY
Bronx Community College
New York

ALEXANDER ECKSTEIN. *China's Economic Revolution.* Pp. xii, 340. New York: Cambridge University Press, 1977. $19.95. Paperbound, $6.95.

In this book the late Alexander Eckstein, one of the foremost authorities on the modern Chinese economy, presents a comprehensive analysis of economic development in the People's Republic. *China's Economic Revolution* concerns itself with broad issues of significance concerning one of the greatest institutional and technological metamorphoses of our time. Eckstein discusses the conception and implementation of economic policy, changing patterns of property relations and economic organization, the allocation of resources under socialist planning, and the degree to which China has successfully reconciled economic stability and growth. These topics are sandwiched between a concise overview of the pre-1949 economy and concluding chapters, which survey Sino foreign trade and assess China's relevance as a model for other developing nations.

Eckstein's conclusions will startle few scholars, but rarely have the problems and achievements of the present regime been set forth with such clarity and objectivity. China's economic heritage conveyed a burden of underdevelopment yet provided the nucleus of physical and human resources for rapid growth. Socialist transformation of that economy entailed persistent conflicts between ends and means, resulting in a succession of grand strategies which alternately accepted, rejected, and finally acculturated the Soviet model of development.

These strategic shifts were mirrored in varying forms of economic organization and resource apportionment. Chinese economic institutions crystallized along Soviet lines between 1955 and 1958, but their operation was infused with a profound consciousness that policy alternatives bore divergent social and ideological consequences. China's leadership assigned changing priorities to material production and socialist values, and oscillated between an emphasis upon centralized control and concern with operational efficiency. Planning in an economy still vulnerable to the ancient harvest cycle was necessarily confined to annual rather than five year periods. Inflation, the bane of Kuomintang authorities in the 1940s, was checked by state regulation of wages, a hyperabundant but controlled labor market, and official denigration of "consumerism." China sustained very high rates of fixed capital investment, greatly enhanced the quality of its labor force, and maintained an economic growth rate impressive in both historical and contemporary contexts. Although marginal to the economy as a whole, foreign trade played, and continues to play, a key role in economic stabilization and providing access to advanced technology.

Eckstein sees China's economic revolution as essentially a sui generis phenomenon, requiring a mix of social controls, ideological motivation, and resource endowments, which has limited applicability to other underdeveloped societies. It is also very much a revolution in process rather than an accomplished fact. As Mao himself acknowledged, tension between the ideal of self-reliance and the need to import foreign techniques, clashes between egalitarianism and material inducements to spur production, and the contradiction between a mass-based and an elitist concept of socialist development remain to be resolved by future generations. Yet it is in the very posing of such apparent dilemmas, as much as in the fulfillment of more concrete goals, that China's economic revolution compels our attention and deserves our continual scrutiny.

ROBERT P. GARDELLA
United States Merchant
Marine Academy
Kings Point
New York

NANCY J. HAFKIN and EDNA G. BAY. *Women in Africa: Studies in Social and Economic Change.* Pp. x, 306. Stanford, Calif.: Stanford University Press, 1976. $15.00.

These dozen essays discuss, on the basis of recent fieldwork, aspects of African women's life besides their domestic activities. This has not been a totally neglected subject. We have heard of women traders in West Africa, of the traditional Igbo women's councils, and of spirit mediumship as a "career" for women. But each of these topics is considered in the light of recent social changes. Margaret Jean Hay's study of Luo women farmers introduces a new subject. She shows that they have been much more open to innovation than is commonly supposed; some effort is currently being made in Britain to urge that agricultural instruction be directed to women rather than their husbands. Margaret Strobel's account of the dance societies created by Arab women in Mombasa and their development into political pressure groups is a new approach. So is Filomina Steady's essay on the church organizations of Creole women in Freetown, essentially conservative bodies strongly insistent on monogamous, indissoluble marriage, to which they look for economic security. Steady by implication, and Strobel explicitly, deplore the fact that these organizations are of but not for women. The Muslim Women's Institute of Mombasa raises funds for a nursery school (children not women) and for scholarships (boys as well as girls). This is not what they ought to be doing. Surely a very maternalist attitude.

Some of the contributors show a lack of proportion and of factual accuracy. "Colonialism" is reproached for employing only men in the industrial centers, but nothing is said about the nature of the work offered or the living conditions. These may be matters for reproach too, but in a different context. Some thought might be given to contemporary systems of migrant labor from one independent country to another. It is curiously naive to treat as peculiarly Victorian the assumption that only men should hold political authority. It is not true that chiefs in the Gold Coast or anywhere else were appointed solely in order to make formal alienations of land, not that District Commissioners in Kenya decided what the limits of African land should be. Nor are we anywhere told what is actually meant by the statement that traditionally African land was communally owned. "Ordered anarchy" is a phrase used not by the British, but by Evans-Pritchard, and not describing the Igbo, but the Nuer, a people who have much less in the way of formal institutions.

LUCY MAIR
London
England

NEVILLE J. MANDEL. *The Arabs and Zionism Before World War I.* Pp. 282.

Berkeley: University of California Press, 1977. $15.00.

The notion that Arab hostility to Zionism and to a Jewish state in the Middle East dates from either the Balfour Declaration in 1917 or from the ascent to power of the Grand Mufti in Jerusalem in the 1930s is clearly a mistaken one. In a meticulously researched monograph on *The Arabs and Zionism Before World War I*, Neville J. Mandel demonstrates quite convincingly that the Arabs in the Ottoman Empire—both those in the Vilayet of Beirut (what is now northern Israel) and those in the Mutasarriflik of Jerusalem—were quite aware of the coming of the Zionists from Europe, and for the most part feared and opposed this renaissance of Jewish nationalism on the site of the ancient Jewish states of Judea and Israel. Mandel's delineation of the relations between the emigrating Zionists and native-born Arabs on the soil of Palestine foreshadows much of the polemics, the economic and political tension, and the international rivalry between Israel and the Arab states since the establishment of Israel in 1948.

In the prewar years, the Ottoman Empire provided the forum for the legitimation of Zionist aspirations, the creation of a Jewish state, and the battleground between the two sides that, after 1945, was to be provided by the United Nations. Other parallels between pre-1914 conditions and those of the post-World War periods abound: the appointment of commissions to investigate the Arab-Zionist dispute and to establish policies for a peaceful resolution of the conflicts; the sense of solidarity between the Palestinian Arabs and those living in Egypt and in the northern areas of the empire (later to become the states of Lebanon and Syria); the Zionist issue as a part of world politics; Arab terrorism and the efforts of the Zionists to overlook the hostility of the local Arab population or to forge ahead in rebuilding the land despite this opposition. Mandel's review of the Arab-Zionist relations in the opening decades of this century leaves little room for optimism

that an easy or durable solution to the Arab-Israeli conflict can be found in the closing decades of the century.

The Ottoman Empire of the 1890s, the decade in which Theodor Herzl gave organization and a voice to the Zionist impulse, was approaching its demise; on one hand, the Ottoman government did not have the strength (or the competence and honesty of administration) to bar Zionists from entry into Palestine; on the other, the Turks were in no position to ignore the protests of their Arab constituency. The result was several decades of vacillation on the part of the Turkish government (much like the British between the two World Wars), on one hand, trying to play off one against the other—with some success—and trying, on the other, to pacify both the Zionists and the Arabs—with little success. The coming of the Young Turks to power in 1908 did little to resolve the issue: the Zionists were not ideologically equipped to become obedient and loyal citizens of the Turkish government nor were they able or interested in halting their purchase of land; the Arabs—whether rural fellahin, Jerusalem patricians, or Christian Arabs—were not about to welcome the Zionist settlers; and the Turks were in no position to mediate or to dictate a resolution of the growing tension.

The mistrust between the Arabs and the Zionists stemmed from three sources: the economic fears of the local Arab population, the religious unity of Islam, and the political nationalism that was beginning to crystallize among Arabs outside of Palestine. Two major efforts to resolve these growing tensions were initiated and both failed. In March and May of 1911, lengthy discussions in the Ottoman Parliament on the Zionist issue failed to resolve the issues; and in 1913 and 1914 a proposed entente between the Arabs and the Zionists proved equally fruitless. By the outbreak of World War I, as Mandel notes, Zionists and Arabs in Palestine were on a collision course. In words that foreshadow the current conflict in the Middle East, Khalil al-Sakakini, a Greek-Orthodox

Christian radical living in Jerusalem added the territorial—and final—element to the economic, religious, and political arguments against the Zionists:

[The Jewish people's] conquest of Palestine is as if it had conquered the heart of the Arab nation, because Palestine is the connecting link which binds the Arabian Peninsula with Egypt and Africa. If the Jews conquer [Palestine], they will prevent the linking of the Arab nation; indeed, they will split it into two unconnected parts. This will weaken the cause of Arabism . . . and will prevent solidarity and unity as a nation.

Reviewing the historical rights of the Arabs and the Jews to the land, he concluded: "[The Jews'] right had died with the passage of time; our right is alive and unshakeable." This position, which over the decades to come developed as the normative one among the Arab nations of the Middle East and a cardinal precept of the Palestine Liberation Organization, could no more be accepted by pre-World War I Zionists than it could find acceptance by the leaders of Israel today.

Mandel's monograph is the product of a prodigious amount of research, well crafted, if occasionally turgid. The findings, 22 "conclusions" Mandel incorporated into a final chapter of his volume, provide the reader with both a summary of the volume as well as a demonstration of the text's stylistic weakness. While this reviewer might have sought a tighter and more interpretative narrative, no criticism can be levelled at the sources, both primary and secondary, employed by the author. Mandel has culled diplomatic material in Vienna, Paris, Berlin, London, Istanbul, and Washington, D.C., Jewish and Zionist material in many of these cities, as well as in Haifa and in Jerusalem, along with hundreds of periodicals and works in Hebrew and Arabic. Mandel's volume will certainly stand as the standard treatment of this theme for all scholars of the Middle East for the foreseeable future.

JULIUS WEINBERG
The Cleveland State University
Ohio

ADRIANO MOREIRA. *O Drama de Timor (The Drama of Portuguese Timor)*. Pp. 142. Braga, Portugal: Editorial Intervenção Lda., 1977. 80 escudos.

Between 1702 and 1976 Portugal officially ruled 7,400 square miles of the East Indian island of Timor. Though this overseas province was completely surrounded by the Indonesian archipelago, Lisbon—halfway around the world—was responsible for its 670,000 residents. As a result of other government priorities, Timor was in every way underdeveloped. At the end of 1974 the per capita G.N.P. was only $40.00. Barely 10 percent of the population was literate, and there were less than a dozen Timorese university graduates.

Until recently the great bulk of Timor's population appeared apolitical if not favorable toward Portugal's negligent rule. Indonesia disavowed any claim to the territory and early this decade refused to support Fretilin, a clandestine group advocating independence. Such was the situation when the April 25, 1974 revolution in distant Portugal resulted in a public promise by the new regime that "Timor will be whatever the majority of its people want it to be."

The subsequent tragic drama for the politically unsophisticated Timorese involved: complex maneuvering by three local political parties, each with completely different goals; abrupt changes in Portugal's attitude toward independence reflecting Lisbon's changing governmental ideologies; concern of Indonesia and Australia over a possible pro-Soviet "Cuba" base in an independent Timor; the critical policy shift toward annexation by Indonesia, resulting in outright occupation and "integration" of eastern Timor in 1976; a consequent civil war involving ideological countercharges, invading "volunteer" armies, and atrocity claims—with at least 60,000 Timorese dead or fled; and ultimately demonstrated frustration and impotence by the United Nations.

The sole problem posed by this fascinating book is publication in Portuguese. Few observers appear better qualified than its author to report and comment upon events in this little-known political unit. Dr. Adriano Moreira was Minister for Overseas Provinces (1961–63)—the only political post of his career—and it is commonly believed that his dismissal resulted from his advocating too advanced a relationship between metropolitan and overseas Portugal. Subsequently he has served in many prominent positions with univeristy and semiacademic organizations related to Portuguese culture and overseas administration.

The author's stated purpose with this publication is to inform the Portuguese public of post-1974 developments in their most remote overseas province. Direct communications from Dili gradually ceased; and due to the political slant of the Lisbon news media, even official reports from the United Nations were largely ignored. *The Drama of Timor*, therefore, includes the full report of the U.N. Political Affairs and Decolonization Department concerning Timor; Dr. Moreira's comments upon various references in that publication; and a concise conclusion analyzing the report and its consequences.

RICHARD J. HOUK
DePaul University
Chicago
Illinois

WALDEMAR R. SMITH. *The Fiesta System and Economic Change.* Pp. viii, 194. New York: Columbia University Press, 1977. $15.00.

The traditional fiesta system of Mesoamerica is one in which an individual household assumes responsibility for organizing and paying for one of the several folk-Catholic religious celebrations which take place in a village each year. What has struck most students of the area is the large expenditure required of the sponsoring household. Smith attempts to refute what he sees as the functionalist interpretation of the fiesta system and the willingness of people to assume the financial burden involved. This view, according to Smith, stresses religious generosity as a cause of

Indian social and economic stability and as a consequence of being Indian. Instead, Smith argues that the "generosity" involved in the fiesta system is, itself, a consequence of economic and social stability and that support of the fiesta system is a reasonably chosen pattern of behavior, given the social and economic isolation of many villages.

Support for his argument is based on his fieldwork in an isolated and highly traditional Indian village, in a modernizing Indian town in the same region of Guatemala, and in two other communities which are more prosperous than the remote village but still ceremonially conservative. The remote village is one in which population has grown rapidly and the available land farmed in the traditional way is no longer adequate to provide sustenance for most households. Most of the residents have been forced to become seasonal laborers on lowland plantations. The number of fiestas per year has been reduced, the fiestas have become simpler, and attempts have been made to distribute the costs of each fiesta among a larger number of people.

In the bustling Indian town of San Pedro, Smith also finds fundamental changes in the fiesta system resulting, he argues, in large part from increased spending opportunities for individuals. In the two "intermediate towns" pressure on land is not intense, there are few new economic opportunities, and the fiesta system is relatively stable. This evidence allows Smith to conclude that economic change and the degree and manner of economic integration in the national economy are primary determinants of stability (and change) in the fiesta system.

Smith's comparative study of the four localities is well done and his argument that economic change causes changes in the fiesta system is persuasive. His interpretation of the mainstream functionalist approach and his insistence upon the novelty of his own approach are less persuasive.

ANNE MAYHEW
University of Tennessee
Knoxville

M. N. SRINIVAS. *The Remembered Village*. Pp. xvi, 374. Berkeley: University of California Press, 1976. $9.50.

This work is a remarkable personal achievement and an important event in the study of rural India. M.N. Srinivas's writing on caste, social change, and rural life in Southern India has long since established him as an outstanding scholar of contemporary Indian society. Here he presents a document at once uniquely human in its warmth and searching personal honesty and especially valuable in the fresh detail and insights it offers on village life. Its tone and value are the products of an extraordinary feat: the overcoming of the loss of the author's field notes at the hands of arsonists in 1970.

The Remembered Village is an account of field work in village Rampura of Mandya district of southern Karnataka state. The recalled material is mostly drawn from Srinivas's residence there in 1948, supplemented by subsequent visits and contact with his informant/friends. It is the necessity of having to re-create the experience of the field work in order to re-establish the writer's findings which gives the account its distinctive quality. Accordingly there is great emphasis placed upon interpersonal relationships and much probing of their subjective as well as their behavioral dimensions. Among its highpoints are portraits of the village headman, of a powerful faction leader who is simultaneously the headman's friend and rival, and of the wiley clerk who served as Srinivas's assistant. The most significant anthropological contributions come in discussions of social relations and in specific analyses of household life, relations between men and women and between castes. Also included is a sharply drawn account of how the agricultural cycle is woven into the life of the community.

Srinivas's treatment of his own role is what makes this study unique. If anything, he pays more attention to his doubts, fears, mistakes, experiences, and subjective reactions as a sociocultural outsider than he does to his analytical accomplishments. What emerges, therefore, is a highly instructive description of the demands of anthropological field work.

The achievements of the book do not obscure the limitations inevitable in the circumstances of its composition. The discussion of Rampura as a social organism is incomplete and uneven. Its weaker families and jatis are admittedly given little attention. The chapters on post-1948 change and (surprisingly) on factions tend to ramble anecdotally. And, as must be expected, the economic data presented are impressionistically descriptive and are much less valuable than the insights into social relations.

Yet, these limitations must be put into perspective. This book will become a guide and an inspiration to students of Indian society and to anyone preparing to investigate small, rural communities anywhere.

RICHARD S. NEWELL
University of Northern Iowa
Cedar Falls

EUROPE

MICHAEL J. DEANE. *Political Control of the Soviet Armed Forces*. Pp. 300. New York: Crane, Russak & Co., 1977. $17.50.

In May 1976 Brezhnev promoted himself to the highest military rank of Marshal of the Soviet Union; and two months later he offered the same rank to his new Defense Minister, professional defense industrialist, rather than professional soldier, Ustinov. Are these two moves signs of the reassertion of civilian Party controls over the professional military? Or are they, on the contrary, symptoms of the growing militarization of Soviet society, including the militarization of high Party officials, which has been expressed in their ever more formidable defense appropriations, their renewed predilection for heavy industry and harsh suppression of political dissenters? In his book Dr. Deane plausibly argues for the former proposition, revealing some friction between the late Marshal Grechko—a truly professional soldier—and Brezhnev on the eve of the last Party Congress in February–March 1976. In such political insights lies the strength of the book: the reviewer learned a lot about the political ties of the somewhat shadowy head of the Main Political Administration Yepishev. The book is certainly up to date.

But on the whole, the work is somewhat uneven. It promises to elucidate "the evolving character of political control, evaluate the changing relationship among the MPA, the Party, and the professional military, . . . and assess the future significance of political control in Soviet party-military affairs" (p. viii). Those themes are indeed touched upon in the book, but nowhere are they fully developed. The author does not give a graphic overall picture of the apparatus of the Main Political Administration, except possibly in the highly condensed Appendix B (pp. 281–83). The book ends abruptly, with the specific events of 1976, rather than with a general conclusion. The author is familiar with the work of Roman Kolkowicz, but does not consider the important, though admittedly article-length, challenge to Kolkowicz by William E. Odom in *Problems of Communism*, September–October 1973. Regrettably, Deane's book lacks a bibliography.

To sum up, the work contains some factual and theoretical gems, but they have not been properly set into a single piece of jewelry. It is a promising first effort rather than a well-rounded book.

YAROSLAV BILINSKY
University of Delaware
Newark

JOHN REDWOOD. *European Science in the Seventeenth Century.* Pp. 208. New York: Barnes & Noble, 1977. $13.50.

From the title of this book one might expect a discussion of the scientific revolution of the seventeenth century, one of the principal intellectual and social phenomena of the modern world.

Rather, this is basically an anthology of extracts from writers of the period, including Galileo, Descartes, and Gassendi, but devoted mainly to English authors. The selections, seldom more than five pages in length, are arranged in four categories: Methods, Achievements, Institutions, and Persons. Brief introductory sections and some biographical sketches are supplied by the author.

In recent years several anthologies of writings bearing on the scientific revolution have appeared, representing a variety of purposes and differing widely in emphasis. The present collection will appeal more to nontechnical readers, who seek a broad sampling, than to students of the history of science. Inclusion of a selection from Kenelme Digby among the medical writings, for example, manifests the author's wish to have the word "science" broadly construed, while his selection of De Chales to represent Euclid in the late seventeenth century is very curious, when Isaac Barrow would seem far more appropriate from the scientific standpoint, particularly in England and as the teacher of Sir Isaac Newton. Galileo's *Il Saggiatore* (*The Assayer*) of 1623 is confused with his very different *Starry Messenger* of 1610 (p. 22), and the assertion that Blaise Pascal himself conducted the Puy de Dome barometric experiment (p. 71) is as mistaken as the accompanying remark that the mercury was found to rise during the ascent. Mr. Redwood's opinion that Galileo's father was neoplatonic in outlook (p. 72) would be very hard to support, since he vigorously opposed musical theory based on harmonic ratios; the same bias is found on p. 171, where the Cimento Academy is characterized as neoplatonic though it published only experimental researches illustrated by the extracts which follow.

From the standpoint of sociology of early science the selections and commentaries are more successful. Extracts from Francis Bacon, Thomas Hobbes, Jonathan Swift, and Thomas Birch are included to represent some philosophical, literary, and historical phases of the impact of early modern science in other cultural fields, while John Ward and John Aubrey are allowed to speak as contemporary biographers of scientists.

A two-page selected bibliography of principal English-language books on the history and philosophy of science published during the past half-century, with running commentary, completes the volume. It is accurately and attractively printed, though the paper used is not of the best.

STILLMAN DRAKE
University of Toronto
Canada

CEILIA S. HELLER. *On the Edge of Destruction: Jews of Poland Between the Two World Wars.* Pp. xi, 369. New York: Columbia University Press, 1977. $14.95.

They were a large and productive community, the Jews of interwar Poland, and their contribution to the culture and economy of that troubled state was a major one. They were a minority, but they had company: nearly a third of the population was non-Polish. There were Germans and Lithuanians who were identified with hostile neighbor states; there were White Russians and Ukrainians who had been beasts of burden for the Polish *pans*; and there were Jews.

Relying upon a variety of published sources and upon epitaphic literature from YIVO Institute archives, Professor Heller has sought to give a glimpse of the thriving, but mortally threatened, society into which, she notes, she was born. The world needs accounts like this, for the old *shtetl* is no more, Yiddish is a dying language, and the victims of the Holocaust will cry throughout time for mankind to ponder their supreme agony. This book will help; but the pity is that it could have done so much more.

There were probably more decent Poles than the author is willing to admit. After all, even Himmler complained that every German had his own good Jew, and that, of course, added up to a lot of Germans and Jews. Poland was not much different. There was unquestionably a great deal of anti-Semitism, unofficial and official; a major party, the

National Democrats, sought that "Hitler class" and won it over easily. But Professor Heller goes a bit far in chiding Pilsudski for not being Masaryk, and few Slovaks—not to mention Sudeten Germans even before 1933—would have agreed with her that Czechoslovakia (which she holds up as a model for Poland) "fully implemented" the 1919 Minorities Treaty. Further, Professor Heller holds the "assimilationists" (called "Poles of Mosaic faith" or "Poles of Jewish descent") in the greatest disregard, and she rejects the mere possibility that even Poles wholly untainted by anti-Semitism might honestly have seen a threat to the Polish state in Zionism. Some reflection upon the Vilnius and Danzig problems might have produced a more balanced assessment.

WOODFORD McCLELLAN
University of Virginia
Charlottesville

HERBERT R. SOUTHWORTH. *Guernica! Guernica! A Study of Journalism, Diplomacy, Propaganda, and History.* Pp. 563. Berkeley: University of California Press, 1977. $19.95.

The subtitle of this book accurately reflects its contents. Mr. Southworth, an historian, journalist, and broadcaster, began this study by asking "How was Guernica destroyed? By whom? Why?" The resulting book, however, tells us little new about the aerial bombing of the Basque town of Guernica on April 26, 1937. Instead, the book is about the powerful role of journalism and propaganda in a world dependent upon the media for its knowledge of "events."

Southworth begins with a painstaking account of the reporting of the event itself. On April 27, 1937, the British public learned that an open town had been attacked by German planes, which had dropped incendiary bombs and strafed the civilian population for more than three hours. That night, in response to world outrage over the bombing, Spanish Nationalist headquarters in Salamanca and Seville indignantly denied that any attack had occurred and falsely attributed the devastation of the town to fleeing Basque arsonists. The initial British press reports and the Nationalists' public disavowals provided material for the controversy that followed.

The purpose of the present book is twofold: (1) to establish Nationalist responsibility for the destruction of Guernica and (2) to expose the faulty logic —if not the deliberate prevarication —of those who have defended the Nationalists' innocence. Because documentary evidence, directly implicating Nationalist headquarters in the attack is not available, the second purpose is more fully achieved than the first. Southworth examines every important contribution to the Nationalist myth of Guernica published during the last 40 years, although he focuses on the Civil War and the late 1960s, when "Neo-Franquista" historians refurbished the myth in response to the revival of Basque nationalism. Of particular interest are the sections in which Southworth links the development of the Nationalist myth to the working conditions of wartime journalists, the hypocrisy of the Non-Intervention Committee, and the ambiguous role of the French news agency, Havas, in reporting news from Spain.

The book enlarges our understanding of the value—or the perceived value—of propaganda in the twentieth century. Southworth argues that the Franco regime could not admit to the bombing of Guernica—either then or later—because of its negative impact on public opinion, especially among liberal Catholics in England and France. Southworth does not develop his analysis fully because his loyalty to the Republicans makes him unwilling to label their exploitation of the Guernica episode as "propaganda" also. A true story, however, often makes better propaganda than a false one. It was precisely the continued Republican success of using Guernica as a symbol that forced the Nationalists to respond with the "lies and propaganda" that Southworth dissects with such expertise in this book.

The book is flawed by its polemical tone. During his long quest for reliable data, Southworth became a participant in the controversy that is the subject of his book. Some of the personal invective that has characterized that debate has been incorporated into the present study, where it diminishes the impact of the documentary evidence and textual criticism that alone would have supported his case.

CAROLYN P. BOYD
University of Texas
Austin

PETER VANNEMAN. *The Supreme Soviet: Politics and the Legislative Process in the Soviet Political System.* Pp. vii, 256. Durham, N.C.: Duke University Press, 1977. $11.75.

RONALD J. HILL. *Soviet Political Elites: The Case of Tiraspol.* Pp. vii, 226. New York: St. Martin's Press, 1977. $16.95.

Peter Vanneman's study is a very thorough analysis of the USSR Supreme Soviet, the most complete treatment of the subject since Peter Juviler's doctoral dissertation on the Soviet deputy nearly twenty years ago. Vannneman examines all aspects of the Supreme Soviet, with individual and very informative chapters on that body's commissions and its Presidium. As far as factual presentation goes, the description and analysis appear to be quite accurate, although, as will be indicated below, a number of his assertions were out of date long before the book was published.

The main difficulty with the book, in this reviewer's opinion, is not the description of the structure and operation of the Supreme Soviet, but with the author's exaggerated assertions concerning the importance of that body in the Soviet scheme of things. While criticizing several authors who find little or no significance in the institution at all, Vanneman moves too far in the other direction, stating that during "the past fifteen years the Supreme Soviet has been gradually but systematically moved closer to the center of political conflict and resolution as the tension between 'legality' and 'legitimacy' increasingly represents competing political forces" (p. 4). Statements of this kind are particularly prevalent at the beginning of the book. In this

reviewer's opinion, a study of the Supreme Soviet does not have to be justified
on the questionable grounds that the
institution has become considerably
more significant in recent years. Whether
a whole book ought to be devoted to such
a study is a question people may disagree
about.

The best chapter in the book is
probably chapter 7, where the author
elaborates on what he sees as the two
major functions of the Supreme Soviet, as
"an organ of legitimation" and as "an
organ of efficiency" seeking to grease the
wheels of government." Also useful are
chapter 9 on the Communist Party in the
Supreme Soviet and the portion of the
final chapter on the differences between
the East European legislatures and the
Supreme Soviet.

The references to constitutional provisions apply to the now-superseded 1936
Constitution, and the author cannot be
faulted on this. But in several other
respects this 1977 publication is considerably behind the times: Chkikvadze
(sic) is identified as Director of the
Institute of Law and Government (read:
"Institute of State and Law"), a position
he left in the early 1970s; Gorkin,
identified as Chairman of the USSR
Supreme Court, retired in 1972; the
Juridical Commission of the USSR
Council of Ministers was replaced by the
Ministry of Justice in 1970; some of the
data, on the size of the Supreme Soviet
commissions, for example, fail to take
into account the changes made immediately after the 1974 elections. Finally, on an unrelated matter, why
should one write about the power "to
enact zakons?" Statutes would be a
perfectly good English word to use.

In conclusion, although this thorough
study constitutes more than most people
would want to know about the Supreme
Soviet, the reviewer had no problem in
this respect. He had more difficulty with
the inflation and misrepresentation of
the rather modest significance of the
Supreme Soviet in the Soviet political
system.

Ronald J. Hill's engagingly written
study of the city of Tiraspol in Moldavia
also seems excessively concerned with

explaining to the reader why such an
analysis is justified. Mr. Hill has no
reason for such concern. His book adds
greatly to our understanding of local
Party and soviet operations.

Hill lived in Tiraspol as an exchange
scholar and had an opportunity to interview local political leaders. But he found
these contacts of little usefulness and
based most of his study on an analysis of
local newspapers for the period 1950–
67. Although he was largely limited to
this source, he maximized its usefulness
and was able to extract a good deal of
interesting longitudinal information
from it such as the growth in the size of
the city soviet and the city Party committee over time and the changes in the
departmental structure of the city soviet
executive committee and the gorkom.

The results of the author's efforts were
obviously based on a painstaking and
time-consuming collection of data. In his
conclusion he acknowledges that little
that is new has come to light. Even this
would be significant and worth the effort,
since it would confirm once more the
tentative conclusions of other scholars.
But there are some small surprises in
Hill's analysis and these nuggets make
the study all the more worth while. He
found, for instance, that the Tiraspol city
soviet has always been made up of a
strong majority of Party members, which
is atypical for both the USSR generally
and for the rest of Moldavia. Likewise,
the Tiraspol soviet has been on the low
side in the proportion of women among
its members when compared both with
Moldavia and the USSR as a whole. Mr.
Hill offers plausible explanations for
these exceptions, and if they are not
completely persuasive, at least he has
done all he could to find reasonable
explanations, including making good use
of available population data.

His analysis of membership turnover
in the city soviet and Party gorkom are
equally interesting. It is a pity, however,
that the study did not go beyond the
mid-1960s, since it would have been
interesting to see whether the rate of
turnover changed in the wake of
Khrushchev's demise and the abandonment of his policy of renewal.

This short review cannot do justice to the completeness of Mr. Hill's analysis. His book amounts to a judicious counterpoint of data against theory, and is a welcome addition to the small number of studies of Soviet local politics.

DONALD D. BARRY
Lehigh University
Bethlehem
Pennsylvania

UNITED STATES HISTORY AND POLITICS

VICTOR BASIUK. *Technology, World Politics and American Policy*. Pp. viii, 409. New York: Columbia University Press, 1977. $17.50.

Rather than producing another "Blue Sky" thesis filled with the world is going to blazes homilies, Victor Basiuk, an operational academician, has written a tempting treatise that is going to create constructive comments among the constituent groups who will read this book. It poses the right questions and provides some new answers with considerable merit. Analyzing the future impact of technology on international relations and societies by focusing on the developed societies, Basiuk works out a response this impact may have for U.S. domestic and foreign policy.

Beginning with now, the time frame is extended 75 years by organizing the book across time dimensions: the first four parts go out to the end of this century and part five continues for 50 years later. Part one orients the reader by explaining the author's view of the sociopolitical impact of technological trends. By employing a definition that permits technology *to do* this or that, readers are assisted in assessing impact that technology can make and quickly note that it may produce certain imperatives of its own because of its very impact.

Those developed societies—the United States, the Soviet Union, Western Europe, and Japan—with most of the world's GNP are exposed to a competent technological assessment in part two. Their strengths, weaknesses, problem areas, and prospects are considered, using thought-provoking scenario models to bring future trends and prospects to the surface.

In part three we are in a position to understand how technology is changing the world arena, particularly how it has changed the distribution of power to make up a "positive sum" process. Also considered is how this process may enhance international stability: its contribution to the integration of world society, to growing interdependence, and to international laws responding to society's reciprocal needs for stability are important in this respect.

The impact of these technological realities on current and future American policy are the subject of part four. Technologically speaking, no difference exists between domestic and foreign policy today. They have become a technological entity. In fact, Basiuk argues convincingly for a new national decisionmaking mechanism, permitting comprehensive planning and implementation of a "technological strategy" for the home front. Success in this area would end the ad hoc and compartmentalized efforts such as we have witnessed in developing an energy policy. Similar initiatives are required for the outside world, and Basiuk proposes an "Adviser to the President for a Future International System" to develop policy for these emerging circumstances.

Part five rounds out the forecast by extending it roughly 50 years into the next century. It analyzes what one day may be referred to as the "postindustrial revolution," in which man battles technology for control of his own destiny. An examination of America's national purpose in an international context provides an appropriate closing for this far-reaching book. Basiuk conceives America's purposes to be as standard as the *Preamble*, and he regrets attacks upon them. New national leadership will be required to defend old purposes, and it may be that we are witnessing the beginnings of this defense today in Mr. Carter's consuming concern for human rights and desire to right old wrongs, as evidenced, especially, in the recent

Panama Canal Treaty. In time these activities may help to recover some of America's ideological appeal and inspiration, both of which are essential for any degree of world leadership.

Russell Baker once said that the future begins in America. He was right, and the greatest contribution that America may make in the future technological world, described so well here, is to demonstrate how mature man can live peacefully within a global, postindustrial society.

JOHN D. ELLIOTT
The George Washington University
Washington, D.C.

CARL M. BRAUER. *John F. Kennedy and the Second Reconstruction*. Pp. vii, 396. New York: Columbia University Press, 1977. $14.95.

This richly documented study of political history is a good addition to the literature of the Kennedy years. The theme of this work is that John F. Kennedy changed from a moderate stance on civil rights and a resistance to the kind of reconstruction imposed on the South following the Civil War, to an activist role and a central position in what the author describes as "The Second Reconstruction."

The irony posed by Carl Brauer is that Kennedy, as an "amateur historian in 1956," castigated Northern radical Republicans for their excesses in the first Reconstruction period; yet, within seven years of his writing on the subject, Kennedy became the most significant political figure in a new movement to abolish racial discrimination. Using the considerable resources of the Kennedy Library, collections from a variety of projects, organizations and people of the period, and personal interviews, Brauer gives full and informative citations to help others trace similar interests.

The book begins with a brief sketch of Kennedy's moderation or lack of interest in racial matters when he was a congressman and senator. His interest in international affairs and his flair for campaigning are noted, as well as his evolving acceptability to blacks and to Southern whites. Despite some argu-

ments with leaders of the NAACP, Kennedy was able to keep on friendly and supportive terms with them throughout his presidential campaign. Southern leaders were attracted by his moderate stance.

Following his election to the Presidency, Kennedy was under pressure from both sides. He was able to satisfy both partially by taking executive action on some discrimination matters and avoiding legislative proposals which would arouse Southern politicians. Brauer draws a number of comparisons with Eisenhower's Presidency in which Eisenhower, despite the Brown Decision of 1954 and the Little Rock confrontation, seemed aloof from issues of civil rights. Kennedy, according to Brauer, was drawn into the issues by a series of dramatic events. Kennedy shifted during his Presidency from limited advocacy and action to a focal position in prodding legislative enactments, which came to fruition after his assassination and Lyndon Johnson's ascendancy.

In presenting Kennedy's movement from peripheral interest in civil rights to central concern, Brauer highlights the roles of leading figures of the civil rights movement, prominent Southern politicians, Robert Kennedy as Attorney General, and certain members of the White House establishment. Most of these portrayals are brief and unidimensional, but Brauer's treatment of Robert Kennedy shows more of the human complexity involved in politics.

The writing style in this book, unfortunately, tends to the dry, descriptive statement in the form of dissertations, which loses the drama of the times. The volume was drawn from Brauer's doctoral dissertation and generally lacks vividness and depth of character development, though it is a scholarly and soundly reasoned work. There are a few portions that are compelling reading: descriptions of Alabama during the Freedom Rides and beatings suffered there and the treatment of demonstrations in Albany, Georgia and at the University of Mississippi. Typically, however, the book provides well-documented detail but little insight into the human condition or complex social situation of the times. The writing is not consistent with the excitement of the period.

In terms of the theme of Kennedy's shift from anti-Reconstructionism to dominance in the Second Reconstruction, Brauer provides no clear definition of Reconstruction, leaving it to the reader's prior knowledge or imagination. The study does show two shifts in Kennedy—from moderation to advocacy in civil rights and from executive action to legislative advocacy. These are not the only defining characteristics of Reconstruction, but Brauer does not provide his definition against which to judge Kennedy. Brauer also gives excessive credit to historians whose writings, he implies, were a major reason for Kennedy's shifts.

Given the volumes of material available, Brauer has done a careful and thoughtful job of pulling out important data and condensing it into a short book. It is worth reading.

JACK L. NELSON
Rutgers University
New Brunswick
New Jersey

DOMINIC J. CAPECI, JR. *The Harlem Riot of 1943.* Pp. ix, 262. Philadelphia, Pa.: Temple University Press, 1977. $15.00.

As the title suggests, *The Harlem Riot of 1943* is an account of a civil disturbance. The event was triggered by an incident involving a white policeman and a black serviceman, on leave in Harlem, on a hot Sunday evening in August. Some 3,000 persons initially collected in front of a police precinct station and later turned to breaking windows and looting. The event was contained by a largely white police force. The disturbance came to an end within 24 hours. It left six dead (all black), 85 injured (mostly blacks), property damage to 1,450 commercial establishments estimated between $225,000 and $5,000,000. A total of 590 persons was arrested.

Capeci covers antecedent events (both remote and proximate), the riot and its aftermath. The narrative begins with description of New York City and Harlem in the 1930s. Capeci describes public leadership with special attention to Fiorello LaGuardia and Adam Clayton Powell. Harlem life during the Depression is reviewed with emphasis on the employment problems experienced by blacks during the period. Capeci reviews black perceptions of World War II and their role in that conflict. A riot which occurred in Detroit earlier in the summer of 1943, and created concern in New York about the possibility of similar outbursts there, is discussed. Various explanations of the riot and reactions to it by public figures in New York are presented. Capeci offers his own view that black frustration about lack of access to social and economic rewards, compounded by their expectation that they participate fully in the War effort, contributed importantly to the outbreak. Capeci also offers the view that containment of the riot was quick. He attributes the success in controlling it to an efficient but restrained effort on the part of police. At the same time, Capeci is critical of the role played by Mayor LaGuardia and the police during the period. He argues that LaGuardia lagged in taking action to alleviate tensions known to have existed in Harlem prior to the riot and is also critical of LaGuardia's insensitivity to black concerns about police brutality.

As a contribution to an understanding of the causes of riots and the means through which racial tensions can be contained, the book is less satisfactory than it is as a historical narrative. Largely implicitly, the author emphasizes the role of public figures and the forces which led to the riot. In so doing he concentrates on matters which were contested during the period between black and white leaders. Public controversy, for example, regarding potential racial discrimination in tenant selection for a quasi-public housing project under construction in the Lower East Side receives attention. The connection between these public issues in black and white relations and the frame of mind of the riot participants is not compellingly made. The historian's problem is that information is available on public leaders and public events; accordingly it is reported. Much less information is available about the ordinary citizens who are potential riot participants. By concentrating on available information, Capeci implicitly appears to overestimate the explanatory importance of the role played by civic leaders in contributing to the forces which led to the riot and the actions they might have taken to more effectively contain civil unrest. An alternate possibility is that riots result from enormously powerful social forces over which public leaders have very little control.

FRANCIS G. CARO
Community Service Society
New York City

EDWARD W. CHESTER. *A Guide to Political Platforms.* Pp. 373. Hamden, Conn.: Archon Books, 1977. $20.00.

This book is an issue-oriented, non-quantitative history of political party platforms from their emergence in the 1830s to the present. As such, it serves as a useful complement to Porter and Johnson's standard compilation, *National Party Platforms 1840–1968*, and other more quantitative works.

Professor Chester draws on a wide range of sources, including scholarly analyses, journalistic reactions of the time, and, of course, the platforms and platform debate accounts themselves. His narrative style is direct and efficient, though not particularly engaging, considering the wealth of interesting characters and issues available for discussion.

The book is organized chronologically, with a section devoted to each presidential election from 1840 to 1976, the latter receiving a "tentative appraisal." Each election is presented in turn through a brief summary of the preceding administration and introduction to the current presidential candidates, a description and comparison of the major party platforms and their continuities and discontinuities with preceding years, a less

extensive review of the minor party candidates and platforms, and finally a listing of the election results. Though this organization serves to present a large quantity of information efficiently, this reviewer found it repetitious. Though the author avoids the tedium of pure quantitative description, the reiterated organizational pattern detracts from the reading enjoyment possible in an issue-oriented narrative.

Despite this, there is no question of the book's comprehensiveness or utility. It contains a lengthy introduction which overviews the major questions and topics to be considered in analyzing and comparing party platforms (e.g., minority planks, third party innovation and reforms, platform rhetoric versus reality), and offers some conclusions based on this and other studies. There is a general and election-specific annotated bibliography of over 400 sources which provides an excellent beginning for future research and reading in this area. As this history shows, though frequently depreciated by commentators and ignored by politicians, political platforms offer an essential insight into the development of the American party system and election process.

JAMES M. GIARELLI
University of Florida
Gainesville

MELVYN DUBOFSKY AND WARREN VAN TINE. *John L. Lewis: A Biography.* Pp. v, 619. New York, Quadrangle, 1977. $20.00.

This valuable book will be must reading for anyone concerned with the history of the American labor movement. Paradoxically I find the biography a failure because it never succeeds in explaining John L. Lewis as a human being. Perhaps no one can. Nothing more indicates this failure than the decision to begin and end the book with the murder of "Jock" Yablonski, which occurred over nine years after Lewis retired and six months after his death. Surely even Lewis, for all his undoubted sins, deserves to have the first and last passages of his biography directed at him. At one point the authors snidely wonder how Lewis could square his well-to-do life style "with his public role as the captain of a mighty host of plebians" (p. 299), while elsewhere they snigger at his "appearing more the striving bourgeois than the emerging proletarian leader" (p. 17). Apart from the obvious conflation of roles, what anyone writing about the mainstream of the American labor movement must understand is that it was never proletarian but always bourgeois. Much (see chapter 13 notes) is based on oral interviews with individuals (e.g., Gardner Jackson) whose reputation for accuracy leaves much to be desired. The authors freely state that "we may have relied on such information too heavily" (p. 593).

Along the way there are confusions —at page 12 the authors doubt Lewis's claim that he attended high school; six pages later they incorporate such attendance into their interpretation. There are also some curious judgments rendered: "most Americans enjoyed prosperity during the late summer and early fall of 1929" (p. 155); "by late summer of 1934. . . . full recovery from depression (was) no nearer than it had been during the Hoover days" (p. 207). The latter is part of the general put-down of FDR now so fashionable, but what inspired the caricature of Sidney Hillman (often from the memoirs of his Stalinist enemies) is difficult to fathom—Lewis would have enjoyed it. Yet, despite all these complaints, this is a book from which I learned much. It fleshes out and demythologizes Lewis's early career, but is best in treating Lewis's "glory years" (1933–1940, pp. 181–388). This part of the work can stand with the best labor history. The overall results suggest that the authors should not have attempted biography, certainly not the biography of a great man who was also a great rogue—or was it the other way around?

ROGER DANIELS
University of Cincinnati
Ohio

DALL W. FORSYTHE. *Taxation and Political Change in the Young Nation, 1781–1833.* Pp. x, 167. New York: Columbia University Press, 1977. $15.00.

Professor Forsythe, a political scientist, investigates the early American national experience to formulate theses relating taxation to political change. Regarding government's power to extract revenue as the key to its dominion, he expects the growth of that power to play a crucial role in developing effective governmental systems.

Before drawing his conclusions, Forsythe provides a summary account of early controversies about federal taxation. He excludes nontax revenue sources from his discussion, although they yielded a significant minority of the government's income. Forsythe emphasizes the tariff, as the available literature does, although the great tariff controversies focused on protection more than on extraction of revenue as such. He relies in his narrative on standard secondary accounts and interpretations. His criticism of Louis Hartz's *The Liberal Tradition in America* (p. 6) suggests that perhaps political theorists value that work more generally than historians do.

In the analytical discussion which constitutes his main contribution, Forsythe presents a sophisticated revision of previous scholars' typologies of political events. Like many of his predecessors, he defines the political "regime" in narrowly constitutional terms and conceptualizes "political development" as a unilinear expansion of state machinery. In his typology an "authority crisis" (suggesting a revolutionary situation) exists when a policy controversy appears to concern the limits of the regime and the survival of the system appears to be in peril. "Normal politics" obtains when neither of those conditions is present; "regime politics," when only the former condition appears; and "environmental crisis," when only the latter does. (To avoid confusion, readers should notice that Forsythe changes the locations of his four categories in the related charts on pp. 114 and 118.)

In addition, the author formulates thoughtful descriptions of the political

structure's "allocative relations" to the
social-economic substructure and its
"authority relations" to the citizens in
their mass political behavior. Forsythe
carefully qualifies his claims for his
models, but he considers them more
useful than other political thinkers' corresponding constructs. His typology deserves careful attention. It leaves the
reader speculating about its applicability
to a wider range of historical events. One
particularly wonders how he might treat
the dynamics of "authority relations"
and "allocative relations" in the origins
of the American Civil War, which he
recognizes as the only unequivocal "authority crisis" in the history of the United
States to date.

JACK P. MADDEX, JR.
University of Oregon
Eugene

HUGH HECLO. A Government of Strangers: Executive Politics in Washington. Pp. x, 272. Washington, D.C.:
The Brookings Institution, 1977.
$10.95. Paperbound, $4.50.

Were you a Republican in Who's Who
in 1968 and thereby assured of consideration for a Nixon appointment? Did you
receive an Atlanta-postmarked letter in
the fall of 1976 bearing the news that
your credentials had been placed in the
Carter "Talent Inventory?" In either
case, that extended moment of truth
between Election Day and Inauguration
sparked questions in the minds of those
awaiting lightening's strike: What can I
read to prepare? There was very little
then—at least for those who assumed
that playing an important part in executive politics means more than "living by
the book." But now the gap is filled, and
the result makes fascinating reading.

If Richard Neustadt's Presidential
Leadership was Machiavelli's Prince for
the American presidency, then Hugh
Heclo's A Government of Strangers is
the comparable handbook for the earl-
doms and baronies of presidential appointees. Helco's intention is to explore
the relatively unknown process by which
high-ranking political executives and top
civil servants interact with one another,

focusing on the people themselves rather
than on institutions, doctrinal legalities,
or jurisdictional boundaries. How do
those interested in political control and
those interested in administrative continuity take the measure of one another?
Why do some presidential appointees do
better than others in getting what they
want? To what extent can any political
leader hope to guide what government
does—programs—by directing and re-
straining those who do it—personnel?

The author uses case studies, maxims,
and telling interview quotations to reveal the little known everyday problems
of executive leadership faced by hundreds of appointees in the executive
branch. An assistant secretary describes
his frustrations and progress in trying to
start a program for minorities: "The
bureaucrats I worked with were competent and hardworking, but damn, if they
couldn't give reasons why any particular
thing couldn't be done. . . . Later I
found out they knew there were ways to
do things, but they weren't volunteering
that information" (p. 174). Heclo also
illustrates why bureaucrats may deal
cautiously or cavalierly with appointees.
A high civil servant is quoted: "When our
last assistant secretary was kicked out, it
didn't affect us. He had no ties outside
his office" (p. 162).

Heclo shows more than a narrow
concern for groundruling effective manipulation within Washington executive
suites. He is constructively interested in
larger problems of democratic leadership theory as well. He contends that the
politicization of the bureaucracy has
been matched by increasing bureau-
cratization of leadership. He asserts that
the changing nature of the political
executive jobs to be filled has generally
favored those with specialized technical
abilities rather than those with broad
political experience. Two important consequences follow from this trend. The
patronage candidates with no technical
training and who are ignorant of complex
policies will be dropped from the final
cut, thereby creating tensions with party
leadership. Second, the changing trend
in elite recruitment, which emphasizes
managerial experience and technical

expertise, generates distance between the electoral coalition with which a president wins office and the executive coalition with which he must try to govern in the bureaucracy.

Having detailed the foibles and short-comings in the face-off between higher level civil servants and political appointees (the Washington strangers), Heclo offers several proposals for change. He suggests reforms that would (1) promote more competent management by appointees, (2) reorganize the administration of the civil service personnel system, and (3) set up a new federal service of public managers. Proposals to create a new kind of federal executive officer, a central personnel agency, and better civil service safeguards should be calculated to insure good faith service from bureaucrats and greater responsibility on the part of top political appointees.

The point is to improve the strategic setting for executive politics. For this is the setting, Heclo convincingly demonstrates, in which statecraft for presidential appointees consists of getting the changes they want without losing the bureaucratic services they need.

RICHARD PIERRE CLAUDE
University of Maryland
College Park

GARY J. JACOBSOHN. *Pragmatism, Statesmanship, and the Supreme Court.* Pp. 214. Ithaca, N.Y.: Cornell University Press, 1977. $12.50.

Should Supreme Court opinions reflect public opinion or should they educate the populace? Williams College political scientist Gary Jacobsohn's well-edited critique places pragmatism and statesmanship in juxtaposition, "pitting them like gamecocks for a test of consequences," as William Y. Elliott said.

Pragmatism loses in the battle, John Dewey and William James notwithstanding. The futuristic orientation of pragmatism is evolutionary. Change becomes "an object of reverence" (p. 49), with creative emphasis on "the accumulation of empirical information" (p. 84).

For the pragmatist, "there are only results" (quoted on p. 175). These results are interest-oriented, seeking "the good" through social engineering of "the spirit of egalitarianism" (p. 94).

Judicial statesmanship, in contrast, imposes restraints on innovations of Constitutional wisdom. It emphasizes prudence, compromise, and great subtlety. Statesmanship adapts to changing socioeconomic conditions without abandoning "the vision of the founding fathers" (p. 190). The statesman weaves a strong, resilient "judicial fabric" capable of withstanding "the wear and tear of modern society" while upholding positive principles of the American testament. Accommodation occurs between "demands of the past and those of the future" (p. 22).

In adversarial fashion, Jacobsohn presents winners and losers: Charles Evans Hughes serves "as a model of judicial statesmanship" (p. 190), while Felix Frankfurter was "not a judicial statesman" (p. 160). Although Wallace Mendelson, Frankfurter's key biographer, must be in distress, he is not alone. Such F. F. friends as Louis Henkin, Albert Sacks, Paul Freund, and Charles Wyzanski also would be prone to point out his greatness.

But greatness is not equated with statesmanship. Frankfurter is lauded for being "an unusually talented judge" with "enduring achievements" (p. 160). His attempt to separate constitutionality and wisdom, though, is criticized. In contrast Hughes, in the *Blaisdell* case on Minnesota's mortgage moratorium law, responded to public opinion "while seeking all the while to inform it" (p. 191).

Jacobsohn's evidence for the pragmatic revolt of our high court is substantial: textual treatment of 24 cases; many more cases in 426 footnotes; and 211 bibliographical sources. The presentation shows clearly that pragmatism has become a positive word, much like democracy, so that modern judges want to be called pragmatic, but many are not, including Frankfurter.

A follow-up volume on judicial statesmanship would serve us well. Jacobsohn notes that few of our justices have been statesmen, but then does not elaborate. Perhaps statesmanship is elusive in "an essentially undemocratic institution" (p. 64) like the Court. Pragmatic faith should convince us, though, to look to the rainbow.

CHARLES T. BARBER
Indiana State University
Evansville

MERRITT ROE SMITH. *Harpers Ferry Armory and the New Technology: The Challenge of Change.* Pp. 363. Ithaca, N.Y.: Cornell University Press, 1977. $17.50.

This study of the Harpers Ferry Armory contains two levels of discussion, each in its own way illuminating. There is first the study of the particular enterprise in its industrial, geographical, and political setting. The story of the Armory is perceptively treated from its founding in 1798 to its demise in 1861. The complexity of the organization, the technology and the labor responses are dealt with in a well-documented and, at the same time, readable way.

But it is on the second aspect of the book, summarized in the introduction and conclusion, that its claim to a place in the more general literature rests. These larger considerations have to do with the role of the state in industrial sponsorship, and the conditions of growth of the industrial capacity of the United States and, indeed, that of the world generally. For the manufacture of arms under government aegis at Springfield, Massachusetts and at Harper's Ferry, West Virginia, played a central role in the standardization of parts and the mechanization of production. But the story is not a simple one; it manifests a duality as exemplified in the two armories. Springfield, set in the industrial Northeast, was the progressive and inventive one; Harper's Ferry, as an implant in the rural context of the Potomac Valley, was derivative and conservative.

The author derives two general theses or lines of reasoning from his study. The first is that it is too simple to accept the judgment of the visiting British inventor and industrialist Joseph Whitworth, that the United States took painlessly, indeed eagerly, to machine technology, free of the resistances, rioting, and machine-breaking of Britain. Harper's Ferry provides an American example, of some importance, of resistance to Yankeeism in the industrial field, even to the murder by gunfire of a superintendent who tried to impose his will. The author, indeed, asks whether the national creed was so receptive to industry as has so commonly been thought, or whether this idea was held by "only a small segment of the population," which "tried to inculcate them through various agencies of economic and social control." There is a call for further "grass roots" investigations of what really went on in particular manufacturing situations.

In the meantime we have the case which Smith sets forth in his book. But the situation at Harper's Ferry seems to have been characterized by special circumstances (which he so excellently brings out), rather than to represent a general syndrome of resistance. It was George Washington, supported by local businessmen, who insisted that the armory be in West Virginia. The president of the new republic, supported by business sycophants, imposed an autocratic decision of a kind and scale that could never have entered the heads of George III and his court. From this a whole set of consequences followed. The works was isolated from the industrialized outlook of the Northeast, the armories insisted on their craft status and resented mechanization, there was a resistance (in the Jeffersonian spirit) to the demands of innovative, machine-governed industry. Politics in the armory and the town produced, through control of key offices in both, a powerful, paternalistic but recalcitrant oligarchy. So was constituted an elite of privileged families who acted as protectors of the community's values against both the new technology and the government which wanted it implemented. It is difficult to see how analogous cases could be found of such complete and intense hostility to new technology to establish a generalized paradigm of resistance. Of course, it is possible to argue that any attempt at a progressive manufacturing establishment in the South would have yielded some such result, but how many such cases were there? The federal government was alone in the scale of its attempt, and this may provide a highly intriguing, but unique case.

The second of the broader implications of the book has to do with the role of the state in the industrializing of an advanced society. The author provides a quite striking example, in the manufacture of armaments, of the state as the great initiator and sponsor of new methods. It was the state, through its Ordnance Department, which impelled American industry toward standardization and mechanization of parts, and which provided the basis for a machine tool industry that was to take the initiative from the British in this critical area. But in so doing, the choice of site was very important: the state's initiative could thrive in Massachusetts, but languish in West Virginia. Even so, however, it was of profound overall importance, though it would presumably have been even more successful if both armories had been in the North.

In this way the obtuseness of the first president has provided the basis for an arresting case study, but one which may exhaust its own category. Professor Smith's study is a highly intriguing account of the relations among business, technology, and the state, brought to a sharp focus by a locational decision made by politicians.

S. G. CHECKLAND
University of Glasgow
Scotland

CHARLES H. TROUT. *Boston: The Great Depression and the New Deal.* Pp. xx, 401. New York: Oxford University Press, 1977. $15.95.

Boston: The Great Depression and the New Deal by Charles H. Trout makes two valuable contributions to American urban and political history. It gives a detailed description of the continuities and changes in one of America's leading metropolitan centers from the coming of the Depression to the coming of World War II. It also uses Boston as a case study of several commonly held assumptions about the impact of the "Roosevelt Revolution" on the nation's cities.

Trout's basic thesis is that continuity and conservatism prevailed over change and liberalism in Boston despite the influence of the Depression and the New Deal. He does not ignore or gloss over changes which do occur in areas as diverse as population and voting patterns, the rise and decline of membership in organizations, from the National Association for the Advancement of Colored People to the Chamber of Commerce, and Boston's economic decline relative to other cities. But Trout believes that this flux leaves Boston's basic institutions and ideologies intact.

One constant factor in city and state politics was the controversy surrounding James Michael Curley, mayor from 1914 to 1918, 1922 to 1926, and 1930 to 1934; governor from 1934 to 1936. His influence, popularity, and ambition helped split Democrats into factions based more on personality than ideology. Other enduring "institutions" included William Cardinal O'Connell, head of the Roman Catholic Church which "instructed three-quarters of the population" (p. 319), Irish political dominance, American Federation of Labor (AFL) control of most union workers, and many self-conscious ethnic neighborhoods. When New Deal programs began pouring new wine into these old bottles, some bent, but few broke. Indeed, Boston shaped the local operation of the New Deal as much, or more than, the New Deal shaped Boston.

Although Trout carefully shows the social and political diversity of Boston, he overemphasizes the underlying ideological unity within the first and second New Deals. He approves this unity and criticizes Boston for lagging behind the New Deal.

Trout correctly emphasizes the importance of a local perspective on the operation and modification of federal programs. But a national perspective on the complex, pragmatic, and developmental nature of the New Deal is also important. A full understanding of the period will necessitate an analytical, comparative integration of such a national perspective with many state and local perspectives such as Trout's excellent, comprehensive study of Boston.

ROBERT G. SHERER

Wiley College
Marshall
Texas

RONALD G. WALTERS. *The Antislavery Appeal: American Abolitionism After 1830.* Pp. xvii, 198. Baltimore: The Johns Hopkins University Press, 1977. $11.00.

This book explores the ideas of immediate abolitionists after 1830, with special attention to those assumptions they held in common with their contemporaries. Ronald Walters joins the debate over whether the abolitionists were anti-institutional, and attempts to resolve it by showing that their style—righteous, sectarian, and evangelical—was after all the style of the whole antebellum reform movement. He also finds abolitionists typical in their religious concerns, not because they shared an orthodoxy, but because they were dedicated seekers, insisting on purity in faith and deeds. He finds their minds precariously balanced between racialism and environmentalism, but opportunistically using both points of view to indict slavery. He finds them dedicated to undefiled and perfectly controlled sexual behavior and to an affectionate and uplifting family life. Finally, abolitionists were conventional Americans in their faith in industrial progress and in their devotion to the historical mission of the United States to redeem mankind (a notion which Walters notes even among the disunionists).

Walters argues quite plausibly that these attitudes defined abolitionist propaganda. Slavery prevented the establishment of true Christianity; it led to sexual vice; it corrupted the families of masters as well as of slaves; it retarded the growth of industry; and it finally poisoned the entire nation.

Except for his discussion of sex hygiene, Walters reworks familiar material. Though less analytical, Alice Felt Tyler's *Freedom's Ferment* (Minneapolis, 1944) remains a richer and more accurate account of antislavery within the context of antebellum reform. Both Tyler and Walters assume rather than prove that reform reflected "the faith of the young republic." Did not the reformers themselves form a subculture, educated and influential, but still somewhat detached from a more lethargic majority? Committed to the methods and philosophy of behaviorism, Walters maintains an admirable objectivity with respect to the personalities of the abolitionists, but when he finds himself discussing issues he, too, often joins their party. He apparently believes that the antislavery movement had been genteel and ineffectual before 1830, that the churches remained silent and inert regarding slavery until the Civil War, that all Americans who supported the Colonization Society were more likely to perpetuate slavery than help emancipation, and that no one besides the immediatists really wished for, or worked toward, the end of slavery.

ROBERT MCCOLLEY

University of Illinois
Urbana-Champaign

JULES WITCOVER. *Marathon: The Pursuit of the Presidency 1972–1976.* Pp. ix, 684. New York: The Viking Press, 1977. $14.95.

This treatment of the 1976 presidential election is appropriately titled. Filled with the detail that makes the book a fascinating one, *Marathon* is an exhaustive, but not exhausting, analysis of the Carter-Ford confrontation.

Jules Witcover, a syndicated news columnist, devotes well over half this book to the complex nominating process, with particular attention given to the impact of the primary elections on the Democratic and Republican candidates. Particularly noteworthy is the author's tracing of the way in which developments within one party had major ramifications within the other. For example, after Wallace's candidacy had been demolished by Jimmy Carter in primary elections in Florida and North Carolina, thousands of the Alabaman's supporters, cut loose from their hero, entered the Republican preconvention struggle and gave Ronald Reagan's sagging candidacy a much needed boost, badly damaging Gerald Ford in the process. Filled with first-hand interviews with candidates and key staff members, the author's analysis of the lengthy preconvention period is an important tool in understanding our most recent national election.

A second significant facet of the volume is Witcover's penetrating examination of the Ford presidency. Those who believe that Gerald Ford was defeated in 1976 essentially because of the Nixon pardon avoid the reality that Ford's presidency was weak and that this unelected president had severe and never corrected image problems. Indeed, the 1976 race was somewhat peculiar since it involved two presidential candidates whose personal style and/or character became important issues in the campaign's final outcome.

Although the book is lengthy, Witcover's appealing writing style makes it readily digestible, with his pungent descriptions of major personalities serving as tasty morsels. Among these, he portrays John Connolly as "eversalivating," Senator John Tower as "sycophantic," George Bush as a man whom "everyone knowledgeable in Republican politics considered incompetent to be President," and Gerald Ford as "one of those big dolls with the rounded base that when hit bobs back up for another punch."

Despite its many strong features, *Marathon* does suffer some imperfections. There is, on occasion, inclusion of detail that is both needless and pointless. The author's reform proposal (regional primaries to be held after a lead-off primary in New Hampshire) is not adequately defended. Witcover seems too eager to defend the media for their coverage of the 1976 race. Understandable, considering his background, this seems out of place here. Finally, the book lacks any broader perspective in which the 1976 election could be set.

Demographic and other changes are largely ignored, although these could have been illuminating.

In all, Witcover presents a valuable historical record of the Carter-Ford election. It should serve as a vital source book for all students of the national political process.

ROBERT E. GILBERT
Northeastern University
Boston
Massachusetts

VIRGINIA YANS-MCLAUGHLIN. *Family and Community: Italian Immigrants in Buffalo, 1880–1930.* Pp. 265. Ithaca, N.Y.: Cornell University Press, 1977. $12.50.

The reader steeped in the ever-increasing volume of literature on the Italian-American experience will find much that is familiar in Virginia Yans-McLaughlin's new book on Italian immigrant families in Buffalo, New York from 1880 to 1930. Indeed it is tempting to say that the book is another case of old wine in new bottles, except that it really is not. Many of the old themes in Italian histography—family l life, attitudes toward women, work, and education—are freshly illuminated by expertly juxtaposing snippets of new and old source materials, plus interview data, in ways that are thoroughly convincing.

The author's point of departure is that the models developed by historians and social scientists that depicted immigrant families as succumbing to the pathological conditions of urban life in the New World are not borne out in the case of Italian families in Buffalo. She presents many persuasive arguments to defend her thesis. A sampler of these include the contentions: 1) that peasants who had eschewed community involvement in Italy created sustaining networks of community relationships in the New World; 2) that familism was so strongly developed a concept among the arrivals from the Mezzogiorno that they were able to resist most of the blandishments of the New World, particularly the individualism of urban life; and 3) that even the lethal threats to family life—

prolonged separation between husbands and wives, working mothers, unemployment, poverty, assimilative pressures from school and charitable agencies—did not cause family breakdown. The reason: the Mezzogiorno peasants had encountered these threats in the Old World and had worked out strategies to deal with them successfully there; thus, what worked in Sicily apparently worked in Buffalo. A particularly fascinating illustration of this claim is Yans-McLaughlin's analysis of the immigrants' adaptation to working conditions in New York. Specifically, she shows that there was a "goodness of fit" between the variegated work pattern of Sicilian peasants (most of whom were primarily agricultural workers, but routinely pursued off-season employment in sulphur mining, town industry, quarrying, and construction) and the employment opportunities for immigrants in Buffalo, which also required occupational versatility.

Much to Yans-McLaughlin's credit, these contentions are not pulled out of a hat and presented as fiat; rather, she provides impressive documentation culled from Buffalo newspaper editorials, scholarly journals, census tracts, and most especially, from the testimonials of the remnants of the immigrant generation and their immediate descendants. Yet anyone familiar with the subject, gets the impression that she acquired the outline for the book by reading the avalanche of materials on Italians (particularly on the way of their family life) and then hammered the Buffalo case into the categories of the outline. The yield from this exercise is generally commendable, but when compared to the corpus of existing materials on Italians, the findings are confirmatory rather than revelatory.

Parodoxically, the author's methodology is vulnerable to criticism on the same grounds that she emphatically wanted to avoid: Throughout the book the reader is told that statistical data often distort and mask the inner dynamics of family life; she hopes to correct this by introducing "literary and oral sources." But it seems to this reviewer that she actually used

many statistical citations and few oral sources. I was surprised to discover that only eleven informants were listed in the bibliography.

Notwithstanding these flaws, the book represents a valuable contribution to the growing recognition that an earlier generation of scholars had erred in their understanding of immigrant families.

ALFRED AVERSA, JR.
Fairleigh Dickinson University
Teaneck
New Jersey

SOCIOLOGY

MARTIN BINKIN and SHIRLEY J. BACH. *Women and the Military.* Pp. vii, 134. Washington, D.C.: The Brookings Institution, 1977. $7.50. Paperbound, $2.95.

Until times within living memory, the soldiery was the least attractive of occupations. Gentlemen chose to be officers, but hunger recruited the rank and file. Reviewing the troops he was about to lead in his victorious Peninsular Campaign, Wellington grumbled: "I don't know what effect these men will have on the enemy, but, by God, they terrify me." To him, the British volunteer army was the scum of the earth, to be flogged to its triumphs. Until World War II, volunteer peacetime armies were drawn from the margins of the labor market. The only women for whom the military had a use were the town whores and the campfollowers.

That has changed. For the last 35 years, women have infiltrated an increasing diversity of military occupations, successfully serving now in nearly every noncombat specialty. They are only barred from duties which call for their taking battle stations. At that point, social sentiment balks, and Congress has legislated their exclusion from combat units. The feminist reaction, as voiced by the National Organization for Women, is uncompromising: "Should women go into combat? To us the question is completely irrelevant. We only need to know that there are capable women who want these jobs . . . (p. 73). The joining of this issue constitutes a national problem, and the Argus-eyed Brookings Institution detailed Binkin and Bach to its dissection.

Marshalling the data, meticulously noting gaps and inadequacies, the authors review the history, summarize policies and laws, and consider the shifting public attitudes. Their foundation laid, they execute an economic analysis. Despite opinions that the costs of sex integration will be prohibitive, they show that the outlay for modified barracks and separate lavatories would be trivial compared to the savings which would accrue from the significantly fewer dependents for whom the government would need to assume responsibility for support, travel, and medical care. The conclusion is startling: ". . . the average annual per capita cost associated . . . with housing, medical care, and transportation . . . is estimated to be about $982 less for military women than for men" (p. 58).

In other contexts the economics would be persuasive. Armies and navies are different; we must know what effect sexually integrated battalions and nuclear submarines will have on the enemy. The indications are not clear. In recent years, enlisted women have been much better educated than male volunteers. Projected trends strongly suggest that the future of the volunteer army must depend on the increasing induction of women. The authors' study of the population pipeline shows that the services will draw from an eligible pool of males in 1992 which will be nearly 20 percent less than the same pool in 1977. The projected enlistments for 1992 will bring in less than 75 percent of the services' need for "highly qualified" males. Clearly, if the military need for technicians is to be met, more women must be attracted.

Whether they can effectively serve in the infantry or the fleet is still an open question, despite the achievements of Boadicea and Jeanne d'Arc. The Israeli army, which has had the most experience with women in combat, has withdrawn them from most fighting units. For tasks requiring great strength, fewer women than men can qualify. The social problems are at least quirky. The Navy's one experiment with women sailors—on a hospital ship—was enlivened with an order that personnel engaging in public displays of affection would be subject to nonjudicial punishment, a nice touch from a perplexed skipper.

Binkin and Bach conclude that the services should experiment with integrated combat units, persevering until women acquire enough experience to qualify as supervisors. Comparisons with all-male units would be indicative, but the final test would be in battle, where points are not allowed for good intentions and sexual egalitarianism.

This short book is an ornament to Brookings. Those questions that can be answered are posed and answered. The authors point to where missing information can be found, and suggest those questions which only experience can answer. As a model of concise exposition, it deserves applause and emulation.

JOHN P. CONRAD
Academy for Contemporary Problems
Columbus
Ohio

RICHARD W. COAN. *Hero, Artist, Sage, or Saint? A Survey of Views on What is Variously Called Mental Health, Normality, Maturity, Self-Actualization, and Human Fulfillment.* Pp. xiii, 322. New York: Columbia University Press, 1977. $20.00. Paperbound, $6.50.

What is the ideal personality? Is there an optimal condition for humans? Professor Coan takes these classical questions as his subject, and offers a rapid survey and evaluation of theories of human nature. Each theory or model of man is considered in terms of its answer to the questions in the book's subtitle: What is mental health, or normality, or maturity, or human fulfillment?

The first third of the book gives a brief introduction to the most significant Eastern and Western positions. With a few pages for each, we are presented with early Greek thought, early Christianity, the Renaissance, recent Western trends, contemporary religious responses, the mental health professions, Hinduism, Buddhism, Tibetian Buddhism, Taoism, Confucianism, Zen Buddhism, and modern Indian thought. Each view is pressed for its answer to some form of the question: What, if anything, is the ideal lifestyle? Of course, rapid surveys have their faults and their uses. We each have complaints about the treatment of our own field. However, there is a service in collecting brief snapshots of each position and in looking for patterns. What patterns emerge? We read that in the West, nature is seen as a domain to be conquered (by science); in the East, harmony with nature is the ideal. The West has an orientation toward the future; the East, toward "the immediate present experience of life." A familiar cliché, for many readers.

Two-thirds of the book is devoted to the Western psychologists and psychiatrists. There are separate chapters on Freud's and on Jung's views of the optimal human condition, and then short pieces on Adler, Rank, Fromm, Erikson, Assagioli, and Eric Berne. A chapter on the Existentialists gives us Kierkegaard, Nietzsche, Heidegger, Jaspers, Marcel, Sartre, Binswanger, Frankl, and Laing. For other contemporaries, we have Skinner, Allport, Rogers, Maslow, and Perls, taking us from behaviorism to gestalt therapy and the human potential movement.

In the final chapter, Professor Coan comments on his own work, presented a few years ago in his *The Optimal Personality*. This was a multivariate analysis of traits involved in concepts of an ideal personality. The work reduced to what the author calls five "basic modes of fulfillment;" efficiency, creativity, inner harmony, relatedness, and transcendence. These few pages make some interesting suggestions, but result in nothing very convincing to Coan himself. Is the question of an optimal personality a scientific matter? Coan raises the issue, discusses several strategies, and concludes that scientific research can provide pertinent information but not *the* solution. Despite a thin

survey, and a vague conclusion, I don't know anything better on this question. Perhaps we should blame the problem and not the author.

SIDNEY AXINN
Temple University
Philadelphia
Pennsylvania

JAMES B. COWIE and JULIAN B. ROE-BUCK. *An Ethnography of a Chiropractic Clinic: Definitions of a Deviant Situation.* Pp. xiv, 167. New York: The Free Press, 1975. $10.00.

This little book, written by two well-read sociologists, seriously studies the "marginally deviant" situation of a small chiropractic clinic which is anonymous, but apparently situated in Louisiana. The deviant status of such a clinic and of its central character, the chiropractor, is said to be imposed on both by the dominant culture, from without. By means of the chiropractor's own learned "methodography," however, this person is said to have "compensatory social power." This is because methodography here means the ability of the deviant person to see himself as both honorable and as uniquely correct in his beliefs and practices, and also to influence his associates and patients so that they constantly impart back to him acceptance of his claims to respect and his own confidence in his ability to remedy practically all human woes.

Since the chiropractor can dismiss patients who do not grant him such acceptance and confidence, retaining only patients who do, and can also surround himself with approving assistants and chiropractic consultants, he can create for himself an environment which sustains his belief in himself, in his "methodology"—here used to mean his methods of both treating and influencing patients—and in the professional excellence and true worth of both.

Of the book's two authors one, Cowie, conducted the study while serving as the paid, part-time assistant of the clinic's central figure the chiropractor. The book is thus largely the report of a participant observer. He views himself as an actor with a role, and sees the subjects of his study, the chiropractor, the other assistants and associates, and the patients, as actors in other roles called for by this drama, while the clinic's rooms, equipment, and many publicity devices are its setting.

To make clear the basis of the chiropractor's beliefs in his own semiscientific philosophy, and hence in himself, Cowie describes at some length the history of the chiropractic movement. This begins with the discovery in Iowa, in 1895, by one, D. D. Palmer, of the "monumental" principle that the restoration of a person's misplaced or "subluxated" vertebrae, to their normal positions relative to one another, and the resulting removal of pressure on the nerves issuing from the vertebral column, cures what are called "diseases." The book reports also Palmer's establishment of the first infirmary and school of chiropractic. Previous to the great discovery, Palmer is said to have had no medical training whatever but to have been an adherent of Anton Mesmer's early conception of what is now called hypnosis: "animal magnetism" to relieve human suffering. The skeptical reader, therefore, can note that as a healer, Palmer had previously practiced a variety of "faith healing," or of what reputable medical authorities today call the "placebo" method, and that this was, and still is, highly effective with many patients. Treatment based on the momentous discovery, therefore, can be viewed as only a more sophisticated variant of placebo treatment, combined, perhaps, with some of the benefits of massage.

The present writer has long seen "straight" chiropractic, such as was practiced by the book's chiropractor, as chiefly such a variant, and of late years has buttressed this view by recollection of a painstakingly careful study of chiropractic's central principle, which appeared in the American Scientist, volume 61, 1971, pages 574–80. This study, "A Scientific Test of the Chiropractic Theory," was authored by Edmund S. Crelin, a highly accredited anatomist at

Yale University's School of Medicine, and it presented the verdict that the principle of vertebral repositioning is clearly false. It should be added, however, that those chiropractors to whom the book's "straight" chiropractor referred scornfully as "mixers"; that is, those who adhere to the subluxation principle but "mix" with it modifications of the patient's diet and health regimen generally, may be using not only placebo treatment and message, but good advice on health related matters as well.

The book ends with a plea for more research studies intended to discover the socioeconomic characteristics of the patients of chiropractors, why they turn to the chiropractor rather than the physician, and how and why they are initially "converted" to a deviant system of beliefs. This plea can only be seconded here. However, before viewing only chiropractors as engaging in self-advertising and deliberately influencing patients to see them as competent, admirable, and trustworthy, the reader is asked to observe that, in the usual physician's office and waiting room, in the doctor's manner and sometimes his impressive equipment, similar devices are also employed. We are all susceptible to such approaches, and doubtless our improved health is in large part brought about by such "methodography." The book, therefore, is well worth reading for these reasons and more valuable than its size suggests.

ELIZABETH J. LEVINSON
Orono
Maine

ROY O. GREEP, MARJORIE A. KOBLINSKY, and FREDERICK S. JAFFEE. Reproduction and Human Welfare: A Challenge to Research. Pp. x, 622. Cambridge, Mass.: MIT Press, 1976. No price.

Massive studies undertaken by blue-ribbon committees of experts often lack depth and coherence and contribute very little to our understanding of key problems. Reproduction and Human Welfare is a happy exception. Although three foundations sponsored the work of no less than 160 scholars in 26 countries, the three primary authors deserve recognition for having condensed this mass of information into a comprehensive, but very thoughtful discussion of a critically important research field.

While this is by no means the first attempt at reviewing the progress of the reproductive sciences, it is perhaps one of the most well-balanced efforts to date. This balance results from the authors' concern not merely with scientific and technological advances, but also with the social and human dimensions of research and population control. The concise and rather technical presentation of scientific discovery appears in the second section of the book; it is preceded and followed by other considerations which place this research endeavor in its proper context.

In the first part of the volume, the authors outline the world population problem and evaluate the effectiveness of our current contraceptive technology in checking unwanted pregnancies. Available birth control methods, it is argued, are questionable not only according to biomedical standards, but according to social and psychological criteria as well. New developments must be safe, but they must also be acceptable and diverse enough to take into account the full range of mores, age requirements, levels of sexual activities, etc., that are found throughout the world.

The third section looks at the institutional and social climate in which contraceptive research is conducted. Here the authors consider the location of research facilities, the increasing role of the public sector, recent concerns with adequate testing and human experimentation, and the relationship of all of these factors to both past and future developments. Since scientific studies do not take place in an abstract world, it is to the authors' credit that they saw fit to investigate this dimension.

Finally, the book discusses financial support for reproduction and contraceptive research. It is very difficult to collect complete and accurate information on available research money, but the authors are conscious of this shortcoming, and what they present speaks eloquently for a reordering of our funding priorities in biomedical research. Progress has been made in the last 15 years, but the preoccupation is still with disease and postponement of death rather than with quality of life. The concluding section, as well as the entire volume, argues in a factual and measured way for a greater concern for life.

CHARLES S. BOURGEOIS
McGill University
Montreal
Canada

ROSABETH MOSS KANTER. *Men and Women of the Corporation.* Pp. 352. New York: Basic Books, 1977. $12.00.

This volume combines a case study of a corporation and a general discussion of the status of women in corporate management. Kanter analyzes the corporation as a male-dominated organization and contrasts the role of the male executive with three roles occupied by women—secretaries, executive wives, and women executives. Both the analysis of the particular corporation and the discussion of the general policy are based on the assumption that the size of the third group, women executives, should be appreciably increased.

Kanter first examines the obstacles for women for achieving executive positions. She discovers three clusters of conditions: blockage of appointments, lack of power, and numerical minority. The importance of each of these conditions is confirmed by reference to current theory and research in social psychology and organization theory. She also shows that the consequences of these conditions lead exactly to those traits which have been used to stereotype women and to throw obstacles into the path of their achievement. Blockage and powerlessness lead to behavior which can be used to deny advancement, and the minority position among executives (frequently a minority of one) has consequences which make it exceedingly difficult for a woman to function in an executive role.

The argument is presented in a convincing way. It combines scientific rigor with compassionate insight and an effective style. The data in the organization were collected through a wide array of techniques, such as formal and informal interviews, group discussions, observation, and inspection of company records. They are woven skillfully into the general analysis of the company. This approach leaves a more convincing and attractive picture than a more pedantic, but traditional, method of data analysis could have.

Kanter excels in bringing to bear the general principles of social psychology, principally derived from laboratory experiments, on the living conditions within the corporation. One almost feels the author's excitement in finding instances of abstract and esoteric principles before her eyes and it is her special skill to recognize them. In addition, this rare link between laboratory restraint and spontaneous action gives better reliance on the data from one case study besides making an important contribution to sociology and social psychology.

Here one might regret that Kanter did not go far enough in generalization. The problems she shows are not unique to women, but are general human problems. For instance, Kanter discusses the conflict women executives experience, especially those promoted from clerical ranks. Either they maintain a special relationship with female secretaries and are looked at suspiciously by their male colleagues or they do not and are looked at as traitors to their sex. Such role conflict is the fate of every person who has an identity in addition to the occupational role. Neglect of this wider generalization leads sometimes to the facile overoptimism of the social reformer, namely that a few new rules and regulations and social inventions can solve intractable human problems. Kanter is too good a sociologist to overlook the essential human dilemmas due to psychological and social constraints. But, especially in the last chapters on contribution to practice, she is in danger of getting carried away with the hope that improvement of women's executive position can overcome tragic dilemmas of human society.

KURT W. BACK

Duke University
Durham
North Carolina

FRED H. MATTHEWS. *Quest for an American Sociology: Robert E. Park and the Chicago School.* Pp. ix, 277. Montreal, Ca.: McGill-Queen's University Press, 1977. $16.00. Paperbound, $7.00.

Intellectual history is at best a difficult undertaking, especially if an author tries to summarize the lifetime work of an important scholar. Historian Fred Matthews has produced an informative book which paints Robert E. Park as an intellectual mixture of Yankee common sense, part-time social worker, and German idealism. Matthews especially admires Park's belief that conflict, rather than consensus, is the basis of social life. Matthews's focus is chiefly on Park, rather than on the Chicago School itself.

Told by William James that he was not intelligent enough to make a contribution to philosophy, Park at age 30 gave up journalism and set off to Germany to study sociology. Park's first book grew out of his dissertation dealing with the crowd, a force he felt was creative and not destructive. He then went to work for Booker T. Washington as public relations man and ghost writer until W. I. Thomas visited Tuskeegee, discovered "ein mensch," and invited Park to the University of Chicago. While there is no rule that an author must like or admire the person he chooses to write about, Matthews has a way of putting Park down as a nice person who just happened to make it to a major university. Unlike Marx, Matthews tells us, Park was not always profound or even particularly levelheaded, failing to see the profoundly reactionary implications of his writings.

There are many interesting insights in this book, such as Matthews's observation that Park's "assumption that value resides in psychic qualities rather than specific ends foreshadows the therapeutic mentality characteristic of a relativistic age . . ." (p. 30), a view more fully developed recently by Rieff. As with many intellectuals of his age, Park was greatly concerned about the potentially harmful effects of city life. Unlike some at the University of Chicago, he believed that reform efforts were probably doomed to failure. Matthews finds Park's intellectual portrayal of the city as a natural social force a serious failure of intellectual nerve, especially since the Chicago in which Park lived had been described by others as the only completely corrupt city in the world.

It is distressing to note that a short book on intellectual history costs $7.00 in paperback and is produced with unjustified lines by photo offset. Corrections are clearly visible; editing, almost totally lacking. I recommend this book because of its wealth of material about an important figure in the field of sociology, for its useful intellectual insights, and its breadth of coverage. But its price and readability probably put it outside its potential market for courses on sociological theory, a pity, since sociologists need to be reminded of the historical development of their discipline.

GEORGE H. CONKLIN
Sweet Briar College
Virginia

WILLIAM MICHELSON. *Environmental Choice, Human Behavior, and Residential Satisfaction.* Pp. xix, 403. New York: Oxford University Press, 1977. $10.50. Paperbound, $6.50.

The assumption underlying this work is that families should be able to obtain the kind of housing which they prefer; the conclusion of a large empirical study is that a substantial proportion of middle-class families settle for something less. Persuasive factual information presented in this book gives the argument substantial weight.

Environmental Choice, Human Behavior, and Residential Satisfaction reports on a five-year study following nearly 800 Toronto families through the housing market. Elaborate questionnaires were employed, requiring as much as 90 minutes of a respondent's time and covering just about everything related to housing—the space and facilities of the house itself, the neighbors and neighborhood, social interaction, commuting by both husband and wife, household chores, shopping and recreation patterns—as well as subjective evaluations and expectations. The author and principal architect of the study is Professor of Sociology at the University of Toronto. His large undertaking was aided in various ways by several Canadian government agencies and a large number of private business organizations. Despite some problems it certainly seems these supporters are well repaid by this volume, and the book will be valuable to policymakers, business people, and scholars concerned with housing issues in many parts of the world.

Participant households were identified when they moved into certain preselected dwelling units; these units were first chosen to represent four basic housing types: downtown apartments; downtown single-family houses; suburban apartments; and suburban single-family houses. Units renting for less than $200 a month or selling for less than $35,000 were excluded, as were luxury-type dwellings. Thus, the households surveyed were middle-income, and families who were not married couples in child raising years were excluded. The panel of respondents, then, was not intended to be representative of all households in the Toronto area, nor can it be assumed to represent the market for all the housing types included in the study, a very significant weakness of the study, depending on who might make use of it. In particular, unmarried individuals, newlyweds, and older persons who might generally be thought to make up the primary market for apartments are ignored, as are postchildraising couples who often predominate in central city single-family house neighborhoods. The author does not misrepresent these limitations, but his conclusions fail to call attention to them.

The book presents a wealth of information about the housing choices and house-related behavior of the panel of households; more than four-fifths of the original panel completed all four of the interview documents stretched out over four years. Some of the responses confirm common beliefs about housing choices, apartments are not considered suitable places for raising children, for example. People moving downtown cite convenience of location and easier commuting as primary considerations while homebuyers are principally interested in the social characteristics of their new neighborhoods.

Other responses conflict with the conventional wisdom on housing choices. While apartment dwellers are less likely than homeowners to make friends among their neighbors, they do have friends—mainly found at work—and they do entertain. Wives in downtown apartments were significantly more likely to begin childrearing than wives in other housing situations, and downtown mothers spend as much time ferrying their children about as do suburban women. Husbands who remained in downtown apartments throughout the study period (many such households moved to the suburbs), had the highest average commuting time at the close of the study; suburban wives, on the other hand, lived closest to their work if they were employed, as many were.

All this has to do with housing preferences, because it tends to support the hypothesis that families move toward the housing situations which fit their individual lifestyles. They do not adapt their behavior to the location or housing type in which they find themselves. Urban designers would thus mislead themselves if they expect high-rise buildings to politicize or socialize people who live in them, or expect suburban houses to induce citizenship. Whatever behavior characteristics are associated with a particular housing type, people tend to adopt that housing type because they already have those characteristics.

But that is a weak conclusion. The author of this book presents a much stronger finding, and one which he apparently did not expect. Substantially all the households in his panel expressed

overwhelming preference for the single-family home, downtown if they were already downtown homeowners, and suburban if they were not. Apartment dwellers among this panel were simply marking time until they could afford a house in the suburbs. Among the more interesting observations in this rich collection of responses is the sense of powerlessness of apartment dwellers to correct anything inconvenient about their present residences except by moving—and they move frequently. Home ownership means the ability to fix and change the residence without moving, and without undertaking collective action.

The study was designed to measure "satisfaction" with different housing types—a reasonable goal of sociological research. It unearthed a paradox, because apartment dwellers did not express great dissatisfaction, even though they earnestly aspired to home ownership. The fact was that these renters expected that in due course they would become homeowners; a large proportion did realize this goal during the study. As for the apartment: "It was a very pleasant place to live and suited our life-style at the time" (p. 334). Housing preference, Michelson concludes, is a dynamic concept.

The final chapter of the book is a nearly polemical cry for more single-family houses to be built in downtown areas. It suggests that Michelson may have learned more from his study than he wanted to know, because the research project did not address the economics of urban land uses nor the spectrum of demographic analysis, two matters closely affecting the reasonableness of his final recommendations. Among his households those with less than about $12,000 in income were likely to become renters, primarily because they could not yet afford to purchase a home. Those families tend to regard apartment dwelling as a reasonably satisfactory interim arrangement, but Michelson seems to feel that the compromise of preference is unnecessary. He does not show convincingly that it is unnecessary; the study was not designed with that issue in mind. He suggests that market processes are at fault, but overlooks the fact that housing markets in North America come closer to providing the kind of housing that families really want than do the largely governmental housing suppliers in so many other nations. This is not a major criticism; the last chapter of the book does not diminish the value of the remainder.

WALLACE F. SMITH
University of California
Berkeley

CAROLINE HODGES PERSELL. *Education and Inequality: The Roots and Results of Stratification in America's Schools*. Pp. v, 244. New York: The Free Press, 1977. $12.95.

The relationship of inequality and education has spawned a vast literature. The challenge now is to integrate these research findings into general theory. Toward this end, Persell synthesizes hundreds of studies into an overall conceptual scheme and she achieves an impressive analytical scope and density in her synthesis. Her sustained liberal value position does not undermine her scholarly objectivity.

After elaborating a four-level flow model of inequality and education, Persell moves incisively from the social stratification system (meritocracy) to influenced educational structures (bureaucracy) and educational dynamics (tracking and teacher expectations). Finally, she extensively investigates educational and life outcomes for students, and thus her exploration completes the causal loop in which educational outputs reinforce the ongoing system of structured inequality.

Her chapters on the "structures of dominance" (a neoelitist perspective) and on bureaucratized urban schools provide Persell with a framework for a thorough treatment of IQ testing, tracking, and teacher expectations. The author not only masses the criticism of IQ tests itself, but also of testing process problems. Similarly, she synthesizes the extensive research on the manifold negative consequences of tracking, such as impaired self-concept and opposition student cultures.

Crucial to her proposed stratification theory of educational inequality is evidence related to the genesis and consequences of teacher expectations about student performance. While it is now commonplace to assert that teacher behavior significantly depresses the achievement of lower class children, Persell provides a needed systematic survey of the sources and impact of these teacher expectations. She isolates and documents the range of the variables and points out useful research directions.

Countering research tendencies to dismiss the effects of the school itself, Persell closely explores 12 interacting correlates of school impact upon children, including integration and school climate. Finally, she analyzes how education shores up societal dominance structures through such supporting processes as insulation and work-setting analogue experiences. The vicious circle of stratification is thereby completed. Persell hopes, however, that growing skepticism about meritocracy will erode this self-perpetuating pattern of social inequality.

Writing with a lucid style, Persell fully controls her analytical direction while exploring multiple research nuances. Substantively, her work can serve as a useful handbook, and several chapters are themselves major bibliographical essays. Conceptually, Persell sets a precedent with a macroscopic model of educational inequality, which in itself deserves critical discussion as a descriptive framework, if not as true analytic theory. This is a major contribution to educational sociology.

EDWARD A. DUANE
Michigan State University
East Lansing

C. J. RICHARDSON. *Contemporary Social Mobility*. Pp. i, 340. New York: Nichols Publishing Company, 1977. $17.50.

As early as 1927, Pitrim Sorokin admonished social scientists for "speculating too much about mobility in American life and studying the facts too little." Given that period's belief in Horatio Alger's rags-to-riches ideology, it fell upon sociologists to take Sorokin's critique seriously and proceed with the task of testing a hypothesis that had somehow attained the status of fact. Today, after four decades of diligent research into "the facts" on rates and directions of social mobility, this area has emerged as one of the most thoroughly documented in social science.

Professor Richardson's study of mobility in Great Britain goes beyond previous work in several important ways. The work is based on sample data gathered in two interview surveys—one conducted in 1970 by the Institute of Community Studies (London), which collected data on 1,928 people aged 17 and over in the London Metropolitan Region. From this initial survey, Richardson conducted second interviews with a subsample of 117 men chosen to represent four different conditions relative to their fathers' experience. The groups were selected to be representative of the: (1) upwardly mobile; (2) downwardly mobile; (3) stable middle class (nonmanual); and (4) stable working class (manual).

The rigor of conducting second interviews and the detail afforded by the subjective accounts of the respondents distinguish this study from the start. A second distinguishing feature is its primary focus on the meaning and nature of downward mobility. This is in stark contrast to the main body of research—especially in the United States—which has as its major focus the nature of upward mobility. A third contribution of Richardson's study is the challenge it presents to the conventional wisdom of U.S. sociology regarding the high social psychological costs of movement up or down the social elevator.

With thematic emphasis on the meaning of mobility to those experiencing it, Richardson analyzes his four groups in three major sections. Part one deals with rates, routes, and patterns; part two

presents a discussion of determinants and conditions conducive to mobility—including an excellent review of the theoretical literature on the social psychology of family life, status striving, and entry to careers; part three focuses on consequences, indicators, and subjective perceptions of what it means to be mobile. The final chapter in this section integrates and highlights the key findings and theoretical insights.

Several of the findings are provocative in that they challenge the main materials on mobility to date. First, it is demonstrated that downwardly mobile men do not necessarily view their experience as failure or loss in any sense. This is so because they come from what Richardson calls "risen working class" backgrounds and are merely responding to their parental socialization. The fathers of these men are predominantly upwardly mobile individuals who have remained on the periphery of the middle class and regret not having chosen a skilled trade.

A second important finding suggests that about two-fifths of the socially mobile travel routes other than those paved with educational credentials. Promotion on the job was one of the most common, though it was noted that this relatively unorthodox route rendered the mobile person peripheral to the middle class and prone to maintain a working class identity. The consequence seems to be downward restoration in the second generation.

A third and particularly challenging finding of this study is that: "Although ability and hard work undoubtedly played a significant part in the determination of who is likely to be upwardly mobile, 'luck,' 'chance,' and 'being in the right place at the right time' were also seen by the respondents as being of considerable significance . . ." (p. 280). What this means is that much of social mobility remains unexplained after all of the variables advanced by sociologists and psychologists together have been exhausted.

One final finding is of interest. The stable middle class men in the study expressed sentiments of relative deprivation in terms of both status and income. In what appears to be a notable case of Marxian "false consciousness," this group seems to direct its hostilities toward the working classes who appear to it to be leading a carefree existence. The irony of this finding is that it exists in a nation of continuing aristocracy, and in spite of the objective reality that middle class incomes in Britain continue to widen the gap between the two classes.

Richardson concludes his book with several policy recommendations, such as expanding apprenticeship programs and reducing academic emphasis. His assertion that the working classes are interested only in economic improvements seems debatable, at least, and should not be accepted at face value. Some other limitations to the study are that Professor Richardson admits to the neglect of women, mothers of the respondents, who clearly played a strong role in shaping their sons' attitudes. He also admits to skirting the issue of the consequences (or lack thereof) of social mobility for a more equitable distribution of resources in industrial society, though he does claim to be "sympathetic" to the radical critique of mainstream mobility studies. I would want to know what sympathy means if it is not reflected in the author's work. Finally, the study must be described as exploratory and in need of replication with much larger sample sizes before generalizations can be deemed reliable. The author seems to be straying too far from the data base in claiming that: "This is a study about the experience of social mobility in industrial society" (p. 19). It is, more accurately, a study about the experience of social mobility in the city of London, England in 1970–71. It is, nonetheless, a fine effort and an excellent contribution to the literature on social stratification.

THOMAS J. RICE

Denison University
Granville
Ohio

PAUL C. ROSENBLATT, R. PATRICIA WALSH, and DOUGLAS A. JACKSON.

Grief and Mourning in Cross-cultural Perspective. Pp. 242. New Haven, Conn.: HRAF Press, 1976. $9.00. Paperbound, $4.50.

The literature on death and mourning has, since the end of the Second World War and especially in the past decade, fortunately included some practically helpful and theoretically stimulating publications in the behavioral sciences. For example, psychiatry's clinical contributions—from Erich Lindemann's to Elisabeth Kübler-Ross's—and sociological studies by Anselm Strauss and Peter Marris have combined careful and insightful observation with conceptual enlightenment. Involving a fitting combination of study methods and theory, such writings have strengthened both our personal and institutional resources for meeting the pains of loss through death.

The intent of the book being reviewed is to add to such understanding and to influence social practices. More specifically, in seeking to discover common aspects of response to death as observed in a wide array of cultures, the writers of this book hope ultimately "to get a perspective on what goes on in the United States when a death occurs." To this end, over 80 variables are rated by readers combing ethnographies on 78 societies, and a host of hypotheses are tested by correlations of these ratings. With the best of intentions, the authors tuck into their appendixes a substantial report on their design and methodology and details on their quantitative work. This material is separated into the latter half of their text so that the first half of the book may be read by persons "without specialized education in the behavioral sciences as well as the behavioral science scholar and the scholarly practitioner." A wide audience of this kind is certainly desirable—if simultaneously addressable—for a subject like death and bereavement.

The most illuminating parts of *Grief and Mourning in Cross-cultural Perspective* are the extracts quoted from ethnographic sources, revealing variations in expressions of feelings in response to the death of a spouse, or "tie-breaking" customs, or "final ceremonies." Such illustrative material is reminiscent of the now quarter-century-old parent study to the one under review, Whiting and Child's *Child Training and Personality*, which drew on the Yale cross-cultural files. But unfortunately the quantitative findings of *Grief and Mourning* add little more to our perspectives on death and bereavement than do some of the questions for study. Ought we, for example, arrange for final ceremonies some months or longer after a funeral service in order to mark publicly the termination of the mourning period? Would such a ritual help to ease or shorten the grief felt by mourners?

The problems with this study's quantitative findings reside basically in its assumptions and conceptual underpinnings. The theoretical approach is baldly behavioral; and while it would be of value to discover, cross-culturally, whether burning or burying the possessions of the deceased with the body is helpful because this procedure removes stimuli that affect the grieving process, no useful criterion variable appears among the 87 strictly "objective" behaviors listed for ratings in the Code Book in appendix 7.0. The pool of ratings available for correlations includes only such items as "crying frequency" or "alcohol at final ceremony" or "isolation of widows," but no independent variables that might tell us what the effects on personal adaptation or on community cohesion are when "crying frequency" or "alcohol" or "isolation" are present in varying degrees. Moreover the meanings of "significant correlations" are difficult to interpret. For example, on page 15 in chapter 1 we are told "Sixty-seven of the sixty-nine societies were rated by both raters as having at least frequent crying at death, and fifty-six of these had the highest rating possible—a rating of 'very frequent' by both raters. Only the Balinese, with a rating of 'absent' and their near neighbors, the Javanese, with a rating equivalent to 'crying rarely present,' deviated from the worldwide pattern." Yet on page 106 the authors say,

"It seems clear from the data presented in Chapter 1 that many bereaved persons in other cultures get along with little or no public crying. . ." What really is the meaning of the high ratings for almost all of the studied societies that could be rated on "crying frequency?" One can certainly learn something about the effects of "stimulus changes that reduce evocation of old response patterns," but not the whole story, if we assume that the stimuli reminding the bereaved of a dead partner lie only out there! And though there may be methodological advantages to studying grief and mourning if one "avoids the question of love" because "without independent measures of love, it seems unproductive and misleading to talk about love and bereavement," perhaps no genuine understanding of responses to death is possible without some reflection on—if not calibration of—the emotional ties that bind partners or other kin or close friends to one another.

Grief and Mourning in Cross-cultural Perspective quotes an Amazonian (Jivaro) woman saying, "O my dear husband, why have you left me alone, why have you abandoned me? . . . who will bring me game from the forest or the gaily-coloured birds which you used to shoot with your blowgun and your poisoned arrows? . . ." This book's many generous, nicely identified and classified excerpts of this kind give us a rich sense of the universality of grief and mourning, as well as cultural variants of custom and personal response to death. This kind of contribution is noteworthy.

HENRY S. MAAS
University of British Columbia
Vancouver
Canada

GAMINI SALGADO. *The Elizabethan Underworld*. Pp. 221. Totowa, N.J.: Rowman & Littlefield, 1977. $10.00.

London and its suburbs form the major setting for this survey of literary accounts of Elizabethan England's social misfits and the institutions that segregated them from the rest of society. Among the misfits discussed are thieves, highway robbers, prostitutes, the mentally ill, and a variety of swindlers sometimes posing as peddlers, tinkers, strolling players, or jesters. That is, the kinds of actors who find a place in the sociology of deviance dominate the pages of this book. In addition, gypsies, witches, astrologers, alchemists, and the poor are covered; and while this latter group is absent from contemporary textbooks on deviance, the activities of all, excepting some of the poor, properly belong in a comprehensive study of deviance.

However, the reader should expect a literary approach, heavily dependent on literary sources, rather than a social scientific one. Shakespeare, Ben Jonson, and Dryden exemplify the writers whose works contribute information. The social scientist will understandably suspect that exaggerations allowed by literary license will make the reliability of many conclusions questionable. However, Salgado in many instances clearly states the nature of the work (for example, chronicle, letter, play), thereby allowing some estimate of accuracy to be made. Of course, a knowledge of English literature would be helpful in judging the validity of claims; but readers with a slight acquaintance with English literature, like this reviewer, will wish that the author had conducted a more systematic evaluation of reliability.

It may be, though, that a careful comparison of Salgado's claims with the findings of more recent studies will show sufficient similarities between the two periods to reassure the most skeptical scientist. For instance, the most extensive involvement in deviance in Elizabethan and in contemporary times is found among the lower classes. Then, as now, prostitution is widely condemned but placed in clearly identifiable white houses (Elizabethan age) or red light districts (today). Also, today's functionalist claim that prostitution has a positive effect on the family is reflected in earlier arguments about prostitution in the suburbs having a positive effect on morality in London. And in both periods, it is suggested that some vices flourish because they are profitable to influential persons. It is also noteworthy that

the institutions intended to relieve Elizabethan England of its misfits resemble in significant respects institutions with a similar purpose in our time. Moreover, there is also a similarity between our situation today and the abuses which occurred in Elizabethan institutions and their poor success record.

In addition, the main reason given for the existence of an unusually large population of deviants in the Elizabethan age is not unlike some explanations of recent increases in deviance. Salgado attributes causal significance to the destruction of many traditional relationships by the prohibition against keeping retainers, the closing of the monasteries, and the enclosure of the land. Likewise, social disorganization resulting from industrialization, urbanization, and immigration is sometimes regarded as a major cause of twentieth-century increases in deviance.

Although the book is relatively short, one tires of it before the end. But the careful researcher, interested in responses to deviance and poverty over time, will find valuable insights. Literary sources of data that are often ignored are suggested as fertile fields of explanatory ideas.

ROY L. AUSTIN
The Pennsylvania State University
University Park

ECONOMICS

FRANCINE D. BLAU. *Equal Pay in the Office.* Pp. xi, 158. Lexington, Mass.: Lexington Books, 1977. $15.00.

"In command this afternoon is Captain John Osgood," said the voice of the stewardess as I read Blau's book; "my name is Marty and I'll be serving you in the cabin." Women occupy different positions than men do; Elizabeth Janeway and others have sharpened our perceptions to this fact (and to the verbs we use). While the number of females employed has soared since 1950, their concentration in "female jobs" is not greatly altered. Francine D. Blau, experienced commentator on women and employment, has moved the discussion beyond occupational segregation (the pilot and the stewardess) to an analysis of intraoccupational and establishment-based sex segregation within industries. A model is presented, tested, and shown to be predictive. The key is not so much equal pay for equal work within a firm as between them. For example, "women employed in firms that hire only women into the occupational category earn less . . . than those employed in firms that employ both sexes . . ." (p. 43). Male advantage is more likely to be found among those firms which offer higher wages; they can, in effect, indulge discriminatory preferences (p. 34).

Blau examines the effect of the wage hierarchy among firms within a given labor market upon female workers. Establishments do not, of course, operate in a free market in terms of employment practices—the size and type of firm and the strength of unionization influences the pay scale that individual firms offer. (The stronger unionization within the manufacturing sector, the fewer the women).

The author argues for greater reliance upon "pattern and practice" attacks on sex discrimination than upon individual case appeals; that is, a showing of the absence of women (related to their presence in the appropriate labor force) greater than would occur randomly should trigger action. It is surely easy to agree with the author that enforcement efforts have been largely unsatisfactory to everyone in the past. Multiple agencies are involved, their regulations deriving from a variety of statutes and executive orders. Individuals appealing to the Civil Rights Commission have waited up to seven years for action (p. 197); employers have been inundated by erratic, overlapping, and arbitrary directives. Blau wisely stresses the need for converting the unions to action (after all they need female-dominated working forces) and for full employment. However, her advocacy of the "establishment of a consolidated agency . . . with broad powers to enforce a single anti-bias statute" (p. 108), as called for by the Civil

Rights Commission, appears to ignore some facts of life. When different agencies are involved in any contentious policy area it is not due to sheer human ineptitude but results from the access of differing constituencies to the agencies in question. The impulse to "consolidate," to be neat, should not blind antidiscrimination proponents to the possibility that the newly minted agency would not necessarily be responsive to their demands. Blau's suggestion of an annual review of a sample of firms "with poor performance records" appears to require political resources which the reform elements may not possess. No one—least of all Blau—will underestimate the difficulties of obtaining the elusive "equal pay in the office."

This book should be a priority addition to the sizeable academic library. It carries the discussion of a complex subject to another level of investigation and does so with clarity. It would be appropriate not only for the specialist, but also for the interested reader with some familiarity in the area and for advanced undergraduates.

JANET HANNIGAN
Lafayette College
Easton
Pennsylvania

VERNON M. BRIGGS, JR., WALTER FOGEL, and FRED H. SCHMIDT. *The Chicano Worker.* Pp. ix, 129. Austin: University of Texas Press. 1977. $9.50.

The Chicano Worker surveys the labor market experience, particularly in the Southwest, of workers of Mexican origin. Its main thrust is to ascertain their patterns of employment and unemployment, the kinds of jobs they hold, the ways they enter those jobs, the incomes they earn, and the relative success of efforts to help them surmount their problems.

The authors are conversant with the kind of data required for a study of this kind; they have identified authentic and up-to-date primary sources of information; and they have utilized meaningful ways of tabulating and analyzing it. Best of all, they have expanded their narrative beyond the area of labor economics, linking it to the history and demography of the Spanish origin population in the Southwest; that population's cultural patterns; international and rural-city migration; American immigration policies; Chicano educational attainment; the goals and tactics of Hispanic interest groups and militants; and public responses to their needs. These rich and varied background materials provide the reader with a depth of understanding of this disadvantaged ethnic group that an outline of their labor experience alone could not possibly offer.

Cross-cultural understanding also enables the authors to develop realistic recommendations for Chicano workers' "public policy needs." They graciously avoid lecturing educators on how to perform their jobs, suggesting that Chicanos will achieve greater academic success only when their educational attainments are recognized by potential employers. The authors also recommend that equal opportunity officials concentrate on ascertaining whether job tests are related to job skills. Their most emphatic recommendations relate to immigration and group culture. They advocate a tight border policy: the flow of illegal immigrants undercuts efforts to improve the lot of resident Mexican-Americans, flooding the labor market with potential workers accustomed to a precarious standard of living. Finally, they request extensive research on the Chicano culture, so that government aid programs may be shaped to match the group's characteristics. Behind the last concept lies the experiences of those whose offers of help were not appreciated. Often barrio leaders were convinced that external assistance would entail loss of self-determination, and the Chicano masses hesitated to accept aid from formal organizations, perceiving it as Anglo attempts to manipulate them. The authors do not wish to convert government officials into sociologists; they are simply trying to avoid counterproductive administrative strategy.

Their concern for Mexican heritage disadvantaged groups is genuine. The reader may well ask, however, whether they are equally sensitive to the group's American-born middle and upper classes. In northern New Mexico, for example, the latter have attempted to disassociate themselves from recent immigrants. Yet in this volume they will find themselves bracketed with "Chicanos."

In summary, the volume fills a genuine need, synthesizing a large body of current census data on labor economics with insights into typical Chicano reactions to labor market conditions.

FREDERICK SHAW
Board of Education
New York City

STEPHEN P. DRESCH, AN-LOH LIN, and DAVID K. STOUT. *Substituting a Value-Added Tax for the Corporate Income Tax.* Pp. vii, 216. Cambridge, Mass.: Ballinger, 1977. No price.

In this monograph, the authors study the economic effects resulting from the substitution of a consumption-type value-added tax (VAT) for the existing federal and state corporation income taxes (CIT). The discussion during the 1970s at the federal level concerning the possibility of such a substitution in itself would seem to justify the research. Moreover, the book may be useful, in a methodological sense, to the public sector economist who has observed the recent trend toward general equilibrium tax incidence analysis. However, what may prove valuable in this regard to the economist could prove tedious to the general reader who is not familar with the economics of public finance.

The research effort is carefully structured with its limitations clearly set forth. Its well-defined objectives are analyzed in a competent fashion. Of course, in testing only the "first-round effects" of the tax substitution (by industry and by final demand component), the study necessarily stops short of a pure general equilibrium methodology. Nonetheless, by entering the realm of relative price effects, it does move some distance away from the traditional partial equilibrium position. Moreover, in selecting an input-output model and data base, an appropriate mechanism has been chosen for extending the analysis beyond pure partial equilibrium effects.

The specific framework of the study involves a testing of the effects of the substitution of VAT for CIT under conditions of both complete (100 percent) substitution and conditions of lesser proportions. These effects are integrated with the effects of several different CIT short-run forward tax shifting parameters, ranging from complete shifting to the absence of shifting. Meanwhile, the VAT is assumed to be fully shifted forward. After chapter 1 provides a broad overview of the study, the second chapter develops the input-output model which is used to test the relative price and profit effects of the tax substitution. The model is then applied to 1969 data in chapter 3 and the major results are described. The remaining four chapters consider some of the income distribution, investment, international trade, regional, intergovernmental, and other effects of the substitution.

Not surprisingly, the VAT is found to be superior to the CIT in terms of allocational neutrality, but not in relationship to distributional and other relevant criteria. Moreover, one clear-cut point emerges from the study; namely, that the substitution of one major tax for another cannot be accomplished without a myriad of complex economic effects resulting.

BERNARD P. HERBER
University of Arizona
Tucson

FRED HIRSCH. *Social Limits to Growth*. Pp. v, 208. Cambridge, Mass.: Harvard University Press, 1976. $10.00.

By the time this number of The ANNALS appears, *Social Limits to Growth* may already be at the center of economic discussion in this country. It will almost certainly intrude on economists' thinking for some time to come. So fundamentally and persuasively does it challenge the truisms and pieties of both right and left that even those who reject its fundamental theses are going to be obliged to justify their rejection by taking considerable note of it. Assuming this, and given the fact that this is a very difficult book (not for speed readers), for Fred Hirsch elaborates these difficult ideas in 200 pages of spare if not Galbraithian prose, it would be a ludicrous effort to attempt here anything more than a statement of the general thesis.

Professor Hirsch sets himself three questions:

—why has economic advance become and remained such a compelling goal when its fruits are disappointing to those who achieve them?;

—why is society so concerned with the problem of distribution when it is clear that most people can improve their lot only through general growth?;

—why does the trend toward centralization dominate economic life while in other realms, such as aesthetics and sexual standards, individual freedom expands and is relentlessly extolled?

Unlike theorists of the physical limits to growth (whose case he regards as "not proven"), Professor Hirsch answers that the problem is social. He points out that as more people are able to afford certain goods previously seen as goals (for example, automobiles or, in our own time and land, a summer place), these are less satisfying. There is none of the pleasure in barrelling down (or sitting hare still) on the freeway that once accompanied motoring alone in the countryside in a Stutz Bearcat. Likewise, the more people able to afford summer cottages, the more crowded becomes "the country" in which they must be built, and the whole point of those goods is lost. In a word, growth is not the philosopher's stone of the good society for all, but destructive of it.

Other "positional goods" (if nothing else, Professor Hirsch has added a valuable concept and its label to economic discussion), include those which are scarce and therefore, by their very nature, unobtainable by the mass and, for that reason, especially coveted: the rewards of being a U.S. Senator (hurry, hurry! only 100 available!); authentic antiques; the mere foremanship of the shop. Then Professor Hirsch deals with that other element of economy, about which exponents of growth must forget in order to sleep in peace, the fact that the individual's wealth is very much valued, not so much in terms of what it is absolutely worth, but in terms of how it compares to that of others.

Many of his ideas are recognizable as the inspiration of others such as J.K. Galbraith, Lewis Mumford, and Sir Roy Harrod. But Fred Hirsch takes his derivations to greater depths, and he has synthesized them into a comprehensive scheme which does explain the profound disappointments and (the word must be used) the contradictions of advanced consumer society. This review, to emphasize the point, barely examines two or three loops of an intricately woven tapestry.

What is to be done? Here, unhappily, the author strikes off in several directions, never pushing on to the end. He dawdles along the way with moral suasion but is too realistic a thinker to take it seriously. He writes of the necessity of people acting in a social way while thinking they are serving their individual self-interests in the old competitive sense, and then he recoils at the idea of thought control and condemns it. The book is a brilliant explanation. But the seeker after solutions will close it disconsolate.

JOSEPH R. CONLIN
California State University
Chico

HARRY MAGDOFF and PAUL M. SWEEZY. *The End of Prosperity: The American Economy in the 1970s.* New York: Monthly Review Press, 1977. Pp. vii, 136. $7.95.

This short book consists of ten essays which originally appeared in the *Monthly Review* between 1973 and early 1977. Devotees of the *Monthly Review* will already have them in their files. Nonreaders of the Magdoff-Sweezy journal will expect to find apocalyptic Marxist pronouncements, and they will not be disappointed.

The essays deal with aspects of the economic crisis of the 1970s: the depreciation of the dollar on foreign exchange markets, stagflation, the shaky financial structure of banks and corporations, the extent of unemployment (estimated by the authors to be at least 13.6 percent of the labor force in early 1975 rather than the official 8.9 percent rate), and the ineffectiveness of Keynesian economic policy. The economic malaise is explained by the Marxist theory of capitalist development: the attempt by monopoly capitalists to maximize surplus value leads to excessive purchasing power in the capitalist class, to the squeezing of the working class, and to the expansion of the reserve army of the unemployed. Keynesian fiscal and monetary remedies for stagnation are futile because they do not resolve the capitalist contradictions inherent in production for profit rather than for use. In the absence of major external stimuli such as war or overwhelming innovations like the nineteenth-century railroad or the twentieth-century automobile, Magdoff and Sweezy forecast continued stagnation. They also forecast a turn to "state capitalism" (apparently beginning with government loans to business), which for some reason will be backed by brutality. The only way out of the stagnation problem is for the working class to be stirred to action and to bring about the revolutionary socialism which is the only hope of a decent existence.

Nobody disagrees that the state of the economy is worrying: Unemployment was around 7 percent at mid-1977; inflation was at an 8.9 percent annual rate in the first half of 1977; the Dow-Jones is down to 1975 levels. What Marxists call bourgeois economics "still has its work cut out for it to come up with a solution to stagflation," as Paul Samuelson put it in the tenth (1976) edition of his *Economics* (p. 820). Will the bourgeois economist find the solution in Magdoff and Sweezy? To him, the Marxist labor theory of value is an ancient relic of by-gone economics and the "whole of *Capital* a long drawn-out *petitio principii*" in its reliance on surplus value, while Marxist social dogma is a "narrow prison of the mind." He will not be persuaded otherwise by this book.

CHARLES E. STALEY
State University of New York
Stony Brook

JACK M. NILLES et al. *The Telecommunications-Transportation Tradeoff: Options for Tomorrow.* Pp. v, 196. New York: Wiley, 1976. $22.95.

For a number of years now, we have been regaled by stories of the revolution in telecommunications and the impact that it will have on our lives. One of the more intriguing suggestions that has been made is the possibility of a telecommunications-transportation tradeoff. Could we substitute telecommunications for transportation in any meaningful way and thus cut down on our use of scarce petroleum products? Until the appearance of this volume, this question, as well as many other interesting ones raised by the observers of the telecommunication revolution, have remained pure speculation.

This book is a documentation of a research program begun in 1973 by an interdisciplinary research team at the University of California with the help of the National Science Foundation. It investigates the possibilities not only of substituting telecommunications for some portion of urban commuter traffic, but also "of the societal implications of widespread adoption of the substitutes" (p. v). The specific case used by the authors is a regional office of a major insurance company located in the central business district of Los Angeles.

After the authors investigate the structure of the insurance company in question and its requirements, especially with respect to personnel, they offer a choice of telecommunications systems which will permit the company to achieve its objective of decentralization in order to take advantage of a desirable work force. A cost-benefit analysis for different types of decentralization is offered as well as an investigation into some of the possible side effects of such a major reorganization, including the ef-fect of a shift to telecommunications by the firm's clerical workers and resistance to innovation. After a survey of a number of other possible tradeoffs and direct and indirect impacts, including problems of security and the effects of widespread use of telecommunications on urban development, the authors discuss the policy implications and offer a number of recommendations for governmental action. The book is completed with appendices containing a survey of related research, a questionnaire used to determine attitudes towards telecommunications and its possible uses, and an index.

The ultimate objective of the book, according to the authors, is "to develop in readers with many different backgrounds an appreciation of some of the alternatives to the developments in contemporary society made possible by technologies that are here, or almost here, today" (p. v). It is the reviewer's opinion that the authors have gone a long way toward meeting that objective. It is a readable book and one that should have a wide circulation.

GEORGE A. CODDING, JR.
University of Colorado
Boulder

WILLIAM WISELEY. *A Tool of Power: The Political History of Money.* Pp. vii, 401. New York: Wiley, 1977. $16.95.

Despite its broad title, Mr. Wiseley's book in essence is a crisis-by-crisis account of how the relationship of gold to the leading monies of the world was progressively, and very likely permanently, broken between the heyday of the international gold standard before World War I and the early 1970s. Two background chapters, comprising a sixth of the text, deal with, respectively, the development of money from ancient times to 1815, and the rise of the international gold standard during the nineteenth century. The remaining ten chapters discuss the breakdown of the gold standard in World War I, the largely futile attempts to reestablish it after the war, the emergence of the gold exchange standard, in which gold continued to serve as money for central bankers but not for ordinary people, the monetary strains of the Great Depression and World War II, the post-World War II Bretton Woods system of fixed exchange rates, the fundamental shift from worldwide dollar shortage to dollar surplus in the 1950s, and finally the abandonment of gold as a monetary base along with the emergence of floating or flexible exchange rates among the world's major paper monies between 1967 and 1973.

Wiseley's detailed account of these events and developments is quite effective in bringing out the personal qualities and beliefs of the major world figures involved, their politico-economic infighting and intrigues, and their ultimate recognition that the force of circumstances in the world economy was more controlling of their actions than a phenomenon they could control. To the extent that the book has any limitations in achieving its purpose, they are sins of omission rather than commission. What I miss in Wiseley's treatment is a discussion of the fundamental drawbacks of any commodity (e.g. gold) standard of money, and an evaluation of the prospects we face now that paper standards and flexible exchange rates have replaced gold. The gold standard was more myth than operating system; it worked only when people did not take very seriously its offer to convert paper money into gold. In principle the paper system of today is more rational. But will it continue to work in practice? That will hinge on whether and how soon the controllers of paper money learn, to paraphrase Wiseley (p. 75), that the real value or purchasing power of a currency is not related in any way to its gold backing or "cover," but rather depends on the quantity of circulation.

RICHARD SYLLA
North Carolina State University
Raleigh

OTHER BOOKS

ALLSWANG, JOHN M. *Bosses, Machines, and Urban Voters: An American Symbiosis.* Pp. vii, 157. Port Washington, N.Y.: Kennikat Press, 1977. $9.95. Paperbound, $5.95.

AMUNDSEN, KIRSTEN. *A New Look at the Silenced Majority: Women and American Democracy.* Pp. ix, 172. Englewood Cliffs, N.J.: Prentice-Hall, 1977. $8.95. Paperbound, $3.95.

ARNOLD, GUY and RUTH WEISS. *Strategic Highways of Africa.* Pp. 178. New York: St. Martin's Press, 1977. $12.95.

The Atlantic Council Working Group on the United Nations. The Future of the UN: A Strategy for Like-Minded Nations. Pp. 58. Boulder, Colo.: Westview Press, 1977. $3.95. Paperbound.

BANKS, ARTHUR S., ed. *Political Handbook of the World: 1977.* Pp. xi, 604. New York: McGraw-Hill, 1977. $24.95.

BARBER, JAMES DAVID. *The Presidential Character: Predicting Performance in the White House.* 2nd ed. Pp. v, 576. Englewood Cliffs, N.J.: Prentice-Hall, 1977. $7.50. Paperbound.

BARNDS, WILLIAM J. ed. *China and America: The Search for A New Relationship.* Pp. ix, 254. New York: New York University Press, 1977. $15.00.

BECK, EMILY MORISON, ed. *Sailor Historian: The Best of Samuel Eliot Morison.* Pp. viii, 431. Boston, Mass.: Houghton Mifflin, 1977. $15.00.

BELL, JOHN D. *Peasants in Power: Alexander Stamboliski and the Bulgarian Agrarian National Union, 1899–1923.* Pp. vii, 271. Princeton, N.J.: Princeton University Press, 1977. $16.50.

BENTLEY, MICHAEL. *The Liberal Mind 1914–1929.* Pp. viii, 279. New York: Cambridge University Press, 1977. $19.95.

BHAGWATI, JAGDISH N., ed. *The New International Economic Order: The North-South Debate.* Pp. vii, 390. Littleton, Mass.: MIT Press, 1977. $9.95. Paperbound.

BIALER, SEWERYN and SOPHIA SLUZAR, eds. *Radicalism in the Contemporary Age: Sources of Contemporary Radicalism,* vol. 1. Pp. xi, 396. Boulder, Colo.: Westview Press, 1977. $15.00.

BIRNBAUM, NORMAN, ed. *Beyond the Crisis.* Pp. v, 233. New York: Oxford University Press, 1977. $11.95. Paperbound, $5.95.

BLACKMER, DONALD L. M. and SIDNEY TARROW, eds. *Communism in Italy and France.* Pp. v, 651. Princeton, N.J.: Princeton University Press, 1977. $9.75. Paperbound.

BLAKE, DAVID H. and ROBERT E. DRISCOLL. *The Social and Economic Impacts of Transnational Corporations: Case Studies of the U.S. Paper Industry in Brazil.* Pp. iii, 133. New York: UNIPUB, 1977. $5.50. Paperbound.

BLOCK, RICHARD. *Violent Crime.* Pp. v, 121.

Lexington, Mass.: Lexington Books, 1977. $13.00.

BLUMENTHAL, ARTHUR L. *The Process of Cognition.* Pp. iii, 230. Englewood Cliffs, N.J.: Prentice-Hall, 1977. $9.95.

BONNER, STANLEY F. *Education in Ancient Rome.* Pp. 416. Berkeley: University of California Press, 1977. $18.50. Paperbound, $10.95.

BRIGGS, ASA and JOHN SAVILLE, eds. *Essays in Labour History 1918–1939.* Pp. 292. Hamden, Conn.: Archon Books, 1977. $15.00.

BRODEUR, PAUL. *The Zapping of America: Microwaves, Their Deadly Risk and the Cover-Up.* Pp. 343. New York: W. W. Norton, 1977. $11.95.

BROWN, ARCHIE and JACK GRAY, eds. *Political Culture and Political Change in Communist States.* Pp. vii, 286. New York: Holmes & Meier, 1977. $24.00.

BUNDY, WILLIAM P., ed. *Two Hundred Years of American Foreign Policy.* Pp. v, 251. New York: New York University Press, 1977. $15.00.

BURCHETT, WILFRED and DEREK ROEBUCK. *The Whores of War: Mercenaries Today.* Pp. 240. New York: Penguin Books, 1977. $2.95. Paperbound.

BUTLIN, R. A., ed. *The Development of the Irish Town.* Pp. 144. Totowa, N.J.: Rowman & Littlefield, 1977. $13.50.

CARELESS, ANTHONY. *Initiative and Response: The Adaptation of Canadian Federalism to Regional Economic Development.* Pp. ix, 244. Quebec: McGill-Queen's University Press, 1977. $6.00. Paperbound.

CARROLL, PETER N. and DAVID W. NOBLE. *The Free and the Unfree: A New History of the United States.* Pp. 448. New York: Penguin Books, 1977. $4.95. Paperbound.

CEDERBLOM, J. B. and WILLIAM L. BLIZEK, eds. *Justice and Punishment.* Pp. 160. Cambridge, Mass.: Ballinger, 1977. $16.50.

CHALLINOR, RAYMOND. *The Origins of British Bolshevism.* Pp. 291. Totowa, N.J.: Rowman & Littlefield, 1977. $16.00.

CHANG, YUNSHIK, and PETER J. DONALDSON. *Population Change in the Pacific Region.* Pp. 206. Vancouver, B.C.: Pacific Science Association, 1976. $4.00. Paperbound.

CLARK, MARTIN. *Antonio Gramsci and the Revolution that Failed.* Pp. viii, 255. New Haven, Conn.: Yale University Press, 1977. $15.00.

COHEN, STEPHEN S. *Modern Capitalist Planning: The French Model.* Pp. 351. Berkeley: University of California Press, 1977. $17.50. Paperbound, $4.85.

COLEMAN, JAMES S. et al. *Parents, Teachers, and Children.* Pp. v, 336. San Francisco, Calif.: Institute for Contemporary Studies, 1977. $5.95. Paperbound.

CONNELL, JOHN and MICHAEL LIPTON. *Assessing Village Labour Situations in Developing Countries.* Pp. 180. New York: Oxford University Press, 1977. $6.25.

COOK, CHRIS et al. *Sources in British Political History 1900–1951: A Guide to the Private Papers of Members of Parliament: A–K,* vol. 3. Pp. 281. New York: St. Martin's Press, 1977. $17.95.

COOK, CHRIS et al. *Sources in British Political History 1900–1951: A Guide to the Private Papers of Members of Parliament: L–Z,* vol. 4. Pp. 272. New York: St. Martin's Press, 1977. $17.95.

COOLING, BENJAMIN FRANKLIN. ed. *War Business, and American Society: Historical Perspectives on the Military-Industrial Complex.* Pp. 205. Port Washington, N.Y.: Kennikat Press, 1977. $12.50.

COOX, ALVIN D. *The Anatomy of A Small War: The Soviet-Japanese Struggle for Changkufeng/Khasan, 1938.* Pp. xxvi, 409. Westport, Conn.: Greenwood Press, 1977. $25.00.

COSER, LEWIS A. *Masters of Sociological Thought: Ideas in Historical and Social Context.* 2nd ed. Pp. 611. New York: Harcourt Brace Jovanovich, 1977. $13.95.

CYR, ARTHUR. *Liberal Party Politics in Britain.* Pp. 318. New Brunswick, N.J.: Transaction Books, 1977. $12.95.

DALLIN, ALEXANDER, ed. *The Twenty-Fifth Congress of the CPSU: Assessment and Context.* Pp. vii, 127. Stanford, Calif.: Hoover Institution Press, 1977. $5.95. Paperbound.

DASGUPTA, BIPLAB. *Village Society and Labour Use.* Pp. i, 229. New York: Oxford University Press, 1977. $6.95.

DEETZ, JAMES. *In Small Things Forgotten: The Archeology of Early American Life.* Pp. 184. New York: Anchor Press, $2.50. Paperbound.

DELUCA, ANTHONY J. *Freud and Future Religious Experience.* Pp. xiii, 263. Totowa, N.J.: Littlefield, Adams, 1977. $4.95. Paperbound.

DE SILVA, K. M. ed. *Sri Landa: A Survey.* Pp. v, 496. Honolulu: University Press of Hawaii, 1977. $22.50.

DOMES, JÜRGEN. *China After the Cultural Revolution: Politics Between Two Party Congresses.* Pp. 293. Berkeley: University of California Press, 1977. $15.00.

DUNG, VAN TIEN. *Our Great Spring Victory: An Account of the Liberation of South*

Vietnam. Pp. v, 275. New York: Monthly Review Press, 1977. $15.00.

DWYER, T. RYLE. *Irish Neutrality and the U.S.A. 1939–47.* Pp. ix, 241. Totowa, N.J.: Rowman & Littlefield, 1977. $16.50.

EAMES, EDWIN and JUDITH GRANICH GOODE. *Anthropology of the City: An Introduction to Urban Anthropology.* Pp. iii, 344. Englewood Cliffs, N.J.: Prentice-Hall, 1977. $8.95. Paperbound.

EBNER, MICHAEL H. and EUGENE M. TOBIN, eds. *The Age of Urban Reform: New Perspectives on the Progressive Era.* Pp. vii, 213. Port Washington, N.Y.: Kennikat Press, 1977. $12.95. Paperbound, $7.95.

ENDICOTT, JOHN E. and ROY W. SAFFORD, JR., eds. *American Defense Policy.* 4th ed. Pp. v, 626. Baltimore, Md.: Johns Hopkins University Press, 1977. $22.50. Paperbound, $7.95.

ENGLISH, JANE, ed. *Sex Equality.* Pp. iii, 250. Englewood Cliffs, N.J.: Prentice-Hall, 1977. $11.95. Paperbound, $6.50.

EZELL, MACEL D. *Unequivocal Americanism: Right-Wing Novels in the Cold War Era.* Pp. v, 152. Metuchen, N.J.: Scarecrow Press, 1977. $6.50.

FAWDRY, MARQUERITE. *Chinese Childhood: A Miscellany of Mythology, Folklore, Fact and Fable.* Pp. 192. Woodbury, N.Y.: Barron's Educational Series, 1977. $10.95.

FEIN, HELEN. *Imperial Crime and Punishment: The Massacre at Jallianwala Bagh and British Judgment, 1919–1920.* Pp. x, 250. Honolulu: University Press of Hawaii, 1977. $12.00.

FELDSTEIN, PAUL J. *Health Associations and the Demand for Legislation: The Political Economy of Health.* Pp. 336. Cambridge, Mass.: Ballinger, 1977. $18.00.

FITZGERALD, C. P. *Mao Tse-Tung and China.* Pp. 197. New York: Penguin Books, 1977. $2.50. Paperbound.

Foreign Relations of the United States: Western Europe, 1950. Vol. III. Pp. 1839. Washington, D.C.: U.S. Government Printing Office, 1977. No price.

FRIEDEN, BERNARD J. and MARSHALL KAPLAN. *The Politics of Neglect: Urban Aid from Model Cities to Revenue Sharing.* Pp. ix, 295. Cambridge, Mass. MIT Press, 1977. $4.95. Paperbound.

FRY, MICHAEL G. *Lloyd George and Foreign Policy: The Education of a Statesman: 1890–1916,* vol. I. Pp. ix, 314. Quebec: McGill-Queen's University Press, 1977. $18.50.

GARVEY, AMY JACQUES and E. U. ESSIEN-UDOM, eds. *More Philosophy and Opinions of Marcus Garvey.* Vol. 3. Pp. vii, 248.

Totowa, N.J.: Frank Cass, 1977. $22.50. Paperbound, $8.95.

GARVEY, AMY, ed. *The Philosophy and Opinions of Marcus Garvey.* Pp. vii, 412. Totowa, N.J.: Frank Cass, 1977. $25.00. Paperbound, $9.50.

GARVEY, GERALD. *Nuclear Power and Social Planning.* Pp. vii, 159. Lexington, Mass.: Lexington Books, 1977. $15.00.

GEERTZ, CLIFFORD. *The Interpretation of Cultures.* Pp. vii, 470. New York: Basic Books, 1977. $5.95. Paperbound.

GLASSCOTE, RAYMOND, JON E. GUDEMAN, and DONALD MILES. *Creative Mental Health Services for the Elderly.* Pp. iii, 190. Washington, D.C.: American Psychiatric and Mental Health Association, 1977. No price.

GOLEMBIEWSKI, ROBERT T. *Public Administration As a Developing Discipline.* Part 2: *Organization Development As One of a Future Family of Miniparadigms.* Pp. v, 209. New York: Marcel Dekker, 1977. $16.75.

GOLEMBIEWSKI, ROBERT T. *Public Administration As a Developing Discipline.* Part 1: *Perspectives on Past and Present.* Pp. v, 246. New York: Marcel Dekker, 1977. $16.75.

GRANT, WYN and DAVID MARSH. *The Confederation of British Industry.* Pp. vii, 226. New York: Holmes and Meier, 1977. $16.50.

GUTKIND, PETER and PETER WATERMAN, eds. *African Social Studies: A Radical Reader.* Pp. ix, 481. New York: Monthly Review Press, 1977. $17.50.

GUY, J. A. *The Cardinal's Court: The Impact of Thomas Wolsey in Star Chamber.* Pp. vi, 191. Totowa, N.J.: Rowman & Littlefield, 1977. $15.00.

HAMMERMESH, DANIEL S. *Jobless Pay and the Economy.* Pp. v, 114. Baltimore, Md. Johns Hopkins University Press, 1977. $8.50. Paperbound, $3.25.

HARMS, L. S., JIM RICHSTAD, and KATHLEEN A. KIE, eds. *Right to Communicate: Collected Papers.* Pp. vii, 136. Honolulu: University Press of Hawaii, 1977. $5.00. Paperbound.

HAWKE, SHARRYL and DAVID KNOX. *One Child by Choice.* Pp. ix, 233. Englewood Cliffs, N.J.: Prentice-Hall, 1977. $8.95. Paperbound, $3.95.

HAYES, DENIS. *Rays of Hope: The Transition to A Post-Petroleum World.* Pp. 240. New York: W.W. Norton, 1977. $3.95. Paperbound.

HERRICK, JAMES E. *Theory Building for Basic Institutional Change.* Pp. iii, 105. San Francisco, Calif.: R. & E. Research Associates, 1977. $9.00. Paperbound.

HIGLEY, JOHN, G., LOWELL FIELD, and KNUT GROHOLT. *Elite Structure and Ideology: A Theory with Application to Norway.* Pp. vi, 367. New York: Columbia University Press, 1977. $17.50.

HINTON, DAVID A. *Alfred's Kingdom: Wessex and the South 800–1500.* Pp. v, 228. Totowa, N.J.: Rowman & Littlefield, 1977. $10.75.

HIRO, DILIP. *Inside India Today.* Pp. ix, 338. New York: Monthly Review Press, 1977. $15.00.

HIRSCH, HERBERT and ARMANDO GUTIERREZ. *Learning to be Militant: Ethnic Identity and the Development of Political Militance in a Chicano Community.* Pp. iii, 145. San Francisco, Calif.: R. & E. Research Associates, 1977. $10.00. Paperbound.

HOLLIS, MARTIN. *Models of Man: Philosophical Thoughts on Social Action.* Pp. vii, 195. New York: Cambridge University Press, 1977. $4.95. Paperbound.

HOWES, ROBERT C. *The Confession of Mikhail Bakunin.* Pp. 200. Ithaca, N.Y.: Cornell University Press, 1977. $12.50.

IDZERDA, STANLEY J., ed. *Lafayette in the Age of the American Revolution: Selected Letters and Papers 1776–1790.* Vol. 1. Ithaca, N.Y.: Cornell University Press, 1977. $18.50.

INBAR, MICHAEL and CHAIM ADLER. *Ethnic Integration in Israel: A Comparative Case Study of Moroccan Brothers Who Settled in France and in Israel.* Pp. 144. New Brunswick, N.J.: Transaction Books, 1977. $16.95.

JACKSON, CURTIS E. and MARCIA J. GALLI. *A History of the Bureau of Indian Affairs and its Activities among Indians.* Pp. iii, 162. San Francisco, Calif.: R. & E. Research Associates, 1977. $12.00. Paperbound.

JALÉE, PIERRE. *How Capitalism Works.* Pp. 128. New York: Monthly Review Press, 1977. $3.95. Paperbound.

JOHNSON, RICH. *The Central Arizona Project, 1918–1968.* Pp. 242. Tucson: University of Arizona Press, 1977. $11.50. Paperbound, $5.95.

KASPERSON, ROGER E. and JEANNE X. KASPERSON, eds. *Water Re-Use and the Cities.* Pp. xi, 238. Hanover, N.H.: University Press of New England, 1977. No price.

KELLEY, DONALD R., ed. *The Energy Crisis and the Environment: An International Perspective.* Pp. v, 245. New York: Praeger, 1977. No price.

KING, ANTHONY. *Britain Says Yes: The 1975 Referendum on the Common Market.* Pp. 153. Washington, D.C.: American Enterprise Institute for Public Policy Research, 1977. $3.75. Paperbound.

KIRSTEIN, PETER N. *Anglo Over Bracero: A History of the Mexican Worker in the United States from Roosevelt to Nixon.* Pp. iii, 113. San Francisco, Calif.: R. & E. Research Associates, 1977. $9.00. Paperbound.

KORBEL, JOSEF. *Twentieth Century Czechoslovakia.* Pp. vii, 346. New York: Columbia University Press, 1977. $14.95.

KRAMER, FRED A. *Perspectives on Public Bureaucracy.* 2nd ed. Pp. 220. Englewood Cliffs, N.J.: Prentice-Hall, 1977. $5.95. Paperbound.

KWARTLER, RICHARD, ed. *Behind Bars: Prisons in America.* Pp. x, 178. New York: Random House, 1977. $3.95. Paperbound.

LAISTNER, M. L. W. *The Greater Roman Historians.* Pp. 203. Berkeley: University of California Press, 1977. $8.75.

LASKY, VICTOR. *J.F.K. The Man and the Myth.* Pp. 883. New York: Dell, 1977. $2.75. Paperbound.

LASSWELL, HAROLD D. *Psychopathology and Politics.* New Introduction by Fred I. Greenstein. Pp. vii, 339. Chicago: University of Chicago Press, 1977. $5.95. Paperbound.

LEVINE, ARNOLD J. *Alienation in the Metropolis.* Pp. iii, 111. San Francisco, Calif.: R. & E. Research Associates, 1977. $9.00. Paperbound.

LEVITAN, SAR A. and RICHARD S. BELOUS. *Shorter Hours, Shorter Weeks: Spreading the Work to Reduce Unemployment.* Pp. v, 94. Baltimore, Md.: Johns Hopkins University Press, 1977. $8.50. Paperbound, $3.25.

LEWIS, EUGENE. *American Politics in a Bureaucratic Age: Citizens, Constituents, Clients and Victims.* Pp. v, 182. Cambridge, Mass.: Winthrop, 1977. $10.00. Paperbound, $5.95.

LINDBORG, KRISTINA and CARLOS J. OVANDO. *Five Mexican-American Women in Transition: A Case Study of Migrants in the Midwest.* Pp. iii, 111. San Francisco, Calif.: R & E Research Associates, 1977. $8.00. Paperbound.

LOSONCY, LEWIS E. *Turning People On: How to Be An Encouraging Person.* Pp. vii, 150. Englewood Cliffs, N.J.: Prentice-Hall, 1977. $8.95. Paperbound, $3.95.

LOWE, ADOLPH. *On Economic Knowledge: Toward A Science of Political Economics.* Enlarged Edition. Pp. v, 351. White Plains, N.Y.: M.E. Sharpe, 1977. $20.00.

MACAVOY, PAUL W., ed. *Deregulation of Cable Television.* Pp. 169. Washington, D.C.: American Enterprise Institute for

Public Policy Research, 1977. $3.75. Paperbound.

MANDEL, ERNEST. *Karl Marx: Capital*. Vol. 1. Pp. 1141. New York: Vintage Books, 1977. $7.95. Paperbound.

MANSFIELD, EDWIN, ed. *Economics: Readings, Issues, and Cases*. 2nd ed. Pp. xvii, 473. New York: W.W. Norton, 1977. No price.

MATRAS, JUDAH. *Introduction to Population: A Sociological Approach*. Pp. iii, 452. Englewood Cliffs, N.J.: Prentice-Hall, 1977. $14.95.

MCCLELLAND, PETER D., ed. *Macro-Economics 1977: Readings on Contemporary Issues*. Pp. 224. Ithaca, N.Y.: Cornell University Press, 1977. $5.95. Paperbound.

MEAD, SIDNEY E. *The Old Religion in the Brave New World: Reflections on the Relation Between Christendom and the Republic*. Pp. 201. Berkeley: University of California Press. 1977. $10.00.

MEAD, WALTER J., GEORGE W. ROGERS, and RUFUS Z. SMITH. *Transporting Natural Gas From the Arctic: The Alternative Systems*. Pp. 111. Washington, D.C.: American Enterprise Institute for Public Policy Research, 1977. $3.25. Paperbound.

MEINECKE, FRIEDRICH. *The Age of German Liberation 1795–1815*. Pp. 154. Berkeley: University of California Press, 1977. $12.50. Paperbound, $2.45.

MENNINGER, KARL. *Numbe Words and Number Symbols*. Pp. xiii, 480. Cambridge, Mass.: MIT Press, 1977. $9.95.

MIDDLETON, LUCY, ed. *Women in the Labour Movement*. Pp. 221. Totowa, N.J.: Rowman & Littlefield, 1977. $13.50.

MILLETT, RICARDO A. *Examination of "Widespread Citizen Participation" in the Model Cities Program and the Demands of Ethnic Minorities for a Greater Decision Making Role in American Cities*. Pp. iii, 151. San Francisco, Calif.: R & E Research Associates, 1977. $8.00. Paperbound.

MINERS, N. J. *The Government and Politics of Hong Kong*. Pp. vii, 333. New York: Oxford University Press, 1977. $13.75. Paperbound.

MISCHEL, THEODORE, ed. *The Self: Psychological and Philosophical Issues*. Pp. ix, 359. Totowa, N.J.: Rowman & Littlefield, 1977. $17.50.

MORAWSKA, EWA T. *The Maintenance of Ethnicity: Case Study of the Polish-American Community in Greater Boston*. Pp. iii, 161. San Francisco, Calif.: R. & E. Research Associates, 1977. $9.00. Paperbound.

MORLEY, FELIX, ed. *Essays on Individuality*. Pp. 380. Indianapolis, Ind.: Liberty Press, 1977. $8.00.

NAGAI, YŌNOSUKE and AKIRA IRIVE, eds. *The Origins of the Cold War in Asia*. Pp. 448. New York: Columbia University Press, 1977. $20.00.

NAGEL, STUART S. and MARIAN G. NEEF. *Legal Policy Analysis*. Pp. vii, 327. Lexington, Mass.: Lexington Books, 1977. $21.00.

NIELSON, DAVID GORDON. *Black Ethos: Northern Urban Negro Life and Thought, 1890–1930*. Pp. xix, 248. Westport, Conn.: Greenwood Press, 1977. $14.95.

NORTHRUP, JAMES P. *Old Age, Handicapped and Vietnam-Era Antidiscrimination Legislation*. Labor Relations and Public Policy Series, no. 14. Pp. iii, 234. Philadelphia: University of Pennsylvania Press, 1977. $8.50. Paperbound.

Nuclear Fuels Policy: Report of the Atlantic Council's Nuclear Fuels Policy Working Group. Pp. ii, 137. Boulder, Colo.: Westview Press, 1977. $5.95. Paperbound.

NWABUEZE, B. O. *Judicialism in Commonwealth Africa*. Pp. v, 324. New York: St. Martin's Press, 1977. $19.95.

OFSHE, RICHARD, ed. *The Sociology of the Possible*. 2nd ed. Pp. ix, 380. Englewood Cliffs, N.J.: Prentice-Hall, 1977. $6.95. Paperbound.

PARSONS, TALCOTT. *The Evolution of Societies*. Edited by Jackson Toby. Pp. vii, 269. Englewood Cliffs, N.J.: Prentice-Hall, 1977. $11.95. Paperbound, $6.95.

PATERSON, WILLIAM E. and ALASTAIR H. THOMAS, eds. *Social Democratic Parties in Western Europe*. Pp. 444. New York: St. Martin's Press, 1977. $19.95.

PECHMAN, JOSEPH A., ed. *The 1978 Budget: Setting National Priorities*. Pp. vii, 443. Washington, D.C.: The Brookings Institution, 1977. $11.95. Paperbound, $4.95.

PEMPEL, T. J., ed. *Policymaking in Contemporary Japan*. Pp. 345. Ithaca, N.Y.: Cornell University Press, 1977. $17.50.

PENNOCK, J. ROLAND and JOHN W. CHAPMAN, eds. *Due Process: Nomos XVIII*. New York: New York University Press, 1977. $17.50.

RADIN, BERYL A. *Implementation, Change, and the Federal Bureaucracy: School Desegregation Policy in H.E.W., 1964–1968*. Pp. vi, 239. New York: Columbia University Press 1977. No price.

RANDALL, JOHN HERMAN, JR. *Philosophy After Darwin*. Edited by Beth J. Singer. Pp. ix, 352. New York: Columbia University Press, 1977. $17.50.

READING, HUGO F. *A Dictionary of the Social Sciences*. Pp. 231. Boston, Mass.: Routledge & Kegan Paul, 1977. $7.95. Paperbound, $3.50.

REYNOLDS, ALLAN G. and PAUL W. FLAGG. *Cognitive Psychology*. Pp. vii, 457. Englewood Cliffs, N.J.: Prentice-Hall, 1977. $13.95.

RITZER, GEORGE. *Working: Conflict and Change*. 2nd ed. Pp. vii, 426. Englewood Cliffs, N.J.: Prentice-Hall, 1977. $13.95.

RIVIÈRE, CLAUDE. *Guinea: The Mobilization of a People*. Pp. 262. Ithaca, N.Y.: Cornell University Press, 1977. $16.50.

ROCKEFELLER, NELSON A. *Vital Resources: Reports on Energy, Food and Raw Materials*. Pp., 187. Lexington, Mass.: Lexington Books, 1977. No price.

ROGERS, JOSEPH W. *Why Are You Not A Criminal?* Pp. ix, 160. Englewood Cliffs, N.J.: Prentice-Hall, 1977. $9.95.

ROSEN, GERALD. *The Carmen Miranda Memorial Flagpole*. Pp. 176. San Rafael, Calif.: Presidio Press, 1977. $8.95.

RUBIN, ROGER H. *Family Structure and Peer Group Affiliation as Related to Attitudes about Male-Female Relations among Black Youth*. Pp. iii, 134. San Francisco, Calif.: R & E Research Associates, 1977. $9.00. Paperbound.

RUBIN, VERA and ARTHUR TUDEN, eds. *Comparative Perspectives on Slavery in New World Plantation Societies*. Vol. 292. Pp. 619. New York: New York Academy of Sciences, 1977. $40.00. Paperbound.

SAFFRON, MORRIS H. *Surgeon to Washington: Dr. John Cochran, 1730–1807*. Pp. viii, 302. New York: Columbia University Press, 1977. $17.50.

SAUGSTAD, PER. *A Theory of Communication and Use of Language: Foundations for the Study of Psychology*. Pp. 263. New York: Columbia University Press, 1977. $12.00. Paperbound.

SCHNEIDER, STEPHEN A. *The Availability of Minorities and Women for Professional and Managerial Positions 1970–1985*. Pp. iii, 280. Philadelphia: University of Pennsylvania Press, 1977. No price. Paperbound.

SCHNEIDER, SUSAN GILBERT. *Revolution, Reaction or Reform: The 1974 Bilingual Education Act*. Pp. iii, 238. New York: Las Americas, 1976. No price.

SCHWARTZ, FLORENCE, FRITZ A. FLUCKINGER and IRVING WEISMAN. *A Cross Cultural Encounter: A Non-Traditional Approach to Social Work Education*. Pp. iii, 134. San Francisco, Calif.: R & E Research Associates, 1977. $8.00. Paperbound.

SELIG, ANDREW L. *Making Things Happen in Communities: Alternatives to Traditional Mental Health Services*. Pp. iii, 99. $8.00. Paperbound.

SHORTER, EDWARD. *The Making of the Modern Family*. Pp. vii, 368. New York: Basic Books, 1977. $5.95. Paperbound.

SIRACUSA, JOSEPH M. and GLEN ST. JOHN BARCLAY. *The Impact of the Cold War: Reconsiderations*. Pp. vii, 208. Port Washington, N.Y.: Kennikat Press, 1977. $12.50. Paperbound, $6.95.

SITHOLE, NDABANINGI. *Obed Mutezo of Zimbabwe*. Pp. vi, 210. New York: Oxford University Press, 1977. $5.75. Paperbound.

SKAGGS, DAVID CURTIS, ed. *The Old Northwest in the American Revolution: An Anthology*. Pp. v, 497. New Berlin, Wisc.: Society Press, 1977. $21.50.

SMITH, DENIS MACK. *Mussolini's Roman Empire*. Pp. xi, 322. New York: Penguin Books, 1977. $3.95. Paperbound.

STEBBINS, RICHARD P. and ELAINE P. ADAM. *American Foreign Relations 1974: A Documentary Record*. Pp. iv, 613. New York: New York University Press, 1977. $26.50.

STEPHENS, JAMES C. *Managing Complexity: Work, Technology, Resources, and Human Relations*. Revised ed. Pp. 331. Mt. Airy, Md.: Lomond Books, 1977. $16.50.

TROLL, LILLIAN E., JOAN ISRAEL, and KENNETH ISRAEL, eds. *Looking Ahead: A Woman's Guide to the Problems and Joys of Growing Older*. Pp. v, 216. Englewood Cliffs, N.J.: Prentice-Hall, 1977. $8.95. Paperbound, $3.95.

TRUITT, NANCY S., et al. *Opinion Leaders and Private Investment: An Attitude Survey in Chile and Venezuela*. Pp. iii, 125. New York: UNIPUB, 1976. $5.50. Paperbound.

TYRRELL, RONALD W., FRANK A. JOHNS, and FREDERICK HANOCH McCARTY. *Growing Pains in the Classroom: A Guide for teachers of Adolescents*. Pp. vii, 202. Englewood Cliffs, N.J.: Prentice-Hall, 1977. $9.95. Paperbound.

TYSE, AGNES M. *International Education: The American Experience, A Bibliography*. Vol 2, part 1: General; part 11: Area Studies and Indexes. Pp. iii, 1094. Metuchen, N.J.: Scarecrow Press, 1977. $37.50. Per Set.

VAN DALEN, HENDRIK and L. HARMON ZEIGLER. *Introduction to Political Science: People, Politics, and Perception*. Pp. v, 275. Englewood Cliffs, N.J.: Prentice-Hall, 1977. $6.95. Paperbound.

VENTURI, ROBERT, DENISE SCOTT BROWN, and STEVEN IZENOUR. *Learning from Las Vegas*. Revised Edition. Pp. xi, 192. Cambridge, Mass.: MIT Press, 1977. $9.95. Paperbound.

WAGNER, RICHARD E. *Inheritance and the State: Tax Principles for a Free and Prosperous Commonwealth.* Pp. 95. Washington, D.C.: American Enterprise Institute for Public Policy Research, 1977. $2.75. Paperbound.

WALDEN, RUSSELL, ed. *The Open Hand: Essays on LeCorbusier.* Pp. ix, 484. Cambridge, Mass.: MIT Press, 1977. $25.00.

WARREN, RACHELLE and DONALD WARREN *The Neighborhood Organizer's Handbook.* Pp. 248. Notre Dame, Ind.: University of Notre Dame Press, 1977. $9.95. Paperbound, $4.95.

WARREN, ROLAND L. *Social Change and Human Purpose: Toward Understanding and Action.* Pp. ix, 348. Chicago, Ill.: Rand McNally, 1977. $9.95.

WEISS, ROBERT S. *Marital Separation: Coping with the End of a Marriage and the Transition to being Single Again.* Pp. vii, 334. New York: Basic Books, 1977. $4.95. Paperbound.

WELBORN, DAVID M. *Governance of Federal Regulatory Agencies.* Pp. vii, 179. Knoxville: University of Tennessee Press, 1977. $9.50.

WETHERBY, TERRY. *Conversations: Working Women Talk About Doing a "Man's Job."* Pp. v, 269. Milbrae, Calif.: Les Femmes, 1977. $4.95. Paperbound.

WILSON, DICK, ed. *Mao Tse-Tung in the Scales of History.* Pp. xii, 331. New York: Cambridge University Press, 1977. $19.95. Paperbound, $5.95.

WONDER, EDWARD F. *Nuclear Fuel and American Foreign Policy: Multilateralization for Uranium Enrichment.* Pp. ix, 72. Boulder, Colo.: Westview Press, 1977. $3.95. Paperbound.

World Armaments and Disarmament: SIPRI Yearbook 1977. Pp. v, 421. Cambridge, Mass.: MIT Press, 1977. No price.

YIN, ROBERT K., KAREN A. HEALD, and MARY E. VOGEL. *Tinkering with the System.* Pp. v, 275. Lexington, Mass.: Lexington Books, 1977. $16.00.

ZELDIN, THEODORE. *The Oxford History of Modern Europe: France 1848–1945.* Vol. II. Pp. vii, 1202. New York: Oxford University Press, 1977. $29.95.

ZIMBALIST, SIDNEY E. *Historic Themes and Landmarks in Social Welfare Research.* Pp. viii, 432. New York: Harper & Row, 1977. $10.95.

EXPERIENCE, ENVIRONMENT, AND HUMAN POTENTIALS

HERBERT L. LEFF, University of Vermont
1978 588 pp. cloth $15.00 paper $8.00

MARXISM AND THE METROPOLIS

New Perspectives in
Urban Political Economy
Edited by **WILLIAM K. TABB,** Queens College, The City University of New York; and **LARRY SAWERS,** The American University
1978 384 pp. cloth $10.00 paper $5.50

FREEDOM AND THE COURT

Civil Rights and Liberties
in the United States
Third Edition
HENRY J. ABRAHAM, University of Virginia
1977 480 pp. cloth $17.95 paper $5.00

CORPORATE AND GOVERNMENTAL DEVIANCE

Problems of Organizational Behavior
in Contemporary Society
Edited by **M. DAVID ERMANN,** University of Delaware, and **RICHARD J. LUNDMAN,** Ohio State University
1978   256 pp.   paper $3.50

KARL MARX: SELECTED WRITINGS

Edited by **DAVID McLELLAN,** University of Kent
1977 640 pp. cloth $12.00 paper $6.00

POLITICAL PARADOXES AND PUZZLES

ARUN BOSE, University of Delhi
1978   256 pp.   paper $5.00

THE LIFE AND TIMES OF LIBERAL DEMOCRACY

C.B. MACPHERSON, University of Toronto
1977 120 pp. cloth $6.95 paper $2.50

AUSTRO-MARXISM

Edited and translated by **TOM BOTTOMORE,** University of Sussex, and **PATRICK GOODE**
June 1978   256 pp.   cloth $18.50
                              paper $6.00

ARISTOTLE'S POLITICAL THEORY

An Introduction for Students of
Political Theory
R.G. MULGAN, University of Otago
1978 160 pp. cloth $10.50 paper $4.00

OXFORD UNIVERSITY PRESS 1478 1978 Publishers of Fine Books for Five Centuries

Prices and publication dates are subject to change.
OXFORD UNIVERSITY PRESS 200 Madison Avenue, New York, New York 10016

West Bank/East Bank
The Palestinians in Jordan, 1949–1967

Shaul Mishal

Two years after the Arab-Israeli War forced hundreds of thousands of Palestinian Arabs to flee to the West Bank of the Jordan River, Jordan annexed the entire area and the Palestinians became a majority in the Jordanian state. For the next seventeen years, the relations between the Palestinians and the Jordanian government posed complex problems for both sides. This detailed study describes what happened on the two banks during the period and explains the explosive aftermath. $9.50

Presidential Impeachment
John R. Labovitz

In this thorough and thoughtful examination of the constitutional issues involved in the impeachment of a president, Labovitz, a lawyer who served on the impeachment inquiry staff of the House Judiciary Committee in 1974, incorporates the Nixon experience into American history over the last two hundred years. $15.00

Secession
The Legitimacy of Self-Determination

Lee C. Buchheit

This probing study critically examines the case for and against application of the doctrine of self-determination to secessionist movements. Buchheit reviews the treatment of this potentially explosive concept from the League of Nations era to the present and analyzes in detail the international reaction to the secessionist struggles in the Congo, Kurdistan, Biafra, Somalia-Kenya/Ethiopia, Nagaland, and Bangla Desh. $17.50

The Supreme Court and the Idea of Progress
Alexander M. Bickel
with a new foreword by Anthony Lewis

Timeless questions about the role of the Supreme Court in the American political and legal system are raised in the late Alexander Bickel's characteristically astute analysis of the work of the Warren Court.
Cloth $15.00   Paper $3.95

The Politics of Propaganda
The Office of War Information, 1942–1945

Allan M. Winkler

The Office of War Information was created during World War II to implement an American propaganda program at home and abroad. From the outset the question of how best to present American intentions was controversial. In this acute and sympathetic appraisal of the aims and achievements of the men who guided OWI's policies, Winkler shows that American propaganda in fact came to reflect something quite different from what OWI's founders had intended. $11.95

Jewish Activism in Imperial Germany
The Struggle for Civil Equality

Marjorie Lamberti

The Centralverein, an association of Jewish citizens founded in 1893, was the first Jewish interest group to be active in German politics and, often allied with the Progressive party, to take part in national elections. Lamberti masterfully reconstructs the policies and tactics of the Centralverein in its struggle to uphold the principles of a pluralistic society and constitutional government. $17.50

Now available in paper

To Be A Politician
Revised edition

Stimson Bullitt
Foreword by David Riesman

"This new version, like its original, is a joy to read. . . . Here abide sensible advice to citizens about political perspectives, pithy observations about the political calling, unpretentious epigrams on successful politicians and their fate. . . . To a political literature filled with exudation of cynicism, indifference, and corruption, these essays are an oasis."—*Perspective*
Cloth $15.00   Paper $3.95

Yale

Yale University Press
New Haven and London

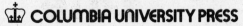

INDEX

INDEX

WATERGATE AND THE CONSTITUTION
Philip B. Kurland
The distinguished legal scholar reviews the essential constitutional issues raised by Watergate and shows that nothing has yet been done to prevent recurrent crises.

"Trenchantly written, full of learning in law and history, and bound to be provocative in its portrait of a constitutionally deranged Republic and its call for a return to ancient moorings."
—Paul A. Freund, Harvard Law School

THE DECLINING SIGNIFICANCE OF RACE
Blacks and Changing American Institutions
William Julius Wilson
"Wilson's analysis of the problem of the black lower class is one of the best I've seen. It is a good and valuable work in defining just where the problem is—and where it isn't."—Nathan Glazer
Cloth   216 pages $12.50   March

THE PERPETUAL DREAM
Reform and Experiment in the American College
Gerald Grant and David Riesman
The Perpetual Dream provides an overview of the diversity of undergraduate education in America to explore a fundamental question: What ought to be the basis of intellectual and social community for undergraduates?
Cloth   488 pages $15.00   April

THE IDEAL IN LAW
Eugene V. Rostow
The Ideal in Law brings together some of Rostow's most significant essays on the role of ethics in law, and of law in ethics.
Cloth   336 pages $20.00   March

NEW STUDIES IN PHILOSOPHY, POLITICS, ECONOMICS, AND THE HISTORY OF IDEAS
F. A. Hayek
Outstanding selections from the Nobel prize-winner's essays and lectures of the last ten years.
Cloth   320 pages $15.00   March

The University of Chicago Press   Chicago 60637

NOW IN PAPER

CULTURE AND PRACTICAL REASON
Marshall Sahlins
" . . . an intensely provocative, inventive, and searching book built on superb scholarship—an event designed to break up the existing structure."—Stephen Gudeman, *American Ethnologist*
Paper xi, 252 pages $4.95 March

OIL RESOURCES
Who Gets What How?
Kenneth W. Dam
"A rich book, thoroughly researched, carefully and rigorously argued, well written."—Norman Metzger, *The Sciences*
Paper xi, 193 pages $4.95 March

LAW, LEGISLATION AND LIBERTY
Volume 1: Rules and Order
Friedrich A. Hayek
This volume represents the first section of Hayek's comprehensive three-part study of the relations between law and liberty.
Paper 192 pages $4.45 February

PURSUING JUSTICE FOR THE CHILD
Edited by Margaret K. Rosenheim
With a Foreword by Robert Maynard Hutchins
"This anthology deserves a wide audience . . . for its exceptional merit in discussing the current issues of reform of the juvenile justice system . . . "—Irving R. Kaufman, *Harvard Law Review*
Paper $5.95 February

DELINQUENCY, CRIME, AND SOCIETY
Edited by James F. Short, Jr.
Reassessing the "Shaw and McKay tradition" of urban sociology, the contributors pursue critical and emerging issues in the study of crime and delinquency.
Paper ix, 325 pages $5.95 March

The University of Chicago Press   *Chicago 60637*

Origin and Purpose. The Academy was organized December 14, 1889, to promote the progress of political and social science, especially through publications and meetings. The Academy does not take sides in controverted questions, but seeks to gather and present reliable information to assist the public in forming an intelligent and accurate judgment.

Meetings. The Academy holds an annual meeting in the spring extending over two days.

Publications. THE ANNALS is the bimonthly publication of The Academy. Each issue contains articles on some prominent social or political problem, written at the invitation of the editors. Also, monographs are published from time to time, numbers of which are distributed to pertinent professional organizations. These volumes constitute important reference works on the topics with which they deal, and they are extensively cited by authorities throughout the United States and abroad. The papers presented at the meetings of The Academy are included in THE ANNALS.

Membership. Each member of The Academy receives THE ANNALS and may attend the meetings of The Academy. Annual dues: Regular Membership—$18.00 (clothbound, $23.00). Special Membership—contributing, $40.00; sustaining, $60.00; patron, $100. A life membership is $500. Add $2.00 to above rates for membership outside the U.S.A. Dues are payable in U.S. dollars in advance. Special members receive a certificate suitable for framing and may choose either paper or clothbound copies of THE ANNALS.

Single copies of THE ANNALS may be obtained by nonmembers of The Academy for $4.50 ($5.50 clothbound) and by members for $4.00 ($5.00 clothbound). A discount of 5 percent is allowed on orders for 10 to 24 copies of any one issue, and of 10 percent on orders for 25 or more copies. These discounts apply only when orders are placed directly with The Academy and not through agencies. The price to all bookstores and to all dealers is $4.50 per copy ($5.00, clothbound) less 20 percent, with no quantity discount. Orders for 5 books or less must be prepaid (add $1.00 for postage and handling). Orders for 6 books or more must be invoiced.

All correspondence concerning The Academy or THE ANNALS should be addressed to the Academy offices, 3937 Chestnut Street, Philadelphia, Pa. 19104.